# Unfinished Business

It's not easy
but it can get easier!

XO,

Amy Yip

11/30/2023

# Unfinished Business

## Breaking Down the Great Wall
## Between Adult Child and Immigrant Parents

# AMY C. YIP

PYP Publish
Your Purpose

For permission requests, write to the publisher, addressed "Attention: Permissions Coordinator," at the address below.

Publish Your Purpose
141 Weston Street, #155
Hartford, CT, 06141

The opinions expressed by the Author are not necessarily those held by Publish Your Purpose.

Ordering Information: Quantity sales and special discounts are available on quantity purchases by corporations, associations, and others. For details, contact the publisher at hello@ publishyourpurpose.com.

Edited by: Brandi Lai & Nancy Graham-Tillman
Cover design by: Cornelia Murariu
Typeset by: Jetlaunch

Printed in the United States of America.
ISBN: 979-8-88797-045-5 (hardcover)
ISBN: 979-8-88797-044-8 (paperback)
ISBN: 979-8-88797-087-5 (ebook)

Library of Congress Control Number: 2023908848

First edition, September 2023.

The information contained within this book is strictly for informational purposes. The material may include information, products, or services by third parties. As such, the Author and Publisher do not assume responsibility or liability for any third-party material or opinions. The publisher is not responsible for websites (or their content) that are not owned by the publisher. Readers are advised to do their own due diligence when it comes to making decisions.

Publish Your Purpose is a hybrid publisher of non-fiction books. Our mission is to elevate the voices often excluded from traditional publishing. We intentionally seek out authors and storytellers with diverse backgrounds, life experiences, and unique perspectives to publish books that will make an impact in the world. Do you have a book idea you would like us to consider publishing? Please visit PublishYourPurpose.com for more information.

*To my incredible parents, Mama and Papa Yip, thank you for being open and patient during the conversations that fill these pages. Your sacrifices over the years have laid the foundation for my journey, and I am forever grateful for the blessings I have today. Your unwavering love, support, and acceptance, even in the face of disagreement, mean the world to me. I want to acknowledge and appreciate all the times you lovingly nagged, knowing it was an expression of your boundless love for me.*

*To my loving husband, Greg, thank you for being my rock throughout this writing process. Your unwavering support and belief in me and your constant encouragement kept me going during the moments of doubt. I am deeply grateful for your willingness to take on extra responsibilities, caring for our son every weekend, allowing me the precious time and space to pour my heart into this book. Your belief in me has been the driving force behind my determination.*

*To my dear son, Logan, you have taught me the true essence of motherhood and shown me love like I've never experienced before. Your presence in my life has ignited my passion to understand the complexities of family dynamics and the depths of parental love. You are my greatest joy and inspiration.*

*To my coaching clients, I extend my heartfelt appreciation for your openness in sharing your personal experiences and struggles with parental relationships. Your stories have inspired me to delve deeper and be curious about understanding and capturing my own parents' narratives. Your trust and vulnerability have been invaluable in shaping the insights within this book.*

*To all those who have supported and encouraged me on this path, thank you from the bottom of my heart. Your presence and encouragement have been a constant source of strength and inspiration.*

*Lastly, I want to express my heartfelt gratitude to the readers who will embark on this literary journey. Your interest and engagement in my work are both humbling and inspiring. Thank you all for being a part of this incredible endeavor. This book would not have been possible without each and every one of you.*

*XO,*
*Amy*

# CONTENTS

BECOMING A MOTHER | 1 |

DATES WITH MY PARENTS: HOW IT STARTED | 7 |

HOW BEST TO USE THIS BOOK AS A GUIDE | 15 |

CONVERSATION TIP SHEET | 23 |

## MYTH 1

**My Success Will Never Be Good Enough for My Parents**
| 27 |

## MYTH 2

**I've Failed My Parents by Not Marrying a Good Chinese Partner**
| 67 |

## MYTH 3

**My Parents Must Not Love Me Because They Never Say It to Me**
| 105 |

## MYTH 4

**I'll Never Be Able to Repay My Parents for Their Sacrifices**
| 143 |

## MYTH 5

**I Don't Belong Anywhere**
| 181 |

**MYTH 6**

**I Must Be Mentally Tough and Never Ask for Help**
| 221 |

**MYTH 7**

**I Don't Deserve to Spend Money on Myself; I Need to Save It**
| 263 |

**MYTH 8**

**It's Better to Be a Boy than a Girl**
| 301 |

DATES WITH MY PARENTS: HOW IT'S GOING | 339 |

AFTERWORD BY GREG MUELLER | 345 |

WORKS CITED | 349 |

ABOUT THE AUTHOR | 351 |

# BECOMING A MOTHER

## February 2023

This is not and was never going to be easy.

I'm writing this on my little guy's first birthday while in the lobby of my apartment building. Yay! Happy birthday kiddo! He's still asleep, so we can all wish him a happy birthday again later when he wakes up.

I live ten minutes from my parents' home in Maryland, the same home I grew up in. I never thought I would say this, but I've fallen back in love with this place and even my parents' weekly visits.

In 2008, at the age of twenty-seven, I left Maryland and went as far away as possible: California. I had finally received the internal transfer approval that I had pushed my manager for. *I'm getting out of here and never coming back*, I thought. Having lived only in Maryland up to that point, I was thrilled to make my escape and explore what was beyond the confines of this state. And exploring is what I did. First I lived in Los Angeles, followed by stints in San Francisco and then New York City.

Just traveling across the country wasn't enough for me. I needed to see the world. So in January 2020, I quit my big corporate job at Google, sold all my belongings, and with my husband took a one-way flight to Ghana to volunteer at a breast cancer nonprofit and travel the world. The pandemic hit the world by storm shortly after we left, and we got stuck in Ghana for seven months. When borders reopened, we lived and worked nomadically all over Europe. I was living big!

In all those years, never for a moment did I consider returning to Maryland.

Then it happened. After more than thirteen years away, I returned. Despite my attempts to never come back, here I am, living just around the corner from where I grew up. I don't regret coming back at all. In fact, I'm grateful that the process of writing this book brought me closer to my parents, both physically and emotionally.

You see, in 2021, when I made the decision to move back, the conversations with my parents that fill this book had already begun. And as much as I want to tell you that the conversations were all beautiful and magical, leading to an immediate rekindling of my relationship with my parents, that's not entirely the case.

The truth is, the conversations felt really hard. Especially the first dozen or so. Oftentimes, the initial conversations would trigger anger, frustration, and hurt in me. At times, I'd leave the conversation feeling deflated, like an old birthday balloon that has stayed up for much longer than it should. Other times, I felt like an eight-year-old child that had just been criticized. *What the hell am I doing? I have no right to be writing this book*, I'd tell myself as tears flowed down my face, completely forgetting my "why" for writing it to begin with (I'll tell you more about that later).

After months and months and months, I wasn't making much progress on trying to reframe my relationship with my parents. And I definitely wasn't making any progress on this book. I mean, how could I possibly write a guide for children of immigrants to start conversations with their parents if I couldn't do it with my own?

## August 2021

I clenched my jaw tight to hold back the tears. My body shook, my heart pounded as if there were a jackhammer gone wild inside, and I couldn't see through the glaze over my eyes. I sat in my parents' kitchen, trying to have a conversation with them as both my mom and my dad wagged their fingers at me. I couldn't hear a word they said. I was trying hard not to explode.

I was five months pregnant. My husband, Greg, and I were trying to figure out where in the US to settle down after having lived nomadically overseas for the last eighteen months. While Greg was in Colorado for his Air Force reserve duty, I was staying with my parents for a few weeks. He and I ping-ponged ideas over email and phone conversations, evaluating our options and building our future plans together. Our discussions were leading us to the West Coast, Las Vegas to be exact. I'm not a fan of cold weather and gray days, so Maryland wasn't even on our radar.

What threw a wrench into our decision-making process was the uncertainty of our financial situation. First there was me, a small business owner about to have a baby without the safety net of maternity leave that a big corporation could provide. For most of our relationship, I had been the breadwinner, rising up the ranks in corporate America as Greg pursued an entrepreneurial venture. When I quit my corporate job to travel the world, I hadn't planned on being a full-time life coach and speaker. But when we got stuck in Ghana, I spent my free time expressing my perspectives in public forums and social media and bringing people together in community. I discovered it's something I enjoy doing. My business boomed.

But now, this small business owner needed her husband to pick up the slack. I needed us to swap places. I mean, we had a baby coming our way for *foxes* sake! I wouldn't have the luxury of taking time away from my business to recover and care for our newborn if Greg wasn't breadwinning.

The pressure on Greg was high. Aside from the four weeks a year of serving his Air Force reservist duty, he was without a steady income. And finding a corporate job was not an easy endeavor. For much of his career, he had either been in a military or government role. Ask anyone who's attempted to switch from military to corporate and they'll tell you it was an arduous transition. It was no different for Greg.

As we tried to plan where we were going to settle down to raise our baby, we had to consider Greg's job prospects. But we had no idea where he'd end up finding a job, if he even found a job before the baby arrived, that is. The baby wasn't going to wait. Time was ticking. My stress levels were high. And here were my parents, lecturing me about my choices.

"Aiya! You play too much, Amy," my mom criticized. "You knew you were pregnant five months ago, but you continued to play in Europe. You should've returned home sooner instead of waiting until you only have four months before the baby arrives. What were you thinking?"

I bit my tongue. My jaw tightened. I wasn't "playing"; I was working nomadically, too, and I only knew I was pregnant three-and-a-half months ago.

"You should've encouraged your husband to start looking for a job sooner," my dad scolded. "You know he's not as experienced or hardworking as you are. He grew up in the White American culture and doesn't have Chinese work ethics."

I gritted my teeth, my lips drew back in a snarl, and my pupils flared. I didn't want Greg to be hardworking the way I was because that mentality had gotten me hospitalized.

"You don't think," my mom accused.

"You don't plan," my dad bristled.

Then it happened. Like a can of soda that had just been shaken hard and then opened, I exploded. I don't even know what I said. As soon as the words came flying out of my mouth, I felt a mixture of shock and shame. I didn't feel any better from my outburst. I paused and from the corner of my eye saw my parents quietly studying me. I couldn't meet their gaze. Instead, I stalked out of the kitchen into my room and slammed the door, feeling ashamed at my outburst. I cried myself to sleep.

The next morning, my mom got up and cooked my favorite breakfast: eggs with avocado. She didn't mention a thing about the night before, nor did my dad. Life continued as if nothing had ever happened.

It wasn't until several days had passed that my dad said anything to me about the explosion. I was lying on my bed reading about baby gear, still feeling tremendous guilt and shame about my behavior, when he walked in.

"Amy," he said.

I looked up from my pastel-colored book and peered at him. He stood at the doorway and eyed my belly, then returned his gaze to meet mine.

"I know you have a lot of pressure right now, but your words were very hurtful. We are just worried about you. We're your parents. Do you know how hard it is for us to see you cry every night because of all the stress you're going through? Especially when you're pregnant. It makes us angry that you've worked so hard all your life, that you're five months pregnant, and your husband doesn't have a job to support his family. As the man of the household, that should be his job. We worry that you're moving all the way to the West Coast. You'll be so far from us. We won't even be able to help you if we wanted to."

He paused and looked at me. Worry lines creased his forehead. Sadness made his entire face droop.

Taking in the sight of him standing at the doorway, I put my book down on the bed, rolled over to my side so as not to put pressure on my pregnant belly, and got out of bed. Walking over to where he stood, I gave him a hug. He received it as I said, "I know you and Mommy love me. I'm sorry for how I acted. I didn't mean to say what I said."

Though I didn't remember what I had said, I didn't ask either, because it didn't matter. Whatever I had said had hurt them, and that's the last thing I wanted to do.

That night I called Greg and said, "We're moving to Maryland." I had decided that I needed to be close to my parents. Something felt right about it.

"We're what?" he asked, completely taken aback. He had just returned to his hotel room after getting off Air Force duty.

Greg was a bit surprised and resistant at first. We had been leaning towards Vegas, a few hours' drive away from his parents, and he had been excited to move closer to his family.

"Why would you want to move back and raise a child in a place you said you'd never want to live again?" he implored.

I had frequently told him that there's nothing in Maryland, but I was wrong about that. There *is* something in Maryland that no other state has: my parents.

In the end, Greg supported my needs. That's what I've always loved about him. He knows how to speak his needs and has always encouraged me to share mine—not something I'm used to doing as a "good Chinese girl."

And so, in October 2021, I officially became a Maryland resident again.

# 2022

After the blowup, I continued to have conversations with my parents. Month after month, hour after hour, each conversation helped me slowly begin seeing them in a different way and understanding them in a new light.

When my baby was born in early 2022, my mom stayed with us for the first two months of his life. She took care of me, her own baby, and she took care of my baby, her grandchild. While she stayed over to help cook, clean, and care for us as I recovered from my emergency C-section, my dad would run errands, picking up the groceries for the family, surprising us with delicious Chinese sweet buns, or taking me to my doctors' appointments while Greg worked (he got a well-paying job in DC before our baby was born! WOOHOO!).

Even after the first two months of my kiddo's life, my parents continue to visit nearly every week. Of course they arrive with an abundance of home-cooked dishes and random groceries in hand, such as navel oranges or broccoli. What warms my heart the most about these visits is seeing how my parents laugh and play with my son. It's as if their inner child is being awakened by his innocence and laughter. They're a gift for him, he's a gift for them, and all of them are a gift for me.

And so here we are in Maryland. I have no regrets. In fact, I'm more than pleasantly surprised. Living ten minutes away from my parents has provided me with a mixture of comfort and joy, and occasional frustration. The process of writing this book and having conversations with them has helped me learn to better handle the moments when we've butted heads.

This is not and was never going to be easy. But it's getting easier.

# DATES WITH MY PARENTS: HOW IT STARTED

The conversations I had with my parents that are included in this book started as a result of coaching sessions with one of my clients. She was a senior vice president at a large bank and was tremendously successful, but unhappy. She had dreams of doing something different, something creative, possibly starting her own business. But something held her back. As we worked together, I coached her to uncover what was beneath that fear.

"I go into little girl mode," Lisa explained.

"And what happens in that mode?" I asked.

"I become afraid. I'm afraid of telling my dad what I want to do with my life. That I want to leave this prestigious job to start a creative business. I'm afraid he'll be disappointed in me. That he'll tell me I've failed him."

"What's the truth here?"

"I don't know."

"How could you find out?"

"I could ask him . . . But I can't. I don't want to. I don't know how to."

Lisa was one of many Asian American Pacific Islander (AAPI) clients I worked with who went into a fear-based mode when we explored their dreams and desires. Some feared disappointing their parents and how their parents would respond. Others held anger and resentment towards their parents for pushing them hard to achieve and succeed yet never showing them love or expressing their pride.

Out of curiosity, I started having conversations with others in the AAPI community; those who weren't clients of mine. They shared similar stories with me: fear, anger, resentment, and sometimes sadness towards their parents. Yet most were unwilling to have an open conversation with them.

"They wouldn't even be open to a conversation," some would say.

"We'd just get into a disagreement and argue," said others. "It's not worth the energy."

I began to wonder about my own parents. I never had the courage to have open, deep conversations with them. My perception of who they are and what they're like was based on my own childhood experiences with and memories of them, all of which were from nearly three decades ago. I'd never actually heard my parents' stories from their mouths; I'd lived only in the stories I created about them, filling in the blanks with my own assumptions.

## The Stories We Live In

The thing is, we all live in stories. Every time we experience something, whether by ourselves or with other people, we create a reality in our heads about what happened, good, bad, or neutral. The stories we create in our heads have little to do with what truly is. They're not reality. It's like looking at the world through stained glass—what you see depends on which part of the stained glass you're looking through.

Why is this so? Research has shown that the thing we are calling our experience "does not only reflect 'what is out there,' but also our previous knowledge and expectation . . . How we perceive our environment is for a large part determined by what we think."[1]

We receive information via one or more of our five senses. We then interpret that information to make meaning of it. How we interpret it is influenced by our emotions, knowledge, previous experiences, and cognitive distortions. In a sense, we're constructing our own lives and the world we live

---

[1]    Jacob Jolij and Maaike Meurs, "Music Alters Visual Perception," *PLoS ONE* 6, no. 4 (April 2011): e18861, https://doi.org/10.1371/journal.pone.0018861.

in. If the world seems unfair, malicious, dull, hectic, or stressful, it's because that's our perception based on something that's happened.

Even now, at this very moment, the way you're interpreting my words is mostly determined by your past experiences and personal model of the world. You might be nodding your head in agreement. You may also be questioning how your reality could possibly be constructed.

Though our stories are not reality, they can act as a lens through which we view it. As Carl Jung said, "It all depends on how we look at things, and not how they are in themselves."[2]

Many of us spend most of our time in our own heads without even realizing it. It's as if we're living life unconsciously in this space. And many people never truly awaken. We see life through our own eyes and rarely from the realities of others' eyes. We can be in the same situation or circumstance as someone else, yet our lived experience of it can be vastly different. The difference is due to how we're piecing bits of information together to construct meaning and make sense of the world. Our stories are the result of this process.

In her book *Rising Strong*, Brené Brown says that we are meaning-making machines. She explains that in the absence of data, we take the bits of information we do have to create something that makes sense to us because we don't like uncertainty, ambiguity, and not understanding.[3]

Oftentimes disagreements, arguments, and misunderstandings arise because our realities are different from those of our parents. We see things only from our storylines, and they see them only from theirs. When their stories differ from ours, we feel the need to defend ourselves (after all, we've created our stories in a way that makes sense to us). We cannot understand their stories at all, perhaps because they have some bits of information that we don't have. More often than not, we choose to not entertain their stories because that would mean ours might be wrong or inaccurate. And as humans, we hate being wrong.

2    Carl Gustav Jung, *Modern Man in Search of a Soul*, trans. William Stanley Dell and Cary F. Baynes (New York: Routledge | Taylor & Francis, 2001), 67.

3    Brené Brown, *Rising Strong* (London: Vermilion, 2015).

So what happens then? We judge their stories. We point out all the holes—all the reasons their stories aren't correct or don't make sense. We may throw out some of our data and facts to prove this. We may even point fingers at them and make up stories about who they are to justify why their stories aren't true:

> "They've always tried to control me, so they must be trying to do the same thing again."

> "They're old-fashioned, so of course they wouldn't understand what I'm going through."

> "They didn't have to grow up trying to straddle two cultures, so they just don't get it."

Then we use all the facts and data we have to support our own stories.

The problem with this pattern is that by continuing to live in the realities we've created in our heads, we stay close-minded. And for many of us, these same old stories are what hold us back. They prevent us from changing, whether the change we seek is to pursue a bigger dream, change a habit, or strengthen our relationship with our parents.

For most of my early life, I too lived in the realities of my own head with stories about who my parents are. I was positive I knew them. I believed they were ignorant and only cared about bragging to others about my achievements, whether it was my grades in school or my various job titles. I was sure they didn't care about love, affection, or any of the mushy emotional stuff. And I was positive they thought I should just spend my life working hard and not having fun.

At times, I loved them. At times, I resented them. Growing up, there were moments when I was proud to have them as my parents just as they were. But more often than not, as a child, I wished they were different. I wished they would verbally tell me they loved me like White American parents do. I desired for them to speak better English without an accent in the hope that my fellow classmates would stop making fun of them. I even begged for a peanut butter and jelly sandwich so that my "weird" lunches would no longer be mocked by my classmates. And I wanted them to understand what it was like to be bullied and made fun of for being a "Chink." But I didn't think they would or could ever understand, so I never tried.

It was a long, silent journey, one filled with guilt, shame, anger, sadness, and plenty of tears and pain, until I found the courage to have conversations with my parents. Deep conversations unraveled the stories I had about them and made space to strengthen our relationship. These conversations led me to understand (or at least try to understand) their side of the story. I could see the twinkle in their eyes as they told me about their lives. I uncovered what gives them joy, happiness, fulfillment, and meaning and learned about their lifelong dreams. And I was able to share myself and my story with them fully, in a way I felt understood.

The journey continues to this day. It's not one of those things where there's a final destination and you're all of a sudden like, *Okay! We fully understand each other now! Mission accomplished.* A relationship is something you're in for the long haul, and as with any relationship, the one with your parents will always need to be worked at and maintained.

## Goals of This Book

My primary goal with this book is to hear our parents' stories, many of which might otherwise never be heard because of the rift in our relationships with them or the misunderstandings between us. These rifts and misunderstandings often stem from the stories in our heads. We believe that our parents don't want to tell their stories, so we don't ask. They believe that we're not even interested in listening, so they don't tell. As Gandhi said, "Your beliefs become your thoughts, your thoughts become your words, your words become your actions, your actions become your habits, your habits become your values, your values become your destiny."[4]

---

4    Kunal K. Ganguly, "Life of M.K. Gandhi: A Message to Youth of Modern India," *Indian Journal of Medical Research* 149, supplement (January 2019): 145–151, https://doi. org/10.4103/0971-5916.251672.

I also want to tell my parents' story because I truly believe it deserves to be heard. When I first shared the idea of this book with my dad and told him how I wanted to help people strengthen their relationship with their parents and cultivate deeper understanding, he loved the idea. Then I asked if he'd be willing to share his stories with me so that I could include them in this book. You know what he said? "I don't have anything to offer. I'm not accomplished. I just worked as a tailor and restaurant manager. Maybe you should ask your uncle. He's a lawyer."

After persuading him that his story matters, my dad finally agreed, but he insisted, "Please leave my name out. I don't want people to know so much about me."

I smiled and agreed, "Sure thing. I won't mention your name." So I won't mention his name in this book and merely refer to him as "Papa Yip." Same goes for my mom, who will be referred to as "Mama Yip."

My second goal with this book is for us to heal. I want to heal myself, heal my parents, and heal our relationship through conversation. I wish the same for you and your parents. By opening up to our parents' stories and the myths we believe about them, us, and our relationships, we can all heal. In this book, I use the word "myths" to describe my stories about myself and my parents, because that's exactly what they are. Though we currently have memories and stories about who our parents are and what our relationships with them are like, they're exactly that: stories. Stories we've created based on memories of the circumstances, not the objective truth of these circumstances. Our memories are not 100 percent reality. They are a valid perspective, but they're just one perspective. Imagine if you got more perspectives to build out your memory bank and what you recall. What might be possible if you could see the bigger picture of who your parents are?

The power in having these conversations and bringing these topics out into the open is that they end up having less of a grip over us. By understanding our parents' perspectives and stories, we can loosen and release our feelings of pressure, heavy hearts, guilt, and shame.

As my parents are aging, I imagine yours are too—if you're lucky enough to still have them around. Time is running out. So I hope we can all take the courageous step towards healing before it's too late.

# HOW BEST TO USE THIS BOOK AS A GUIDE

This book is structured in sections, each one focusing on a different myth (or story) we have about our parents, from "My success will never be good enough for my parents" to "I must be mentally tough and never ask for help" and everything in between. Each myth is a stand-alone section, so you don't have to read this book from front to back. Pick each topic as it's relevant for you. You might be surprised, though, what you can learn by checking out the myths that you don't think are relevant.

The first part of each myth is a personal reflection of my story and the experiences that formed my beliefs around the myth. The second part of each myth is my parents' side of the story, based on the conversations I've had with them. Though this second part might read like it was an easy conversation, what you'll be reading is the second, third, fourth, or even fifth attempt at a conversation without a blowup or a need for a pause. Like I said earlier, this is not and was never going to be easy. But it can get easier.

At the end of each chapter, I include a framework for a "Date with Your Parents." Much like the structure of my own reflections and conversations with my parents, this framework is a three-parter:

1.  Pre-Conversation Personal Reflection

2.  The Conversation

3.  Post-Conversation Contemplation

The personal reflection exercise should be done prior to having a conversation with your parents. For the conversation itself, I've included suggestions and questions you can use as a starting point to get the conversation going. Following the conversation, there are questions for you to do a post-conversation contemplation. Some include an activity as well.

The exercises are all in English. If language is a barrier for communicating with your parents, you can use Google Translate to translate the questions into a language your parents understand.

Worksheets, along with additional supporting materials, are available on my website for download. These include a warm-up questions guide for those who are just beginning their journey of having conversations with their parents. You can start with these foundational questions before delving into the topic-specific conversations covered in this book. Visit my site for the latest book resources and to sign up for updates: https://amyyipcoaching.com/UnfinishedBusiness-Resources.

As you embark on this journey, here are three tips to keep in mind:

1. **Shift your mindset to openness and curiosity.**
When I started writing this book, I was not yet pregnant. The conversations with my parents were decent. We had surface-level discussions about their lives, but I couldn't get them to fully open up. Anytime difficult topics arose or we disagreed on something, it would mark an impasse and the conversation would abruptly end, oftentimes with intense emotions for both parties.

Towards the end of my pregnancy, I took a pause from writing, which meant I also paused the conversations on topics covered in this book. I didn't pick up writing again until my little guy turned three months old. Upon returning to the book, I spent time revisiting the recorded conversations I had with my parents pre-baby. What I heard was shocking. There was often judgment and defensiveness on my end. While my choice of words may not have explicitly conveyed it, my tone revealed my impatience and abruptness. This wasn't how I wanted my conversations with them to go.

I imagined what it would feel like if my kiddo grew up and spoke to me the way I initially spoke to my parents. It would hurt really bad. This realization led me to understand why my parents wouldn't open up as much as I'd hoped; I wouldn't either if I were in their shoes.

Post-baby, I returned to my parents to revisit many of those conversations. This time, having a baby of my own and recognizing the challenges of parenting, I approached these conversations with greater empathy, curiosity, and openness. In turn, my parents were more willing to share and go deeper.

So approach the conversations with your parents with an open mind about what you believe to be true. Shift your mindset from who you believe they were and be open to who they are now.

2.  **Don't try to change them.**
We always want to change the people and situations around us. We can't. The only thing we have the power to change is ourselves. The sooner you accept this, the sooner things will change for you.

"How well do you know your partner today?" John Gottman asked from the stage.

I looked at Greg, my fiancé at the time, who was sitting next to me. We were at "The Art and Science of Love" workshop in Seattle with the Gottmans, a psychologist couple who have devoted their life to "the research and practice of fostering healthy, long-lasting relationships."[5]

John Gottman continued by explaining that, as humans, we're constantly evolving.

---

[5] "About John & Julie Gottman," The Gottman Institute, accessed April 13, 2023, https://www.gottman.com/about/john-julie-gottman/.

One of the biggest misnomers and problems in relationships is to assume the person you're seeing in front of you is the same human being from a decade or two ago. Or even the same person as a year or two ago. People are constantly evolving and growing. In order for relationships to thrive, it's important to realize that your partner is changing just as much as you are. In order for a relationship to evolve and thrive as each person in the relationship evolves, we need to continuously relearn who they are and who they are becoming throughout the relationship; to see them with fresh eyes and open curiosity each and every day.[6]

Though your relationship with your parents isn't the same as a romantic relationship, this notion that they are constantly changing still holds true. Who they were decades ago when you were a child is not who they are today. The same is true of you. You can't control how *they* change, but you can control how *you* change.

3. **Turn towards your parents.**

When things get hard, it's easy to turn away. There were more moments than I can count when I wanted to give up. What kept me going? I reminded myself of why I was doing this. I wanted to heal myself, my parents, and our relationship before I lost the chance to do so forever. With a strong why, we will persist.

And so I would take a breath, take time for myself, then return. At times, I'd return to the conversation minutes later. Other times, it might be days, weeks, or even months before I'd return for the next round of conversations.

As you embark on this brave journey, acknowledge that it takes courage to have these conversations, both from your end and from your par-

---

[6]  John Gottman, "The Art and Science of Love" (presentation, the Gottman Institute, Seattle, WA, October 20–21, 2018), https://www.gottman.com/couples/workshops/art-science-of-love/.

ents' end. It can feel scary, and that's okay. It might take weeks, months, or perhaps even years to get through a topic. That's okay too. There's no rush. Just remember the phrase, "for the sake of what?" For the sake of what does strengthening your relationship with your parents matter? For the sake of what does understanding and hearing their stories matter? And for the sake of what does being understood and having your story heard matter?

I hope you find the courage to continuously lean in and turn towards your parents. Using this book as a stepping stone, I hope you can start cultivating a stronger relationship and deeper bond with them. You matter. They matter. It matters.

## The Journey Ahead

Many people, not just those in the AAPI community but really of any race or ethnicity, never get a chance to hear their parents' stories. They never get a chance to intimately talk and learn about the lives of their parents. And sadly, their parents never get to experience the joy of sharing their stories. Those who do get the chance to engage their parents and hear about their lives (and share their own with their parents) realize how similar they really are. They learn that as human beings we desire much of the same thing: to love and be loved, to need and be needed, to belong and to matter.

As a Somatic Life Transformation and Mental Fitness Coach who works with AAPI women, I've realized that the relationship I have with my parents today, after many failed attempts at these conversations, is a rare one. But I promise you that it isn't because my parents are easier to talk to or more open-minded than other parents. Our relationship is different today because of my willingness to let go of my stories and my willingness to hear them and see them for who they are.

Many of my clients started out struggling to engage with their parents. They felt frustrated, misunderstood, guilty, and at times even resentful. A mere conversation with their parents left them feeling as if they'd just left a battlefield.

The output of our work together has helped my clients strengthen their mental fitness, their capacity to respond to life's challenges with a positive mindset rather than get upset and stressed. With stronger mental fitness, they're able to leave interactions with their parents feeling calm and collected instead of overwhelmed and stressed. Many have taken it a step further and managed to strengthen their relationships with their parents, learning stories about them that they never would've known had the conversations not happened.

Ida, a client of mine in her mid-50s, sent me this message, which touched my heart and further inspired me to write this book:

> I wanted to share that some of the ideas of talking to one's parents and asking historical questions about their experience helped create one of the best conversations I have ever had with my father . . . it wasn't a mansplaining or an "I'm telling you what to do" conversation . . . I asked questions about experiences and history, and he shared. If it weren't for that time last Saturday and listening to all those amazing people you had on the call, I would have missed out on this opportunity while my father is alive and somewhat healthy. I am going to drive more of these conversations for our family. Thank you from the bottom of my heart . . . all the way to the tippy top part of it too.

Remember: this is a journey, not a one-and-done process. You can continue to revisit these conversations and dive deeper with your parents. Just don't give up. And keep bringing the magic of empathy and compassion to your conversations.

Be persistent. Be consistent.

With love and light,

XO
*Amy*

P.S. Papa Yip asked me to share his advice with you as well: "There's nothing to be afraid of when talking to your parents. They raised you. They love you. Trust me, they do. When you embark on the conversations, try to bring lightness and humor. If they criticize you or judge you, say something in a playful tone like, 'I learned it from you!' or 'If I'm so bad at everything, then you must not be proud of anything I've done.' Then smile really big. If you relax, your parents will relax too."

# CONVERSATION TIP SHEET

These conversations can be hard. They can be triggering. I encourage you to revisit these tips ahead of each conversation to remind yourself of how best to approach them. I've also left you with some blank lines. After each conversation, come back here and add your own tips as you learn about what works and what doesn't when it comes to engaging your parents in these discussions.

◈ **Have the conversation in person or via video.**
Ideally, you want to be able to see your parents and have them see you. Nonverbal language speaks volumes more than verbal language. Plus, if you bring photos or other items as conversation starters, you can show them in person or over video.

◈ **Pick and choose questions from the list provided that allow the conversation to flow naturally.**
You don't have to ask all the questions, nor do you have to go in order as listed.

◈ **Use Google Translate if English isn't the primary language you converse with your parents in.**
That's what I used. It's not a perfect translation, but along with my second-grade level Chinese, it worked well enough that my parents understood what I was trying to communicate.

◈ **Your goal is to understand your parents, not to try to change them or their beliefs and worldviews.**

You may not agree with their beliefs, nor do you have to. They also don't have to agree with your beliefs.

◈ **Give your parents the greatest gift: listening.**

Approach the conversation with patience, openness, and curiosity to listen to their stories. Put yourself in their shoes, see the world from their eyes, and acknowledge that, just like you, they have a right to their beliefs and opinions.

◈ **Gently encourage them to share.**

If they don't say much, or if they go silent, then smile and say, "Tell me more" to encourage them to continue.

◈ **If at any point you strongly disagree, consider holding that thought and letting them finish before you share your perspective.**

Be sure you're sharing from a grounded, centered state rather than a triggered one.

◈ **If you feel triggered, call a time-out.**

This might mean taking a bathroom break if you're in person or telling them you have to call them back later if you're chatting virtually. During your time-out, take three deep breaths, jump up and down, and shake your body and the triggers away until you feel composed enough to return to the conversation, even if that's another day. (This is what helped me!)

◈ **Revisit these questions over multiple "dates" with your parents.**

No need to rush through all the questions in a single date.

◈ **Don't give up. Keep trying.**

◈ _____

_____

_____

_____

_____

**MYTH 1**

My Success Will Never
Be Good Enough
for My Parents

# My Story

## Dealing with Expectations and Misconceptions

No pain, no gain. For most of my life, I 100 percent believed this. No way could anyone possibly reach their full potential unless they put 100 percent into everything they did.

For me, 100 percent meant 15+ hour workdays plus working on weekends. It meant rolling out of bed at 5 a.m. to catch my shuttle despite not having fallen asleep until 1 a.m. from insomnia because work had been running through my mind all night. It meant drinking coffee every few hours, working at my desk during lunch breaks, and developing permanent eye bags. And it meant skipping friends' birthdays, forgetting to call my parents back, and needing to postpone date nights because there were things that "needed" to get done. After all, how else would I realize my dreams and achieve success in life?

This misconception of working hard and not deserving a break was ingrained in my psyche as a child. You see, my parents, particularly my dad, were your typical, traditional Chinese parents: strict, controlling through punishment, and subject to placing high standards and expectations on their children. Growing up, I witnessed these expectations and what it meant to work hard through their actions, day in and day out.

My mom worked two full-time jobs. She worked eighty hours across six days. Her only day off was Sunday. What did she do with her day off? Play chauffeur by taking us to and from the dreaded Sunday Chinese school, as well as doing the grocery shopping, cooking, cleaning, and laundry. Not much of a day off in my opinion. My dad worked long days at a Chinese restaurant. Neither one of my parents had free time, much less time to get a good night's rest.

There were telltale signs of their constant exhaustion. During visits to my grandma's house, as the rest of us would engage in food and conversation, my dad would nod off. In fact, he would fall asleep nearly anywhere, including while watching TV, reading his newspaper, and even sitting in the waiting room of the doctor's office. One time, he even fell asleep on the toilet. After an hour and a half of him being in there, we knocked on the door to check on him.

My mom was no better. She had purple bags under her eyes and would constantly ask me to step on her back or use my fists to pound on her sore, aching muscles. She was often impatient and had a short fuse.

My parents' actions taught me about hard work and success, but they also verbally taught me what it means.

"Amy, if you don't work hard, you will become homeless," my dad would threaten me.

"You must focus on your studies so you can do better than us," my mom would explain.

"Try to get into an Ivy League school," my dad would advise. "Become a doctor, lawyer, or engineer. That will set you up for success."

Though I tried to rebel and resist their teachings and expectations throughout my teens and young adulthood, I can't say I was successful. More often than not, I caved to their expectations.

## Rebelling Against College Decisions

"You are *not* permitted to attend NYU," my dad said to me. "This isn't even a college campus. It's right in the city!" He waved his hand around at the sky-scrapers around us as we followed the group of high school seniors and their parents who were also on the NYU campus tour.

"So? What's wrong with that?" I demanded, irritated that he was trying to control my life choices. Again.

"The city is dangerous! You'll be robbed, raped, or murdered! And you'll play too much. You won't focus on your studies. You cannot attend this school. You should go to Harvard or Yale or another Ivy League school instead. Those are prestigious."

Thank goodness nobody on the tour was Chinese. They couldn't understand the ridiculous things that my dad was saying.

"I'm paying for school myself," I retorted indignantly. "You can't tell me where I can and cannot go. I'm applying to NYU just because you're telling me I can't come here. And I'm not applying to any Ivy Leagues." I felt a lump in my throat and angry tears burning my eyes. I blinked my tears away, refusing to show my hurt. Without looking, I sensed my dad's eyes boring into me with disapproval.

I resented having to live by my parents' ridiculous rules and expectations. Throughout my teenage years I developed a deep longing for freedom of choice and independence. I wanted to pursue my own dreams, not theirs. I felt that by refusing to apply to an Ivy League school, I was standing my ground and living my own will.

But in the end, I caved.

My craving for my parents' approval, especially my dad's, was more powerful than my longing for independence. And so I applied to both Harvard University and the University of Pennsylvania. I persuaded myself into thinking that I was still rebelling because I intentionally submitted half-assed, shitty applications. As suspected, those half-assed, shitty applications didn't render an acceptance from either school. *Whew,* I sighed to myself. Not getting into either school relieved me of having to engage in a debate with my dad about whether I should attend an Ivy League. Though admittedly, deep down, a part of me still felt as if I had let him down.

I further attempted to rebel against my dad's expectations by applying to NYU despite his forbiddance to do so. I got in, but I chose not to attend. To be honest, I didn't really want to go to NYU to begin with. I just wanted to piss off my dad.

After all was said and done around NYU, Ivy Leagues, and piles of college applications and acceptance letters, I made my decision on where I was headed for college.

"I'm attending the University of Maryland," I announced to my parents.

"Good choice," my dad remarked. "NYU wouldn't have been good."

I clenched my jaw. I could tell he was glad I was staying close to home. Close to them. *Maybe I should've chosen NYU.* "Well I'm going to live on campus."

"What? Why? School is only thirty minutes from here. Why would you live on campus? There are parties and boys. You need to live at home," my dad demanded.

"No. I'm paying for school. I get to choose where I'm living, and I've decided that I'm going to live on campus. I'm already attending the University of Maryland instead of NYU. You should be happy enough about that." I stomped off, proud that I didn't surrender to their demands. At least not all of them.

## Declaring "Undecided" to Piss Them Off

The pattern of rebelling, resisting, but eventually caving continued into my college years. Be a prestigious doctor, lawyer, or engineer? No thanks.

"I want to study art," I announced to my parents.

"You cannot study art, Amy," my dad wagged his finger at me. "Artists die poor. It isn't until after they die that their artwork becomes valuable. Do you really want that for yourself? To be poor all your life?"

Like clockwork, I eventually relinquished my dream to study art, but again, I refused to fully comply. No way was I going to be a doctor, a lawyer, or an engineer. So I started freshman year at the University of Maryland with "undecided" as my degree of choice. This upset my parents. Actually, that's an understatement. It pissed them off.

"How could you not know what you want to study? You're eighteen! Who spends all this money to go to college undecided?" My dad was livid.

"I guess a stupid eighteen-year-old is who goes to college undecided," I said smugly, knowing I had hit his nerves.

I proudly stood my ground. Like a solid tree rooted to the ground, I refused to budge. That is until a month later when I caved under my parents' influence and declared my major.

"What operating system are you running?" my friend Paul asked me over the phone. It was the first semester of college, and my new computer had already completely crashed.

"Umm . . . what's an operating system?" I asked.

"Uhhh . . . really Amy? When you turn on your computer, what does it say? Windows 93? 98?"

"Oh!" I exclaimed. "It says 98!"

"Okay. I'll be right over with the startup disk."

Startup disk? I had no idea what he was talking about, but I trusted him. After all, Paul was a computer science major.

A few weeks later, Paul and I, along with a few other friends who all happened to be computer science majors, were enjoying late-night cookies and ice cream at the dining hall.

"This coding assignment is impossible. I'm going to have to pull an all-nighter again," Andy complained.

"Yeah, me too," Paul nodded in agreement.

I studied both of them and shook my head. "Guys," I started, "it can't be that bad. I mean, sure it's probably not easy, but you guys are always talking about how hard it is. I doubt it's that bad."

Five heads turned all together and surveyed me inquisitively. I leaned back, feeling uncomfortable with all their stares.

"You know, Amy, for a girl who doesn't know much about computers, you really shouldn't be talking," Paul retorted.

I pressed my lips together and tapped my chin as Paul's words surfaced an idea for me. Eyes sparkling, I exclaimed, "You're right! I don't know anything about computers. I bet they're going to be a big thing one day." Nodding my head in agreement with myself, I continued, "I really should learn more about these computers. I'm going to declare computer science as my major!"

And so I did. Perhaps I had unconsciously cracked under the pressure of my own parents wanting me to figure out what to do with my life. Or perhaps it was the influence of all my friends who were computer science majors at the will of their Asian immigrant parents. Regardless of the reason, I caved. I didn't even make it an entire semester as "undecided."

During the first semester of my freshman year, I elected to double major in computer science and communications. I later topped it off with a minor in Asian American studies and entrepreneurship.

As if two degrees and two minors weren't enough, I returned to school several times after that, first to get a masters in science, then to get my MBA. And after that I got not one, not two, but three coaching certifications. I suppose that resisting my parents' expectations to work hard and achieve never really worked out the way I planned.

## Fueling My Hyper-Achiever Bug for the Sake of Acceptance and Love

As I progressed in my career through several large companies, I eventually found myself at Google. But increasing job titles and salaries, and even the prestige of the company itself, didn't matter to me. I just wanted to be happy at my job. At least that's what I'd say aloud. I truly believed it too. But with the values I was raised with, I could never half-ass anything (except those Ivy League college applications). If I was going to do something, I would always put 100 percent into it or not do it at all. That hard work led to rapid promotions and salary increases over the course of my sixteen years in the corporate world.

These "successes" are what fueled my "achievement bug." And, if I'm being truly honest, what was most rewarding about these achievements was the feeling of love and acceptance from my parents after sharing my successes with them. Conversations would typically go something like this:

"It's the end of the year. Have you found out about your salary increase? Bonus? Promotion?"

"Yes. I got [insert the wins from that particular year]," I'd tell my parents.

"Wow! That's good!" they'd say to me.

The simple "Wow! That's good!" was like a hit of dopamine for me. My addiction to hearing their affirmations and feeling like I was good enough for them had started in elementary school. But the desire for approval became greater and greater over time, like a snowball accumulating in size as it rolls down a hill of snow. This fueled my endless years of working literally non-stop. I had to do more, achieve more, be able to brag more, just for that sweet hit of parental approval.

My work-hard mentality was further reinforced by the media and corporate work cultures. Phrases such as "I have so much on my plate at work," "I've been working ridiculous hours," and "I'm completely swamped at work" have become a bragging right of sorts—a Badge of Honor. We're not achieving enough unless we can boast about how busy and swamped we are.

Sucked into the vortex of these bragging rights, I was always busy. Always swamped. I wore my "Medal of Honor" with pride. I survived off caffeine, was Theraflu's best customer, and would mindlessly eat through boxes of cereal as I worked. Oftentimes I felt so exhausted that I'd fall asleep in the oddest of places, including my dentist's office in the middle of getting a cleaning. Insomnia was like a family member that I didn't want around but would always show up at the most annoying times, including the nights before big presentations and meetings.

Friends would say things to me like, "You're amazing, Amy. I don't know how you do what you do and get so much shit done" and "You're on a whole other level. There's everyone else's level of productivity and delivery, then there's Amy's."

Despite what other people said, despite how much I worked, despite being miles ahead of others, I still felt behind. There was always more to do; always more things on the list to check off. It's exactly as people call it: a hamster on a perpetual wheel.

## Hitting My Breaking Point

Perhaps it was because I was so caught in the midst of societal and parental expectations for reaching success, or perhaps I just didn't recognize what was happening to my own health. Or maybe I didn't believe it could happen to me at the young age of twenty-six.

On an otherwise typical Thursday morning, I awoke to my alarm going off. After hitting the snooze button a few times, I yawned, stretched, and finally dragged myself out of bed. I hated mornings; it always felt so hard to get out of bed. On this particular morning, it felt even harder to get up. As I stood, I noticed a slight dull ache around my right rib. I thought nothing of it and just continued my day.

As the day wore on, the pain increased. I ignored it. I was too busy with things I had to get done to worry about it. I popped a few ibuprofens to ease the discomfort, but by evening the pain had become excruciating. I popped a few more ibuprofens and lay on the floor of my apartment, curled up in a fetal position to ease the stabbing sensations. I couldn't pinpoint the source; it was all over. It was as if a little hedgehog had curled up and started rolling around in my insides, the full brunt of its sharp spines poking every square inch within me. With my work phone in one hand, I finished responding to a few more emails.

When the ibuprofen finally kicked in, I fell asleep on the floor, still in a fetal position. But once the painkiller wore off, I woke up to a stabbing on my insides that was so painful it made me whimper and my eyes tear up. I finally conceded that I needed to see a doctor. But it was 2 a.m. *Maybe I can make it until morning*, I thought. But a sharp stab on my insides, as if a Roman warrior were inside jabbing away with her sharp sword, changed my mind. I called a taxi to take me to the hospital.

The rest of the night was a blur. I was given an IV and morphine for the pain and passed out almost immediately. Nobody could tell me what was wrong. Even after X-rays, scans, multiple blood draws, and poking and prodding by doctors, the results showed that I seemed to be fine.

"How can there be nothing wrong?" I demanded. "I was in so much pain. There has to be something."

"There's nothing visibly wrong," the doctor reassured me before studying me for a moment. "How are your stress levels?"

"They're fine. Nothing I can't handle," I replied.

"I'm sure you can handle it," she said empathetically, "but this might just be your body's way of telling you that you need rest."

As she walked out, I muttered, more to myself than her, "I don't need rest. I'm fine."

This was the first of three hospitalizations. I didn't learn from my first trip. The second trip was no different. I refused to accept the doctor's advice to rest. You can say I was stubborn; that's probable. More likely, though, it was because my desire to achieve success was so deeply embedded in me that I didn't know any other way of being. And I was stubborn.

On my third hospital visit, my dad took me. He had stopped by my apartment to drop something off and saw my face, which was pale as a whitewashed wall.

"You don't look okay," he gasped as I opened the door for him.

"I'm fine," I whimpered. "It's just some pain. I'm okay."

"You're not."

After some back-and-forth, my dad insisted we go to the ER. Similar to the first two visits, I was placed on an IV, given painkillers, and was knocked out.

Again, they couldn't figure out what was wrong. When I awoke, feeling groggy with a head throb, the doctor told us that everything seemed normal and that I'd be released as soon as I felt ready to get up.

"There has to be something," my dad insisted. "She can't be in so much pain and there's nothing wrong."

"Daddy it's fine," I began, speaking in Cantonese to him. "The doctors just suck. This happens every time. They can't ever figure it out."

"What do you mean 'every time'?" his eyes got big.

"Oh I've had pain before and came to the ER. They can't ever figure it out. They say things are normal. That's why I told you I was fine and didn't want to come in."

My dad gazed at me quietly, then shook his head. Finally, after a long, uncomfortable silence, he sighed, "You work too hard. You have eye bags. You never sleep. You need to take care of your health. You need to rest. You need to have fun."

My jaw dropped. I nearly shouted, "What?!"

"You heard me. You don't have to work so hard. Enjoy life!" His eyes twinkled and he had a cheerful smile on his face.

"I don't understand," I whispered, thinking of all the all-nighters I'd pulled, the insomnia I'd endured, and the visits to the ER I'd made. *What was it all for?*

We had a long conversation after that. His words set me free from the unspoken assumption I had of what I believed were his expectations of me. His words gave me permission to let go of constantly gathering achievements to gain both his and my mom's approval.

My body sank into the bed I was still lying in. I listened to the beeping of the machines attached to me. The IV dripped slowly. Something let go within me. I was finally able to admit that maybe the doctors didn't suck. The pains were signals from my body telling me to rest. To chill the fuck out.

## Knowing, Yet Still Unable to Do Differently

This was the start of a new beginning for me. With the encouragement (and confusion) of my dad's comments to take care of my health and have fun, I was motivated to find a better way of living—to unlearn all the things I thought I knew about how the world works and what truly shapes happiness within us.

I started to question: *What is success anyway? And what is "enough"? When do we have "enough" salary? A high "enough" job title? A prestigious "enough" company name to put on our resume? When will we know we've reached the mountain top and that's "enough"?* It felt like once I reached one mountain top, it was time to find the next, bigger, higher, harder mountain to climb. All there seemed to be was a never-ending cycle of mountains.

For most of my life, I had been driven by a definition of success that didn't even reflect who I truly was, what I wanted, or what brought me joy. At the same time, I had no idea what I even wanted anymore.

I felt lost. I felt like the entire ground beneath me had dropped and I was floating with nothing to hold me. I never paused to think about why I was doing the things I was doing; I just did them because I thought I should; because I believed I was clear on my unspoken assumptions about what my parents expected of me. And I believed that if I succeeded and achieved "enough," I would get the love, acceptance, and recognition from my parents that I had craved for decades, especially from my dad.

Though my dad's words released me from the grips of believing that my worth to him was predicated on my successes, I continued to struggle to let go of this ingrained dependency on constant performance and achievement for self-respect and self-validation. As much as I questioned success and achievement, as much as I knew I needed to change, I just didn't know how to let go of my conditioned way of responding to life. In moments when I knew I should choose differently, working hard and checking things off my to-do list felt like a strong magnet drawing me in towards the deep, dark hole where the achievement monster lived. I'd cave and choose work over other choices. It was hard to let go.

## The Choices We Make

On February 8, 2019, Michael, a good friend and colleague of mine, was visiting New York City from San Francisco. We had plans for dinner and drinks, but work got busy. Then again, when was it not busy?

"I'm swamped," I texted him. "Need to bail tonight. Dinner + drinks when I'm in SF in 2 wks?"

I watched the dots going on my phone, indicating that Michael had read my text and was responding.

"Sure, no problem at all!" he responded. "See you in 2 wks! I'm excited. Don't work too hard! :)"

I put my phone down and returned back to what I was working on.

Five days later, I was sitting on a comfortable chair in a little nook of the Google NYC office with a small mobile desk in front of me. My belly growling uncontrollably, I removed the earbuds from my ears and set them down to go grab lunch. Just as I stood up, my phone rang.

*That's weird,* I thought when I saw who was on the other end of the line. "Hey James. What's going on?" I asked.

"Hi Amy, it's James," he said before trailing off.

I waited for him to say something more, but he remained silent. Something was clearly wrong.

"Hey Amy. I need to share some news with you. It's about Michael," he finally continued.

"Yeah?" My brows furrowed, waiting for more information.

"He had a heart attack this morning."

"Oh!" I gasped, falling back into my chair. "Is he in the hospital? Is he okay?" I stammered.

"Well no. No he's not. He passed away this morning, Amy. I'm sorry to have to be the bearer of this news. I wanted to let you know personally," James breathed. "I'm really sorry. I know you were close."

My heart stopped beating. The world stood still. I held the phone away not knowing what else to say or do.

Swallowing hard and feeling breathless, I stammered, "Um . . . Okay. Thanks. Thank you, James. I appreciate it." We hung up, and I sank into my chair, unable to move.

I had always heard about how each moment matters. Choices matter. We never know when someone will be gone, so we need to value them while they're here. I understood this concept in my head, but I never, not once, thought that I could lose someone by making the wrong choice. Nor did I think that I could miss a chance to say goodbye.

Had I made the choice to leave my work and see Michael, I would've had a chance to give him one last hug, have one last laugh together, share one last meal. I chose work, and I never got to see Michael again.

At that moment I made the decision that I would never choose work over people I care about ever again. Success was no longer about how much I worked or how much I accomplished and achieved. Success was being able to enjoy the life I created and the people in it while I still had the chance.

## A Journey to Self-Acceptance and Unconditional Love

I wish I could say that after losing Michael I changed my behavior immediately. I didn't. I knew in my head that I should prioritize people over my to-do lists, but just because it makes sense in the head doesn't mean it's easy to do. I really wanted to change, yet it was as if I were addicted to my unsustainable workaholic tendencies. I couldn't shake the notion of how I perceived what was worthy of my time (work and my to-dos) and what wasn't (relaxing, resting, playing). Anytime I felt a pull to do something enjoyable, the achievement monster would tug me back into the dark hole where my hamster wheel sat waiting for me to get back on.

"I'm frustrated," I sighed during a session with my executive coach. "I feel like I'm losing my freedom and independence. Greg wants me to travel less for work, to be home more, to not stay at the office so late, and to stop doing work when I'm home, but he doesn't realize how much is on my plate and how hard it is to just stop. I don't know how to balance all of it. Work, friends, him, my own well-being."

"What would make you feel like you had freedom and independence?" she asked calmly.

"Choice!" I exclaimed, throwing up my arms. "I want to have choices. I feel like I don't have any choices right now. He just wants it his way."

"Was being with Greg a choice?"

I bit my lower lip and glanced at the floor as I processed her question. "I guess so," I murmured. "Yeah, he was a choice."

"And what choices do you have right now?" she dug deeper.

I closed my eyes. "I guess I can choose to stay with him. Or I can choose to leave him."

She stayed silent, just holding space for me. I opened my eyes and tapped my forefinger on the table in front of me. Tap tap tap. My finger stopped and I gazed up at her. "I also have the choice of how much I travel, how much I work, when I work, and when I shut down. Just like I had a choice to shut down and go meet up with Michael for dinner, but I didn't." A single tear ran down my cheek as I choked out those last words.

"What do you want to choose?" she asked softly.

"I want to have balance. I want to shut down work by a certain time. I want to be able to have fun without feeling guilty. But it's hard. It's like I'm addicted to it. I think 'Oh I'll just respond to one more email' or 'Oh I'll just do this one last thing,' and I end up repeating this statement over and over until I've done ten emails or ten things. Next thing I know, it's late. It's like I can't get out of this loop."

We began exploring how I could have balance. How I could shut off and leave work at work. How I could have fun without the guilt.

Weeks bled into months, which bled into years, as I explored my inner self with my coach and through medicinal plant ceremonies. I dug deep into questions such as What is success to me? What matters to me? What is my relevance in this world?

Sustainable change takes more than having the knowledge and insight that we want to change. For example, everyone says they want to get healthier, and a majority of people know what it takes to get that way: eating well, moving, resting, and hydrating. We all have the knowledge and insights about what it takes to be healthier, so why is it that most of us still struggle to do so?

Change seems to elude us regardless of all the knowledge we have. This is because change requires transforming our embodied states. You see, our bodies are an essential place of change, learning, and transformation. Our muscles have memory, and our tissues have intelligence. From a young age, we developed embodied patterns and automatic tendencies to protect our safety, belonging, and dignity. We've been practicing these ways of being for so long that they've become hard to change. Despite the knowledge in our heads that we *want* to change, our default patterns kick in when we're under pressure because it's easy for our bodies to access.

To get off the hamster wheel and out of the grips of the achievement monster, I needed to let go of these decades-long, embodied patterns that I'd been practicing and replace them with a new practice. Though it's not an easy thing to do, it's not impossible. Anything learned can be unlearned.

When I finally gave myself permission to rest, I began literally high-fiving myself. I put myself on a "'no' diet" and would hug myself every time I said no. I even left my laptop at my office at the end of the day. If I fell off the wagon, and I did, I graciously forgave myself. *I'm unlearning a habit that I've been doing for decades upon decades*, I'd remind myself, then hop back on with my new practices.

And through it all, Greg stood by my side, cheering me on. He'd high-five me back when I'd tell him I let myself rest. Anytime I'd grumble, "I've done nothing today," he'd lovingly remind me that "Nobody does nothing. Maybe not everything we want to get done, but we always do things. So what did you do today?" And he'd always be there unplugging the router and turning off the lights when it was time to go to bed, forcing me to shut down.

After years of practicing and unlearning, how do I define success today? I define success as unconditional self-love. Success is not conditioned based on my performance or anything else, nor does it mean needing to earn love, work for love, or prove anything. Success is true, unconditional self-love.

What does unconditional self-love look like? Unconditional self-love looks like showing up as my authentic self. It means I can take off all the armor I've worn for most of my life (and boy that shit was heavy!) and just be me: playful, silly, curious, creative, and a bit awkward. It means telling my stories without a need to emphasize all the things I've achieved and bury parts that might feel "less than."

Unconditional self-love also looks like nurturing my body, this one vessel I have that does amazing things for me. By treating this vessel as not just a machine to carry me around but a sacred temple, I can rest, nourish myself, and connect with people I care about. When I'm able to do that, I feel greater joy, my relationships are deeper, and, ironically, my vessel is in a healthier state to do more and be more productive. Unconditional self-love has also allowed me to fall back in love with this vessel, regardless of how it looks on the outside.

And finally, unconditional self-love looks like prioritizing what truly matters to me rather than following the "shoulds" of others. Unconditional self-love is based not on how others have defined what should or shouldn't matter to me, but on what I really value. It means catching myself about to write another email and remembering the cost of that: waking up tired or not being present with my husband. My reward for intentionally choosing to close the lid of my laptop is being excited to get to bed so I can spend some time chatting and holding hands with my husband before drifting off to sleep.

Unlearning my beliefs that success and achievement are the only ways to gain my parents' approval and make them proud has been a tough journey. I know it's possible, though, because I'm there.

Many of us children of immigrant parents grew up believing that we must have a specific job title, own a specific car, or live in a particular neighborhood in order to be truly happy and accomplished. We believe it would bring honor and face for the family. Our parents' teachings have shaped our understanding of happiness and success. But I can tell you that everything that can be learned can be unlearned. Everything is a choice, including how we view success.

# *Mama & Papa Yip's Story*

**每人手上 有不同尺.**
*měi rén shǒu shàng yǒu bù tóng chǐ.*
Every person has a different measuring stick.

## Setting the scene

It's a warm day in May. The sky is still bright, and I can see it from the window in front of the writing desk I'm sitting at. I just got back to our Airbnb from dinner with my husband. Pizza. It is the cheapest and fastest thing we can get in the atrociously pricey Dubrovnik, Croatia, (where *Game of Thrones* was filmed!). I had rushed back, not wanting to miss my conversation with my parents.

And here they are, on my phone via WhatsApp video. They're both sitting at their kitchen table in the home I grew up in. The familiar aluminum foil covering the stove area is fresh. They must've just changed it. My parents have used aluminum foil since I was young. Apparently it keeps the stove free of oil splatters. My mom's right eye is all I can see in the video on my phone. I laugh. They're not the most technologically savvy people. My parents fuss about whether I've had dinner and what I ate before we settle into the meat of the conversation about success.

# Our Life Experiences Impact How We View Success

一百個人, 一百個性.

*yī bǎi gè rén, yī bǎi gè xìng.*

One hundred people, one hundred personalities.

"Our life experiences are no different than many other Asians in our generation," Papa Yip states matter-of-factly. "It's one of suffering. Back when we were growing up, there were many Asian countries that were poor. We grew up not having enough food to fill our belly and oftentimes would have to wonder when and where the next meal would arrive."

Mama Yip chimes in, "When I was a baby, our family was poor. My mother, your grandmother, had to sell her breast milk to buy rice for the whole family. So I had no breast milk to drink. I don't really remember this since I was a baby, but I was told that your great-grandmother would cook rice, then scoop the top layer of liquid, the rice milk, for me to drink. That's what I grew up on as a baby."

From a young age I remember Mama Yip's health being quite poor. Perhaps it had a lot to do with being raised on rice milk as a baby. She was sick a lot, yet she'd somehow power through and keep working despite being ill. I honestly don't know how she did it. I suppose she didn't really have a choice. Every hour she missed work was money lost. Our family couldn't afford that. My heart feels tender as I see Mama Yip through a new lens.

"I used to love apples when I had stronger teeth that could bite into them," Mama Yip smiles, showing two holes where her teeth are missing. "Especially when I was a young girl. But apples were only a special treat. One time, my dad brought an apple home. One apple split among six kids, but we were so elated to have even one-sixth of that apple. Those experiences of hunger and scarcity have become so ingrained in us," Mama Yip murmurs. "We remember them deeply in our hearts: the fear, the worry, the empty bellies. It motivated us to want to constantly do better and have more to avoid ever having to worry about where the next meal would come from."

My parents glance at each other in deep understanding.

Papa Yip turns his gaze towards me as he leans back in his chair and says, "That's why, for your mommy and I, our criteria for success has always been to have no worries. No financial worries. No health worries. Being able to afford the basic necessities of life, feed our kids, put a roof over our heads. And when our kids are sick, be able to take them to the doctors, buy medicine without wondering how we could afford it."

"We know what it's like to have nothing, not even your next meal," Mama Yip puts forth. "And we wanted things to be different for our daughters. We wanted you to never have these types of worries."

I feel warmth flood over my body as I peer into their eyes through my phone screen and choke back a tear.

## Our Perspectives of Success Are Limited by What We Know

活到老, 學到老.

*huó dào lǎo, xué dào lǎo.*

Live until old, learn until old.

"That's why we always insisted that our children become a doctor, lawyer, or engineer," Papa Yip states. "We knew those jobs provided a good future, high income, and stability. People will always need a doctor, lawyer, or engineer. We wanted safety and security for our daughters. That's all."

"I'm not a doctor, lawyer, or engineer," I point out. "What do you think about that?"

"I'd like to point out that I never cared if you were a doctor, lawyer, or engineer," Mama Yip protests. "I just wanted you girls to have financial stability. Decent job and no debt was good enough for me!"

I nod. It's true. Mama Yip was always laxer. It was Papa Yip who had pushed us. Even with Chinese school he demanded 100 percent. He'd make me stand against the kitchen wall reciting my speech for a Chinese school speech contest until I got through it with zero errors. Mama Yip would often argue with him, saying, "Chinese school doesn't matter for their future success in America." He wouldn't budge. It made me resent Chinese school.

"No, you aren't a doctor, lawyer, or engineer," Papa Yip agrees. "But you've had some impressive jobs at respected companies."

I close my eyes, then open them wide. I still see Papa and Mama Yip on my WhatsApp. I pinch myself. Nope. Not a dream. Papa Yip really did just acknowledge my achievements, albeit in a roundabout way. "Yeah? So you admit you were wrong?" I tease.

Papa Yip laughs as he shakes his head and says, "No! I'm never wrong." He points his finger and continues, "We had limited knowledge when our kids were growing up in the '80s and '90s. We didn't know what other good jobs existed outside of doctor, lawyer, engineer. And how could we possibly predict what jobs could exist in the future? Who would've guessed back in the '80s that one day there would be a company called Google with all kinds of unique jobs like the one our daughter got? Who would've ever predicted that one day books would be sold on-the-line and that company would turn into Amazon? These are things we couldn't have predicted."

My mind wanders to the moment I opened up the email from a Google recruiter asking if I'd be interested in a global marketing, communications, and engagement manager role on the Food Team at Google. I had to do a double take and even forwarded the message to a friend to confirm it was real. A marketing role to help people live happier and healthier lives through food? Who would've known such a role existed? I can't blame Papa Yip for not having guessed it, because I couldn't have imagined its existence myself.

"That's true, Daddy. You couldn't have predicted those things, but there were other well-paying career paths too," I argued. "Like acting or politics."

"When we first moved here, Amy, we thought it would be nearly impossible for Asians to break into politics or Hollywood," Mama Yip explains. "Hollywood was mostly White. American politics, same thing. It wasn't until recently that you started to see Asians in those fields."

*That's exactly why representation matters*, I think to myself, *and why the AAPI community as a whole needs to get out of the doctor–lawyer–engineer mentality and spread their wings into other fields.*

Papa Yip nods his head as if he read my mind. "Times are different," he says. "Opportunities are different. The US is different. Growing up in China and even living in British-owned Hong Kong, things like bank loans, social security, 401(k), and health insurance just didn't exist. Cash was king. That means you had to work and save for anything you wanted. No credit cards. No credit scores. What we knew and what we had access to decades ago impacted what we believed about success. Ours was a time of scarcity and fear. Times are different, society is different, so your perspective also has to be different."

Papa Yip sighs as he meets Mama Yip's eyes. "We are old. We don't know many things about how the world works today. It's hard for us to think differently because of how we grew up. But even if it's hard for us to think differently, the younger generations need to think differently. It's the only way to move our world in a positive direction."

I study my parents' faces, seeing the wrinkles at the corners of their mouths, the age in their eyes, the years of hard work across the creases in their foreheads. I can't help but wonder what their lives might've been like had they been born in different circumstances and not had to share a single apple among six kids. A heaviness sits in my belly like a cement block.

As he prepares to get on his soapbox, Papa Yip wags his pointer finger and nods his head up and down, an all-too-familiar pattern of his. "I do want to add though, while being a doctor, lawyer, or engineer isn't as important these days, we still believe school is important. School has always been an important foundation throughout China's history. Back when China was ruled by emperors, in order to work for the emperor and hold any sort of power, you needed an education. With greater knowledge, you learn to be a better human being; you learn about morals, life skills, like how to manage your finances and invest for the future. School increases your chance of success. It doesn't guarantee it. Your character also matters. But it's a starting point. So you must teach your own children to value education, Amy."

"Yes sir," I salute him with a grin.

## How We View Success Changes over Time

姜还是老的辣.

*jiāng hái shì lǎo de là.*

Aged ginger is stronger and more spicy.

Papa Yip gets up to heat some water in the kettle for Mama Yip. As he putters back to his chair at the kitchen table, his phone tips from its upright position and lands horizontally.

"Old man!" Mama Yip yelps loudly as if he were hundreds of feet away rather than five feet away. "Amy's upside down now. What's wrong with the phone?"

Cantonese is a harsh language. As a teenager, I was embarrassed by Mama Yip's voice. I would often be on the phone with a friend while she'd be saying something in the background. My friends would always think she was yelling at me. "No, she's not yelling at me. It's just how she talks," I'd have to explain.

Papa Yip sets the phone back upright, his finger in the camera of the phone as he does so. "Where were we?" he asks.

I remind him.

"Oh yes," he begins. "Our life experiences have changed. Our knowledge has changed. So with those changes, how we viewed success also changed."

Papa Yip surveys the kitchen. "We didn't have all this before. We came to the US in 1978 with a thousand seven hundred US dollars in our pockets. We had to make that money last as we established ourselves in the US. Rent, food, healthcare. Some of that money also had to be sent back to your grandparents in Hong Kong because they were taking care of your sisters while we were gone. And we needed to save money so we could bring your sisters to the US. Do you know all the things we had to save for?"

Though I have an idea of what that might entail, I shake my head to give Papa Yip the space to share.

"Okay. Then let me tell you," he replies. Lifting his hands, he counts off on his fingers as he lists out all the things they needed to save money for: "One, we needed a place big enough for four people to live in. We didn't have you yet, so your two sisters and your mommy and I. We couldn't all fit comfortably in the room your mommy and I were renting in our friend's house. So we needed to save to afford a bigger rent. Two, we needed to save enough for a car. Three, we needed to buy flights for your mommy to go back to Hong Kong and get your sisters. Do you know how expensive flights were back in the early 1980s?"

Papa Yip doesn't pause to let me respond.

"Nearly a thousand dollars for your mommy's roundtrip ticket to Hong Kong. Then another five hundred dollars each for your sisters' tickets. That's two thousand dollars! This was in the 1980s. Imagine how much that's worth today! Now put yourself in our shoes, with our circumstances. How would you define success?"

Without waiting for a response, Papa Yip answers his own question: "For us, the most important thing was to reunite with our daughters. Reunite and give them a good life in America."

I do a quick Google search for an inflation calculator and plug in $2,000 in 1980. Holy shit! That's the equivalent of over $7,000 today. They arrived in the US with only $1,700 in their pocket and somehow had to save more than that just to buy plane tickets! Jeez. My heart wrenches. My sisters were only seven and two when my parents left Hong Kong for the US. I can't imagine the agony of being separated from your two young children—the immense motivation to do anything and everything to reunite with them, counting down the days until you can hold them in your arms again.

Papa Yip gazes out the window, deep in thought as if the scenes from decades ago are slowly flitting in front of his eyes. He sighs loudly as if releasing all the years of pain. "We immigrated to the US with the help of a fellow in my tailoring community," he starts. "He had left for the US a few years prior and set up shop here. We stayed in contact, and he later helped your mommy and I get a green card to come to the US. In return, I was contractually obligated to work for him for three years."

Mama Yip's eyebrows narrow, and her head shakes back and forth like an angry lioness. She growls, "We appreciated his help, but he paid your daddy a measly three hundred dollars a month. Even forty years ago it was extremely low. And the worst part was that he didn't have any work for your daddy to do, but he wouldn't let your daddy get another job. Not even a part-time job to fill his empty hours." I could tell Mama Yip was not pleased. She's not one to hide her dislike of people or things.

"I often had no work," Papa Yip agrees. "During my breaks I used to frequent the pizza shop next to our tailor shop. The pizza shop owner would always ask me, 'Do you need a job? I will pay you three dollars an hour!' I was overjoyed at the thought of three dollars an hour. At forty hours a week that would be over four hundred eighty dollars a month! A lot more than the three hundred dollars I was making. But I was contractually obligated to the tailor shop owner. He refused to let me get another job. It was so frustrating. All I wanted to do was to make more money so I could reunite with my daughters. But he was making it impossible to do so."

Papa Yip pauses and gazes at me. A huge grin crosses his face. It's so big you can see all his teeth. I'm already prepared for a cheesy joke. And here it comes.

"Amy, back then you were not part of the plan yet! So we didn't save money for you."

Mama Yip rolls her eyes and shakes her head, typical of their relationship. I smirk, "But I was the best surprise for your plan!"

Papa Yip smiles and says, "The tailor shop owner and I eventually got into a disagreement. I told him how unfair he was being and told him I quit. Then I walked out. Thankfully, he didn't come after me to return to the job." Papa Yip's grin widens as he reminisces. "I ended up finding a job that paid me six dollars an hour. Can you imagine how happy I was?" he asks, throwing his hands up as if celebrating that moment. "From a measly two dollars an hour to six dollars an hour! And I only had to work six days a week instead of seven. You know what else? The sixth day was considered overtime. So I got paid nine dollars an hour. That was a lot of money for me. After paying taxes I took home about a thousand dollars a month. More than I had ever made."

"That time was good for us," Mama Yip beams. "Your daddy found a good job. And shortly after, I also got a better job. When we first arrived, I worked in housekeeping at the Ramada Hotel in Arlington, Virginia. It took me an hour and a half each way using public transportation. Then I got a job closer to home at a Chinese restaurant. It didn't pay me more, but I had a shorter commute. They fed me and gave us free housing. We were both able to bring in more money and save faster."

"Forty years ago, that's how your mommy and I defined success," Papa Yip explains. "Working hard. Making a bigger salary. Saving more money. Less overstretched when it came to finances. And finally being able to reunite with our kids and give them a good life. Over time, our life circumstances changed. We made more money and established ourselves. Our knowledge also changed. We learned that you can sell books on-the-line and turn it into Amazon. We realized that you can be a global marketer of the free food that's given away to employees at a company like Google." Papa Yip nods at me. "As our experiences and knowledge changed, so did our perspective on success. Now that we're older, it's time to enjoy life and all that hard work. To be happy with all that we have in the remaining years of our life."

The words "to be happy" linger in my thoughts. Are they truly happy? I see them doing the same thing day in and day out. Mama Yip still refuses to spend money on things she wants because they're not on sale. Papa Yip has constant aches and pains. During the pandemic, they were too afraid to leave their house. Perhaps it's my biased perspective, but I want to see them happy. In these last few years, how can I help them live a more joyful life?

One thing comes to mind: quality time with me; moments when I'm fully present, not distracted by my to-do lists, and listening with an open heart and patience. They often tell me they don't want to bother me, but I know they enjoy my presence. Even if I can't physically be with them, a phone call means the world to them. I make a mental note to call them at least once a week.

## A Strong Beginning Is Crucial to Later Success

良好的開端是成功的一半.

*liáng hǎo de kāi duān shì chéng gōng de yī bàn.*

A good beginning is half of the success.

The kettle whistles. Papa Yip gets up to pour Mama Yip her hot water. As he fills her white mug, a mug I custom-printed for Mother's Day with a photo of us all at McDonald's, Papa Yip notes, "There are phases in life. What is required for success evolves with those phases. The phase of life while you're young is when you must work hard because you still have energy. You're also probably still single. So this is the time to focus on your career. It's the initial investment you're making towards a better future."

Papa Yip returns back to the table and sets Mama Yip's mug down in front of her. "It's like planting a garden," he says, pointing out the window to their backyard. "Initially, you have to put in a lot of effort to set the foundation. You have to choose the right location, pick the type of plants, prepare the soil, plant the seeds, water the soil, and fertilize and weed around the garden. Then finally, after all the work, you get plants in bloom! When the plants bloom, you can harvest the fruits and vegetables to enjoy. Extra work at the front end allows you to reap the benefits later."

"So how come you always tell me to rest and not work so hard?" I inquire, curious about his constant reminders for me to rest and sleep.

"Okay. Let me be clear, Amy," Papa Yip says as he moves closer to the screen—so close that I only see his two eyes and his nose. I can tell he's trying to look me in the eye and explain something he deems to be extremely important. "When I say 'work hard,' I don't mean to put your health at risk. There's a fine line between working hard and overdoing it to the point of overexhaustion. Work hard, but don't kill yourself."

"But you and Mommy both never took breaks," I point out. "You always worked multiple jobs. You barely slept. You'd sleep talk, saying things like, 'Welcome to Hunan Express' or 'Fried rice and sesame chicken with a large coke.' You were always dreaming about work. That wasn't good for your health."

Papa Yip shakes his head as he explains, "Amy, working hard for survival like we did is not the same as working hard for things like titles, achievements, and luxuries. We had blue-collar jobs. Very different circumstances from many of today's Asians in America who are working to exhaustion in white-collar, salaried jobs. If we work an extra hour, what do we get? We get paid more. An extra hour of work equals extra money, which equals our family being able to move out of our two-bedroom, roach-infested apartment into a new-build, three-bedroom townhome that we own."

Papa Yip then asks rhetorically, "What do you get when you work extra hours in a white-collar, salaried job? You still get paid the same salary. Maybe you get bigger titles, promotions, people praising you for how wonderful and smart you are. But that is not worth your health. When I say to set the foundation while you're young, that means yes work hard, but not at the expense of your health."

"So when can you be happy?" I ask pointedly. "You said now is the time to be happy with all that you have. When did that start mattering?"

"We always had happy moments," Papa Yip starts, then pauses as he goes down memory lane. A large grin, like the Cheshire Cat from *Alice in Wonderland*, appears on his face. "My happiest memory was when we were living in the apartment. I'd come home from work and the three of you would run towards the door. Annie, the oldest, would be on one leg; Jenny, the middle, would be on the other leg; and you'd be in the middle, arms up wanting to be picked up. All of you would happily shout 'DiDi! DiDi! You're home!' That made me happy."

I smile, fondly remembering those days. I loved when Papa Yip came home and smothered my face with kisses.

"We had happy moments," Mama Yip chimes in. "We just didn't prioritize happiness and enjoying life until later. Much too late. Maybe it was after we retired, then happiness became increasingly more important."

"In truth, our biggest regret is working so hard," Papa Yip breathes. "Your mommy worked two jobs. I worked a part-time job on top of my full-time job. I think just one job each would have been enough. We might not have saved as much, but we would have enough to pay basic expenses with a little to go into savings each month. But at the time, we could only think from a survival mindset. We always worried about the 'what ifs.' So we gave up spending time with our children. We gave up playing more and enjoying life. We gave up relaxing and sleeping and taking care of our health. If I could go back, I wouldn't rush rush rush. I would be more intentional with my time. I would spend more time with my kids before they grew up and left. But that time is already gone."

Papa Yip's eyes glisten. He peers away and swipes at his face.

"You're in your forties now, Amy," Mama Yip speaks up. "You've worked hard, you're financially stable, it's time to start enjoying life more. Don't wait until you're older to be happy. You won't be able to enjoy life the same way. Look at us. We can't eat the foods we love anymore because of health issues, or like me, I'm missing my teeth! We can't walk the way we used to because of muscular and joint pains."

"So start to relax and enjoy life now," Papa Yip advises. "And by the time you're in your sixties, don't focus on trying to increase the money in your bank. If you want to eat something or buy something, just do it. Don't wait for later, because by the time later comes you might not be able to eat it. You might not be able to walk to it. You might not be able to wear it. You might not even be here. You might have a lot of money, but so what? If you can't enjoy it, then what's the point?"

As I process Papa Yip's words, I start to feel the day catching up to me. I gently rub my neck and lean back into my chair.

Papa Yip picks up the phone and studies my face before saying, "Okay, it's getting late there. You need to go relax and go to bed."

I nod. "Yes sir. Good night."

# My Reflections Post-Conversation

I hung up and stared out the window at the darkness that had overtaken the sky during the ninety minutes I had been chatting with my parents. I felt stunned as I silently absorbed my parents' words. It had been six years since my last hospitalization due to overworking, and it felt as if everything I had known and believed about success from my parents' early teachings had been blown up.

I breathed deeply as I started to piece things together. I sensed a profound connection to my parents and their story, a story that's probably familiar to many other Asian immigrant parents.

The word that stood out in my mind was "suffering." That's what many of our immigrant parents have experienced. War. Scarcity. Trauma. Things being taken away. These life experiences have made them focus on climbing the ladder—climbing for more, climbing to get better, and climbing in fear of falling back down to the land of scarcity, the place where lack of food, shelter, and freedom were commonplace.

Their stories are those of survival. Their traumas live in them and never really go away. The best my parents could do was try to teach me that I don't have to carry that trauma; I can live a different way. And perhaps the best thing I can do is ask them what they need from me—how I can help them—rather than always asking them for things.

For us children of immigrants, times are different. We have our basic needs of food, shelter, and clothing met. Unlike our parents, we don't live from a perspective of survival. We have the freedom to redefine success for ourselves in ways that our parents couldn't. At a finger's tap, we have access to as much information as we want. And with that knowledge, we all know that there's more to our world than doctors, lawyers, and engineers. In fact, new career paths and ways of working are sprouting up with each passing year. No longer do we have to physically be in an office. No longer do we have to work for one large company our entire lives. No longer do we have to put our roots down in one place. We have flexibility and choice that our parents didn't, and that gives us flexibility and choice in how we want to define success for ourselves.

I also recognize that our life perspectives change with age. My parents of today are not the same parents they were when I was a teenager. At a young age, they were fighting to just survive and support their children. Success for them meant money and stability. Now they're older and have that money and stability, yet they can't physically do the same things they used to. No longer can my dad swim, row boats, and ride a bike like he used to. No longer can my mom eat the same foods she used to enjoy, due to health issues.

Success for my parents has become about happiness and enjoying life. Enjoying life in their remaining years means taking more cruises and spending more time with their kids, things they gave up while they were younger.

I made a note in my calendar to call my parents every week no matter where I am physically. I know they enjoy these long conversations when I'm fully present with them, just listening to them. But these conversations have also provided me with a gift—a gift of connection to my parents, and a gift of freedom. My parents' words have freed me from working so hard and from feeling immense guilt when I take a break. They've given me permission to enjoy my life right now rather than waiting until later.

Perhaps the choice we can all make right now is to put ourselves in the shoes of our own elder, wiser selves. What would that version of you tell you about what living a meaningful, purposeful, successful life looks like? What matters? Who matters? What doesn't matter so much? How could you live your life today to make that possible?

# A Date with Your Parents

## PRE-CONVERSATION PERSONAL REFLECTION

### Overview

Success can be defined in many different ways, but it's up to you to choose the definition that fits you. As you explore how you define success, it's important to acknowledge the influences of the world around you on your thoughts, your beliefs, and your actions. These influential experiences might include where you grew up, the significant people in your life, your experiences related to your race and gender, the institutions that surround you, and more. By understanding how you've been shaped, you can start to let go of what no longer serves you to make space for a definition of success that's truly authentic to you.

### Instructions

1. Take some time to reflect on these questions and journal your answers to them:

   ◈ What gives me joy?

   ◈ What gives me meaning?

   ◈ What are my core values?[7]

---

[7] Visit https://amyyipcoaching.com/UnfinishedBusiness-Resources for a values worksheet and other book resources.

◈ When I was young, I wanted to be a ＿＿＿＿＿＿＿ when I grew up.

◈ Where did I learn about what success means? What was I taught about success? (Consider influential experiences or people such as caretakers, teachers, schools, institutions, or communities you were a part of.)

◈ What is the greatest accomplishment of my life?

◈ What are the most important parts of my life right now? Consider the following:

✦ Career

✦ Community (family, friends)

✦ Finance

✦ Fun and Recreation

✦ Health and Well-being

✦ Partner / Spouse / Significant Other

✦ Personal Growth

✦ Spirituality

◈ Why do those parts of my life matter?

◈ Moving forward, what do I want the most important parts of my life to be?

2. Take a look at what you've written. Now set a timer for five minutes and answer this prompt: "Success to me is . . ." Here are some tips:

◈ Write as if your life depended on writing as much as possible. Don't put your pen down! Fill the page!

◈ If you get stuck, keep writing the prompt "Success to me is" until other words flow out.

◈ Here's some inspiration if you're feeling stuck about where to begin:

✦ Success to me is finding my true calling.

✦ Success to me is being my own best friend.

✦ Success to me is celebrating all my wins, big or small.

✦ Success to me is leveraging my creative side.

✦ Success to me is trying something new despite my fear.

✦ Success to me is helping others.

✦ Success to me is a happy, healthy family.

✦ Success to me is making enough money.

◈ As you write, try to get increasingly detailed. For example, if you first write "Success to me is making enough money," the next thing you might write is "Success to me is making enough money to support my family."

3. Take a look at what you've written. Notice if anything stands out for you. You might even read it aloud to yourself to see how it feels. Pick out the key themes you're noticing and turn that into a succinct, one- or two-sentence summary of what success means to you.

How you define success may change over time. That's natural. The most important thing is that your definition of success is authentic to you; it's aligned with who you are and who you want to be, not how others have defined success for you.

## THE CONVERSATION

### Conversation Topic

How your parents define success and how this definition has shifted over time.

### Tips

These conversations can be hard, and potentially triggering. Priority number one is to take care of yourself. Remember to review the Conversation Tip Sheet on page 23 before your conversation.

### Conversation-Specific Suggestions

Just as the world has shaped your thoughts, your beliefs, and your actions, it has done the same with your parents. During this conversation, consider how the world has shaped your parents' thoughts, beliefs, and actions around success. If it feels right, bring your written definition of success to share with your parents.

If you have access to old mementos of your achievements (e.g., trophies, report cards, graduation hat, diploma) or your parents' achievements (e.g., certificates from promotions, their graduation photos, the key to their first home or car), bring them as a conversation starter. For example, you might say, "Remember the time I won this trophy? What did you think about it then? How about today?" or "I remember when you first bought this [car or home]. How did it feel to buy it?"

## Questions For Your Parents

### *Lighter Questions*

- ❖ When you were a child, what did you want to be when you grew up?

- ❖ What were your hobbies or special interests when you were a child? What did you like about them?

- ❖ What were your dreams as a teenager? What did you want to do with your life?

- ❖ What options did you consider when you were deciding on college or a career?

- ❖ Are you happy with the profession you chose? Why or why not?

- ❖ If money weren't a factor, what career would you have chosen? How come?

- ❖ How would you describe success in the workplace?

- ❖ What was the greatest accomplishment of your life?

- ❖ Where did you learn about what success is or isn't? Were there certain people? Certain experiences?

### *Deeper Questions*

- ❖ What does success in life mean to you?

- ❖ What do you believe are the metrics of success? How do you know when you're successful?

- ❖ Reflecting on your life and looking at where you are today, how successful do you believe you are? What makes you believe that?

*You might want to further dig into the different parts of their lives by asking the following:*

- ✦ What made you successful at work?
- ✦ At home?
- ✦ As a parent?
- ✦ As a partner / spouse?

◈ How has your definition of success changed over time?

◈ What gives you joy?

◈ What gives you meaning?

◈ What are the most important parts of your life? *You can use this list to guide your parent(s) if they're stuck:*

- ✦ Career
- ✦ Community (family, friends)
- ✦ Finance
- ✦ Fun and Recreation
- ✦ Health and Well-being
- ✦ Partner / Spouse / Significant Other
- ✦ Personal Growth
- ✦ Spirituality

◈ What regrets do you have? If there's one thing you could change in your life, what would it be?

◈ What mistake have you made that you never want me to make?

## POST-CONVERSATION CONTEMPLATION

After the conversation with your parents, contemplate and journal on the following:

◈ What new insights have you gained about

✦ who your parents are,

✦ what their definition of success is, and

✦ where they learned about success?

◈ How might you help your parents live more aligned with what gives them joy and meaning?

◈ What beliefs about success do you want to keep?

◈ What beliefs about success are you ready to let go of?

Using the new insights, go back to your own definition of success from the Pre-Conversation Personal Reflection.

◈ What changes do you want to make to your definition of success?

◈ How might you live a life more aligned with what gives you joy and meaning? If you don't know, how might you start to find out?

Mark your calendar to return to what you've written in a month, a year, or even years later, and see how that definition of success has evolved for you.

*It is better to fail in originality than to succeed in imitation.*
~ Herman Melville ~

# I've Failed My Parents by Not Marrying a Good Chinese Partner

# My Story

## Study Hard. Don't Date.
## Be a Good Chinese Girl.

"Who was that?" my dad asked after I hung up the phone.

"A friend," I stated.

"It was a boy."

"Yeah?"

"Why is he calling you?"

"Nothing."

"What does he want?"

"Nothing. We're just friends." I resisted answering his question despite the fact that all Mike wanted to know was what time we were meeting to play basketball.

Throughout middle school, I played basketball nearly every day, weather permitting, at the community outdoor courts. Boys would often call my house or come knocking on our door asking for me, which I'm sure gave my dad many heartaches. The good news for him was that they weren't calling or visiting because they wanted to date or kiss or anything like that. They just wanted to play basketball. The bad news for him was that they were still boys, and my dad remembers what boys in their preteen years are like.

My dad shook his head and wagged his forefinger as he started the same lecture again. "You have too many boys always calling and knocking on our door. Good Chinese girls don't have so many boys around. And good Chinese boys don't go calling and knocking on young Chinese girls' doors!"

"Okay," I responded with a resting bitch face. I had heard this same lecture one too many times.

"Amy!" my dad nearly shouted. "Boys will get you pregnant. No boyfriend. Only study. If you get pregnant, then no good Chinese boy will ever want you later. You will bring us shame! We will lose face. Don't ever do anything that would bring shame to the family."

"Okay! I'm going to study now then," I muttered as I walked towards my room. Basketball would have to wait until the next day when my dad was at work.

Throughout my teenage years, I heard the same lecture as if it were a bad song on repeat: "Study hard. Don't date. Be a good Chinese girl." Desperately wanting the song to stop playing, I succumbed to my dad's demands. So in middle school and most of high school I didn't date anyone. Sure, I had plenty of crushes, but my focus was on doing well in my academics, keeping the lectures at bay, and of course, making sure I didn't cause my parents to lose face. Though, truth be told, the video my ninth-grade sex ed teacher showed of a woman giving birth certainly helped persuade me to stay at arm's length from boys. I had no interest in an accidental pregnancy anytime soon.

## Not Good Enough for Our Daughter

"He looks like Mickey Mouse. Why would you date someone that looks like Mickey Mouse?" My dad stared at me, creases across his forehead. He was referring to my college boyfriend.

I had just returned home for a weekend visit from college and showed my parents a photo of my boyfriend and me. Ever since I'd left for college, they'd been pestering me about my dating life, probably because they were worried about what I was doing while living on campus away from the safety of their home and wanted to know what I was up to. After avoiding their questions for months, I finally gave in and shared that I was dating someone from a different college. The reaction I received upon showing them a photo of my boyfriend was less than welcoming.

"He's Chinese," I defended.

"We're happy that he's Chinese, but he's not good enough for you," my mom stated.

"You're the same height," my dad said, starting to list all the areas my boyfriend fell short.

"He's an inch taller," I argued.

"He's younger than you."

"By five months."

"He's attending a lousy college," my dad bellowed as he threw up his arms. "That's already an indicator of his future lack of potential."

A wave of fury crashed through me. All these years, I had internalized their words. I didn't date while I was younger, I found a Chinese boyfriend, yet none of that was enough for them. It felt as if nothing I did could ever meet their expectations and gain their approval. It was like I could never win.

I glared at my parents and growled under my breath, "I'm not going to let what you think impact my decisions." Little did I know, it still did.

Case in point, in an attempt to prove my parents wrong and piss them off, my relationship with "Mickey Mouse" lasted longer than it should have. When it finally ended, my parents were thrilled that I, in their words, "finally realized he wasn't good enough" for me. I didn't want to admit it at the time, but they were right. He was immature, jealous, and controlling, and he had a lot of growing up to do. I also got tired of always having to tutor him.

Patrick, the next Chinese boyfriend I brought home in my early twenties, didn't fare any better when it came to my parents' acceptance of him.

"He doesn't have a college degree?" my dad exclaimed. "Aiya." He shook his head in clear disapproval.

"He's still enrolled in college," I argued, which was the truth. What I didn't mention was that Patrick had told me he had no interest in finishing school and was considering dropping out.

"He's twenty-four!" my dad exclaimed. "He's older than you and still hasn't graduated college with just one degree. You've already finished with multiple degrees! He's clearly just failing at school."

"You said to date someone older and taller! He's older and taller!" I bellowed.

"He's taller, but he's not exactly good-looking," my mom inserts. "I don't understand why you like him. You're pretty. You're smart." She sighed heavily.

"It's like Beauty and the Beast," my dad agreed.

I felt a lump in my throat and blinked away the tears. *Will they ever like anyone I bring home?* I thought to myself. It seemed like no matter who I dated, they weren't happy. They were nice enough to the "Beast" in front of him, but they continued to remind me that I could do better.

During the two-and-a-half years I dated Patrick, I tried to prove to my parents that he was a great match for me, but our relationship didn't survive our constant fights about money. He had quit school, was barely making ends meet, and loved to gamble. I was heartbroken when it ended. At the time, I thought the throbbing tightness I felt in my chest was a result of the breakup. Reflecting now, I wonder if the hurt came from the fact that my parents were right, yet again. I felt as if I had failed. As if I'd always be the little girl that got it wrong.

During the months after the breakup, I was like a zombie, walking aimlessly about. I had no appetite, and my mind was a constant blur. Somehow my mom and I ended up on a road trip together from San Diego to Los Angeles. I don't even know how we ended up going on this trip together. What I do remember is that my mom wanted to be with me as I worked through my pain and hurt.

It was a beautiful San Diego morning on the second day of our road trip. I was lying in bed, still groggy from one too many cocktails the evening before. Eyes still shut, I grumbled as I tried to process the faint sound of sniffling I heard in the background. I finally mustered the energy to open my eyes. As I blinked to adjust to the sunlight streaming in through the windows, I saw my mom standing by the balcony door, hands in prayer position in front of her heart, head bowed, whispering words I could barely hear. The sniffles were coming from her. My heart jumped out of my chest with worry.

I bounded out of bed towards my mom. Placing one hand on her back I asked, "Mommy, what's wrong?"

She paused. Hands still in prayer, she opened her eyes and turned towards me. Tears shimmered in her eyes.

"What's wrong?" I breathed.

"I don't like seeing you so sad and upset Amy," my mom sniffled. "I just want you to be happy. I'm praying to Guanyin Pu Sa, the bodhisattva of compassion, to let you be happy."

My heart tightened as I looked into my mom's downturned eyes. I hated seeing the sadness and worry she felt because I couldn't get over some stupid guy and a failed relationship. Her love warmed the depths of my belly.

"I'll be okay, Mommy. I am okay."

She nodded, I held her shoulders, and in that moment I vowed to put a pause on my dating life. I didn't want to risk another heartbreak, especially if it would impact my mom like this. I never dated a Chinese guy again.

## All the Good Ones Are Disappearing!

As I headed into my late twenties, the barrage of questions from my parents increased.

"Are you dating? Any prospects?" they would ask.

"The older you get, the harder it'll be to find someone, Amy," my dad would comment. "All the good ones are already taken!"

"You're not getting younger," my mom would state. "Stop being so picky."

Wait a second. Me? Picky? Weren't *they* the ones who called my ex-boyfriends things like "Mickey Mouse" and the "Beast"? How did we go from "Don't date, just study" to "Stop being so picky"?

When I finally did start dating someone, my parents were still discontent.

"You too?" my dad nearly shouted, his mouth wide open in disbelief. My eldest sister had married a Korean guy, and my middle sister had been dating White guys consistently with no "good Chinese boy" on the horizon. I was their last hope for a good Chinese son-in-law. So when I told them I was dating a White guy, it was as if all their hopes and dreams had fallen into an abyss. "It's hard to connect with someone who's so different culturally," my dad tried to explain.

Back to swiping right. Swiping left. OkCupid, Tinder, Bumble, and everything in between. The whole process felt like job interviewing, except at least with job interviews there's a general timeline and you know where you're trying to go. Dating was more like hopping into a boat and sailing into the horizon with no sense of what the weather would be like, what the water conditions would be like, or where I was even headed.

Once I hit my early thirties, the comments became increasingly irritating.

"Good men won't want an old maid."

"Stop playing so much. Settle down and have grandkids for us."

I got so annoyed I retorted, "What race would you like your grandchild to be? Half Asian, half White? Half Asian, half Black? Or maybe full Asian, but a blend of Chinese with something else? I'll go find a man to impregnate me once you tell me what kind of grandchild you want."

They stopped badgering me about grandkids after that, but their jabbing at me about my marriage prospects continued.

"I'm going to pray to Guanyin Pu Sa that you will find a good man," my mom sighed.

## The Chinese Way

"Okay, so remember these rules," I began as I counted off on my fingers. "First, no shoes in the house. Take them off at the door. Second, eat everything my mom cooks, even if you don't want to, then compliment her cooking and say it's the best you've had, even if it isn't. But don't ever take the last of something on a plate. If my parents offer it to you, kindly decline and tell them to enjoy the last piece. They'll decline and insist you can have it, at which time you can accept it. Third, when dinner is over, offer to help. Maybe collect the dirty dishes or take out the trash. They'll never accept, but offering is a sign of respect and shows that you're considerate."

Greg's brows drew together, and his forehead creased as he looked at me quizzically and said, "You serious?"

After going through business school together, Greg and I lost touch for a few years before recently reconnecting and dating. I had told my parents about him and, despite Greg not being Chinese, they seemed to approve of him so far. He was taller than me, older than me, and a military guy, which, in my dad's words, "means he's disciplined and an honorable man." Plus we had met in business school so, "he must be smart and motivated," my dad had said approvingly. "Bring him home to visit," my mom requested.

And so here we were, visiting Maryland together and on our way to my parents' house for dinner. I was giving Greg a rundown of the "rules," which were completely new to him. His family is from Wisconsin and are classic Cheesehead Packers fans. Greg grew up in Arizona during the '80s when the population of Asians was less than 1 percent,[8] so his exposure to Asians and Asian culture was limited. The week before we took off for this trip, he had even practiced using chopsticks.

Pursing my lips, I sighed, "Yes. I'm serious. Oh, and no PDA with me in front of them. Like zero PDA."

"Okay. If you say so," Greg agreed. "But only because I love you," he winked. Greg has always been a good sport.

When we arrived at my parents' front door, I shoved a box of Chinese pineapple cakes into Greg's hands. "Give this to my parents," I whispered as the door opened. "Just do it."

My dad greeted us. Greg took off his shoes and handed the box to my dad who beamed, "Oh, you didn't have to. Thank you, Grace." I saw the big smile across my dad's face. He's always had a huge sweet tooth, so I knew he'd be enjoying those pineapple cakes later. One point for Greg!

"Grace?" Greg whispered to me, as my dad led us towards the kitchen.

---

[8]    "Arizona - Race and Hispanic Origin: 1860 to 1990," U. S. Census Bureau, internet release date September 13, 2002, accessed March 1, 2023, https://www2.census.gov/library/working-papers/2002/demo/pop-twps0056/table17.pdf.

"He can't pronounce your name," I explained. "And trust me. It's better than the nicknames he's given to my exes! Count that as a point for you."

That night, Greg ate everything served on the table. My mom even cooked a second round of food after asking, "Do you want more?" and Greg responded, "Sure!"

"He sure eats a lot!" she praised. Another point for Greg! My mom loves people who can eat.

My dad even commented, "You eat almost as much as I did when I was young. Close, but not as much." They ended the evening with promises for a future Chinese bun-eating competition. My dad inviting Greg over again? Score.

I later found out that Greg misunderstood what I meant by "eat everything my mom cooks." He thought he was supposed to keep saying yes when she asked if he wanted more, even if it meant she had to cook a second round of food.

"No babe," I explained. "You just have to eat what's on the table. You don't even have to finish it. Just try it all and say it's good."

That night, his belly hurt from overeating. But overall, the first meeting with my parents was a smashing success—even though he made a mess with his chopsticks, called my parents by their first names instead of Mr. and Mrs. Yip, and gave them bear hugs as we were walking out the door. Oops. I forgot to warn Greg that the "no PDA" rule was applicable to my parents as well. They just laughed awkwardly at Greg's hugs.

The pros of the night outweighed the cons, and my parents seemed content that I was finally dating someone. I suppose the fact that I was in my mid-thirties eased their pickiness. I also commended Greg for not questioning and just doing. Not his usual style. Unlike the Chinese way of never questioning, Greg grew up learning to question everything. Over time, he slowly learned about the Chinese way. Little did I know that this was the easy part of teaching Greg about how we did things. The harder parts were yet to come.

## Cultural Differences in Our Upbringings

"We were confused about what he was saying," my dad chuckled. "It sounded like, 'I want to be famous and powerful.'"

I gazed at Greg, who was sitting across from me on the couch. My parents were visiting us in New York and were recounting Greg's secret visit to them in Maryland a few months prior. He had asked for their permission to propose to me. "I practiced!" Greg exclaimed. "Amy, your sisters told me I was saying it right."

"We finally figured out what he was trying to say," my dad laughed, shaking his head. "Greg was trying to say that he loves our daughter very much and wanted our permission to propose to you."

"How'd you respond?" I leaned in with curiosity.

"I said he should be asking you!" my mom blurted in a no-nonsense tone. "This isn't the old-fashioned days of arranged marriages. It's not our choice if you marry him or not. You're the one that has to say yes."

I sank into the sofa, laughing so hard that my belly hurt.

"Then we opened a bottle of red wine and made a toast!" Papa Yip raised his arm with an imaginary glass in hand. "Our thirty-seven-year-old daughter is finally going to get married."

"Aiya lo yeh," my mom exclaimed.

"Aiya lo yeh," Greg mimicked.

Slapping Greg on his arm playfully, my mom shook her head and said, "That's not for you to say! That means 'old man.' Only I can say that, okay?"

"Okay, Mom!" Greg responded with a smile.

Greg and I were compatible in many ways. We both had a lust for life, love for adventure, and dedication to learning and growth. We both cared about our families and had a longing to make the world a better place. But the things that brought us together didn't override the struggles we had in understanding each other's life experiences—like the time at the New York Botanical Garden.

"Where's that flower from?"

I turned my head and saw an older White lady dressed in a gray, knee-length wool coat standing next to me and pointing to the water lily in front of her.

"It says Thailand," I responded, confused at how she missed the big bold letters on the sign.

"No," she bristled. "*Where* in Thailand?"

I paused, feeling a familiar storm building inside of me. After a long, deep breath I questioned, "Why would I know where it's from?"

"Well you're from Asia, aren't you?"

I clenched my jaw and said, "Asia is a big continent." Without waiting to hear her response, I stalked off to find Greg.

After I recounted the incident to him, he advised, "It was just an innocent question. Don't take it so personally."

I fumed. "You don't get it do you?"

He didn't.

He didn't understand why everyday, subtle, sometimes unintentional comments, like someone saying "Wow, your English is so good" or asking "where are you *really* from?" could trigger deeply embedded frustration and anger within me. Greg never had those questions asked of him.

He also didn't understand why it was so hard for me to say no, ask for my needs, and put myself ahead of others. Greg was taught to be independent and speak up, while I was taught to prioritize family and community and follow the rules. Putting myself first equated to being selfish.

And he didn't understand how my fears of disappointing my parents drove my addiction to achievement. It was near impossible for me to put down my work, get rest, and prioritize my health, even after I got hospitalized from exhaustion. Greg couldn't comprehend this because his parents never pushed him to achieve or criticized him for only getting an A and not an A+. They supported him in whatever endeavors he was interested in.

But these things. These were little things.

## For the Sake of Love

"I feel uncomfortable," I whispered to Greg. I could feel the eyes of strangers walking by boring into me. I gripped harder onto Greg's hands.

It was September 2017, the year Trump took office as president of the US. We were walking through a small town in Kansas during our cross-country road trip, a town where there probably weren't many Asians, judging by the looks I was getting. It made me uncomfortable.

"Why?" Greg questioned.

"Because of all the increased hate crimes towards Asians. I just don't want to be stared at."

"It looks safe here to me," he observed. "Middle America is one of the friendliest places in this country, Amy!"

I sighed, feeling a hollow darkness in my torso. I was tired of trying to explain to him the fear that sat in the depths of me. Every time I tried to communicate, I felt like I was talking to a wall. So I didn't bother trying to help him understand. I just let it go. But in the coming years, as the Asian hate crimes in America increased alongside the arrival of COVID-19, our arguments and my frustration around his lack of understanding also increased.

"I can't believe this happened," I gasped as I read the headlines on my phone.

Greg looked over at me from the driver's seat. "What happened?" he asked. It was March 2021, and we were driving through the mountains in Albania during a period of our nomadic life.

"There was a shooting in Atlanta and six Asian women massage workers were killed by this guy. The amount of violence happening in America right now towards Asians is horrifying."

"Is there any evidence it was racially motivated?" Greg inquired. "I saw that news. I don't think they know much about the killer's motive yet. We shouldn't jump to conclusions until there's actual evidence."

*There he goes with his rational thinking. Doesn't he understand that fear isn't rational? Clearly no. He doesn't get it.*

"There doesn't need to be evidence," I bellowed.

"What do you mean? Of course you have to have evidence before you start calling something a hate crime!"

"You just don't understand me!" I shouted. "You don't understand what Asians have been through in this country. The racism in this country. How much Asian history do you even know? The little paragraph in your high school history book? Do you know about the Chinese railroad workers? The Japanese internment camps? Vincent Chin's murder?"

"Who?"

"Exactly!" I seethed. "You don't know anything about the history of my people, of Asians in America. You don't know what it's been like for our ancestors and certainly not us right now. Maybe you should do your own research and learn a little since you're married to a Chinese woman!" Tears streamed down my red-hot face. I sobbed as anger, frustration, and sadness erupted out of me like a dormant volcano that had just come alive.

I spiraled down thoughts, wondering if life would've been easier had I just listened to my parents and married a "good Chinese boy" instead of this White Cheesehead from Arizona. *A good Chinese boy would get it without me having to explain everything. A good Chinese boy would understand my fears and frustrations without a debate.*

Greg stared out the front windshield. He was silent for what felt like an eternity. Then he grabbed my hands, glanced over at me, and said, "You're right. I don't understand. I don't know much about your history. But I love you, and I want to understand you. I promise I'll try to learn and understand if you'll be patient with me."

I gazed down at his hand holding mine. It reminded me of our wedding day, holding hands as we said our vows to always love each other and stand by each other. The life we'd created and the experiences we'd had since our wedding day came rushing through me. *Life may not always be easier with Greg, but life is certainly better with him.*

"Thank you," I sighed. I breathed deeply and felt a buzzing aliveness awaken within me as I said, "I will no longer stand for this. I was born in this country. My parents have lived here for decades. They've contributed to this country to make it a better place. My sisters and I have contributed to making it a better place. We all belong here."

"You do belong," he said softly, turning his head away from the road to smile at me with love twinkling in his eyes.

To Greg's credit, he kept his word. The very next day he had his nose buried in his Kindle, reading away at *The Making of Asian America: A History* by Erika Lee. Good thing he reads fast! That was a 560-page book. After finishing it, Greg asked me to join him in watching a five-hour PBS docuseries called *Asian Americans*.

Greg began to understand the context of why I am the way I am and why my parents are the way they are. We began to teach each other new ways of being. I taught him to be more attentive and mindful of others' needs, while he taught me to speak up for my own needs. I taught him to face his fears and go after his dreams, and he taught me how to prioritize my self-care.

He still doesn't always get it, but I've realized that it's okay if he doesn't. He's learned to listen, take in what he can, and figure out what he doesn't know. Same goes for me. And we're both better for it and better together. White guy from Arizona. Chinese gal from Maryland.

**羅拔青菜, 各有所爱.**
*luó bo qīng cài, gè yǒu suǒ ài.*
Every man loves to his own taste.

## Setting the Scene

It's a warm July afternoon. I'm sitting at a wooden desk in the spare room of our two-bedroom Airbnb in Porto, Portugal. I have my phone propped up against the wall as I gaze at my parents on the screen. It's still morning for them. My dad is preparing his Folgers instant coffee in the same mug he's used since before I was born. My mom is making toast in the toaster oven that has sat in the same position on the kitchen table for the last four decades.

As I wait for them to finish preparing breakfast, I pat my pregnant belly. I'm only ten weeks pregnant so there's no bump yet, but I've been feeling constantly drained. The first trimester has not been easy for me, particularly because Greg and I have yet to come to an agreement on our plans for where in the US to settle down before our baby's arrival. I haven't told my parents I'm pregnant yet either because I'm positive they'll lecture me. "How can you not know where you're going to settle down?" I hear them saying. "You have to start planning and stop playing!" I hate lying to them, though, so I'm grateful that their small talk today hasn't entailed asking me when I plan to end my nomadic life and return to the US to give them grandchildren. They've only asked whether I've had lunch and what I ate.

My parents finally bring their toast and coffee to the kitchen table and settle into their seats.

# Dating Back in Our Day

執子之手, 與子偕老.

*zhí zǐ zhī shǒu, yǔ zǐ xié lǎo.*

Hold hands with you, grow old with you.

"My father passed away when I was young," Papa Yip starts. "So he never taught me anything about dating. Nor did he share his opinion about what type of girl I should marry. The only thing he ever taught me was to be a good person, keep good people close, and keep bad people at arm's length."

"Your grandmother had opinions for your daddy though," Mama Yip chimes in.

"What did Grandmother teach you?" I inquire.

"Your grandmother insisted I marry a girl from Ningbo, the city she was from," Papa Yip shares. "She said that Ningbo girls are more reasonable." He breaks into a grin and raises his forefinger. "But my number one criteria was to *not* marry a Ningbo girl."

"How come?" I tilt my head curiously.

"Because Ningbo girls are hostile!" Papa Yip exclaims. "You should've seen how contentious your grandmother was when she argued with your grandfather. I got scared growing up by how she yelled at him. So I decided that I didn't want to marry a girl like your grandmother!" Papa Yip shrugs and turns to Mama Yip with a grin, "But I ended up with a girl from Ningbo anyway."

Mama Yip responds with an eye roll. My heart hums with joy. I love seeing them be playful together.

"Your grandmother also insisted that I not marry a Cantonese girl," Papa Yip notes. "She felt that their language was harsh and sounded awful."

"Didn't you date a Cantonese girl though? Are you saying that you were disobeying your own mother?" I tease.

Papa Yip smirks, "Yeah, my first girlfriend was Cantonese, but by then your grandmother didn't object. The girl was educated and skilled. Her family was well-off. They even had a maid." As he takes a sip of his coffee, a memory seems to float into his mind. He laughs as he shares, "Her family maid always called her 'Gau Siu Je.' My Cantonese wasn't so good at the time, so I thought her maid was calling her 'Miss Dog.' You see, 'gau' can mean 'dog,' and it can mean the number nine. She had to explain to me that the maid was calling her 'Miss Nine' not 'Miss Dog' because she was the ninth child in the family."

Mama Yip shakes her head at Papa Yip as she nibbles on her toast.

Papa Yip beams at the funny memory, then goes on. "Your grandmother didn't mind that she was Cantonese because the family was well-off. Her dad owned a pharmacy and her siblings taught at a college, which was a big deal back then. By then, your grandmother cared less about whether I dated someone from Ningbo or Canton. She just wanted me to marry a woman that cared about me and was concerned for my well-being. My girlfriend was very kind to me. She would bring cakes, and when I was sick, she would have her maid make me soup. So your grandmother liked her."

"What about your parents?" I nod towards Mama Yip.

"My parents didn't have as many opinions," Mama Yip replies. "They never mentioned anything about dating to me, and they seemed indifferent whether their children married someone from Ningbo, Canton, Shanghai, or from another province of China. I have always been old-fashioned, so they knew they didn't have to worry about me dating when I was too young or being irresponsible with a boy."

"They had an opinion about your sister though," Papa Yip reminds her.

"Oh yes!" Mama Yip remembers. "My younger sister was in her early twenties, and this guy was courting her. He had just returned to Hong Kong from New York. His hair was on the longer side, and they said he looked like a thug, so they didn't like him. But instead of saying they disapproved, they demanded a ten-thousand-dollar dowry. I forget if it was in Hong Kong dollars or US dollars, but it was a ridiculous amount. They thought the guy wouldn't be able to pay it, but he said okay. In the end they had to admit they just didn't like him."

"I had hair like that too," Papa Yip beams. "It was fashionable back then. Your mommy's parents never disapproved of me though. They liked me." He winks at Mama Yip.

*What's going on here? They must've drunk some happy juice this morning. They're so playful and silly today. Maybe they're finding joy in going down memory lane of their dating years.*

"Your daddy was very fashionable back then," Mama Yip says as she gazes at Papa Yip. "He wore custom-made shirts, skinny slacks, and boots."

"Not shabby like now," Papa Yip points to his T-shirt and ruffles his own hair. "Back then I had to look good to court the girls, but now I have a wife, so I don't have to look so good." Papa Yip pokes his elbow at Mama Yip.

I've seen many photos of my parents in their late teens and early twenties. They were both extremely dapper and, if I do say so myself, really good-looking. Papa Yip, up until recently, used all kinds of hair products and constantly kept a comb in his shirt pocket. Because, you know, how your hair looks matters.

"So how did you meet?" I lean towards the screen, interested to hear more of the juicy details.

"Your mommy's auntie catered the lunches and dinners for the tailor shop I worked at," Papa Yip explains. "Her auntie organized our first meeting at a local restaurant. Everyone attended. Mommy's auntie, Mommy's parents, my mother."

"They were all there for your first date?" My jaw drops. I can't imagine Greg's parents and my parents going on our first date with us.

"Of course," Mama Yip replies. "That's how things were. The two sides have to meet each other."

"And what did the two sides think?" I question, leaning further towards my phone screen as if that'd give me an answer quicker.

Mama Yip snickers, "Your grandfather said to me, 'He's decent enough for you, good enough.'"

"Your grandfather said to your mommy that she better hurry and marry me or she'd lose a treasure," Papa Yip says, pressing both eyes shut and grinning so big I can see all his teeth. "Back then your daddy was good-looking, polite, and hardworking, so of course they approved of me. Who wouldn't?"

"Yeah, and such a good temperament too, right?" Mama Yip comments sarcastically. Then she adds, "Your daddy actually did have a good temper back then. Better than now."

Papa Yip's smile doesn't fade as he says, "My mother didn't have much of an opinion, but I knew immediately that this Ningbo village girl was going to be my wife."

"Oh yeah, old man?" Mama Yip gives Papa Yip a once-over, unable to hold back her giggles.

"What'd you think when you first saw Daddy?" I ask.

"Of course she liked me!" Papa Yip jumps in.

"I thought, 'Oh what a handsome man!'" Mama Yip gushes with a hint of sarcasm. But I see the twinkle in her eyes.

The corners of Papa Yip's mouth quirk up as he says, "And your mommy delivered herself to me!" He peers at her. There's clearly some inside joke here that I'm not getting. "I took your mommy to Lai Yuen, an amusement park in Hong Kong, for a date. They had a haunted ride."

"It was scary!" Mama Yip interjects as she throws up her arms. "We passed this coffin and this person jumped out of it! So I got scared and jumped towards your daddy."

"And that's how your mommy delivered herself to me," Papa Yip proclaims with a wink. "Obviously, I had to take the opportunity with her jumping onto me. So I kissed her cheek, and I knew she was the one."

"Your daddy always joked that he would eventually marry me," Mama Yip beams.

"And so we did," Papa Yip notes. "Our wedding was the first big celebration in Hong Kong for both my family and your mommy's family. So my mother and your mommy's parents said that we have to do it right. And 'do it right' meant I had to spend a lot of money. Twenty tables, two hundred people, and the finest food and beverages."

"Your daddy didn't skimp," Mama Yip admits. "There were twenty bottles of brandy, even the whole fish dinner plate was adorned with expensive cured meats, and he had to pay my parents a dowry of three thousand Hong Kong dollars to marry me."

"In all, I spent twenty thousand Hong Kong dollars," Papa Yip exclaims. "In the '60s, that could buy you a decent apartment." He studies Mama Yip as he asks, "She was worth it though, wasn't she?"

I nod and give him my best toothy grin. "Without her," I say, "you wouldn't have your amazing daughters."

"Or our wonderful grandsons," Papa Yip adds.

I touch my belly and whisper to myself, "And maybe a granddaughter too." Greg and I don't know the gender of our baby; we had decided to let it be a surprise.

# Permanence of Marriage

生米做成熟飯.

*shēng mǐ zuò chéng shú fàn.*
Raw rice is now cooked to become cooked rice.

Papa Yip sips his coffee and takes on a more serious tone. "All we ever wanted for our daughters was for each of you to have a good, stable life. A happy marriage, financial security, and a healthy family. That's why we discouraged you from dating as a teenager. I read in the newspaper that your brain doesn't finish developing and fully mature until your mid-twenties. So you're more likely to make poor decisions that lead to negative long-term consequences. Like picking an incompatible husband or getting pregnant too young."

Papa Yip sits up straight and wags his finger at me. "Dating too young is also a distraction from focusing on your education and setting yourself up for future success. No parent wants that. When you finally have a child, you'll understand why we didn't want you to date before you finished college."

*Oh boy. If only they knew that I was going to be a mom sooner than they were anticipating. Even when this child arrives, I wonder if I'll ever understand their beliefs about not dating until after college.*

Greg's parents' perspectives were the opposite of my parents'. They often questioned why he wasn't dating anyone during his high school years. His mom even tried to set him up with her friend's daughter, but he was shy and always resisted.

"Your grandfather wasn't overprotective of your daddy at all," Mama Yip puts forth. "Yet your daddy is so protective of his own children."

"That's because I was a boy!" Papa Yip defends.

"And you are girls," Mama Yip finishes. "If you were sons he would say, 'Just go and do whatever you like.' But because you're girls, he's afraid you'll be tricked by boys."

"I know what boys are like!" Papa Yip professes.

I laugh as I shake my head. Greg makes similar comments about having a daughter. He often jokes, at least I think he's joking, that if we have a baby girl, he'll have to invest in a shotgun. *Maybe the reason Greg's parents were more lenient when it came to dating had more to do with the fact that he was a boy than because of our cultural upbringing,* I think to myself.

"I just wanted you girls to find a good partner," Papa Yip explains, cutting into my thoughts.

"Like a doctor, lawyer, or engineer?" I blurt out with a raised eyebrow.

Seeming to not notice my sarcasm, Papa Yip answers, "Yes. Those jobs are an indication that the person is skilled and ambitious. They're not easy fields to study. We just wanted to know that our daughters would be taken care of. Have a safe, secure future."

"I always wanted my daughters to be successful on their own," Mama Yip jumps in. "Not have to rely on a man to feel safe and secure."

I see Papa Yip glance at her from the corner of his eyes. "Well yes," he says, "but I still don't want your husbands freeloading off you. They need to be successful in their own right."

Mama and Papa Yip have often disagreed about their beliefs about a woman's role versus a man's role. Mama Yip is forward-thinking and in some ways a feminist. I want to dive into this gender topic another time, so I pivot our conversation: "So why did you always insist on us dating and marrying a Chinese boy?"

Papa Yip rests back into his chair. "Because culturally you're more similar, which makes it easier to understand each other. There's more in common with your upbringing, your thinking, your way of living. For example, debt versus debt-free. In Chinese culture we like to be debt-free. We don't like using credit cards. You don't spend what you don't have. Cash is king. In contrast, in America, you have to use credit cards to increase your credit score and take out loans to buy homes and cars and pay for school."

"Another example is marriage," Papa Yip continues. "Chinese believe that marriage is forever. Divorce is not a good event. There's even a saying, '寧教人打仔, 莫教人分妻 [*níng jiào rén dǎ zǐ, mò jiào rén fēn qī*],' which means 'I would rather teach a man to discipline a child than to teach a man to divorce his wife.' But in America, it seems that everyone is getting married today and divorcing tomorrow. They go into marriages dividing their money, having nuptials laid out. It's as if they're going into marriage assuming divorce is imminent. People just give up so easily on their marriage."

One of my Asian American clients surfaces in my mind. Her parents have similar beliefs about divorce as mine do. She struggles in her marriage. Both she and her husband are miserable, yet they're still together out of guilt and shame from their parents' pressures to make it work. They've been trying to make it work for over five years. They've gone to therapy. Their unhappiness is now having an impact on their young children. In my mind, only the couple knows what's truly in their hearts and what's best for them. The external world has limited perspective about what's happening behind the scenes.

"What if the couple truly is unhappy?" I wonder aloud.

"What's the source of unhappiness, and can they honestly say they've tried?" Papa Yip questions. "If there's abuse, that's an automatic divorce. If it's disagreements, then they have to really try before they give up. Chinese believe that marriage is permanent. It's like raw rice boiled to cooked rice: permanent. You cannot change it back to raw rice. That's why choosing the right partner is something to be treated with caution. It's why we didn't want you to be dating so young and making a mistake."

From my screen, I see Greg poking his head in the door of the room I'm in.

"Want to go out for dinner?" he asks.

I indicate that I'm chatting with my parents.

"Oh! Hi Mom and Dad!" He waves at my parents.

My parents lean towards their screen to get a better look at Greg. They're so far forward that all we can see are their eyes. "Hi Gray!" Papa Yip shouts loudly—you know, just to be sure Greg can hear him. At least "Gray" is an improvement on "Grace."

Before Greg leaves, my parents ask him how he's doing and what he's eaten. I do a lot of translating for them.

"You know why else we wanted our daughters to marry Chinese?" Papa Yip inquires after Greg leaves.

Before I can answer, he admits, "We wanted to be able to communicate with our son-in-law. Right now we can't understand our sons-in-law very well, and they can't really understand our broken English."

I fall back into my chair, a heavy pang of guilt in my belly forming like a black cement ball. My mother-in-law loves having conversations with me. We often chat for hours without Greg around. It's something my parents don't get the privilege to do with any of their sons-in-law. I gaze silently at my parents as I process what it must be like for them to need every word translated in conversations with their sons-in-law.

## Hopes and Dreams for Our Daughters' Marriages

人逢喜事精神爽.

*rén féng xǐ shì jīng shén shuǎng.*
A happy occasion gladdens the spirit.

"None of your daughters married Chinese," I say. "How do you feel about that?"

"At the end of the day, it's your choice who you marry," Mama Yip asserts. "You know I never cared as much as your daddy about what race or ethnicity you married. I always told you that you are the one that will be with your husband for the rest of your life. Not us. So as long as you're happy and your husband treats you well, then that's what matters to us most."

I feel a warm love enveloping me.

"We used to want you to marry Chinese, but that's not to say that Chinese people are better than others," Papa Yip clarifies. "No matter what race or ethnicity, there are always good people and bad people."

"It always feels like there's animosity between the Black and Asian communities," Mama Yip remarks. "But just the other day, your daddy and I were walking around the Rio Pond. We decided to go into the building to use the bathroom. There were two young Black men. It looked like they were in their early twenties. They were walking much faster than us two old people. So your daddy and I let them pass us. One of them pushed the door open and they walked in. Just as I was approaching, the door swung shut. The young man immediately turned around and pulled the door open as he apologized for not holding it open for us. Very polite."

Papa Yip adds, "Then there are Chinese shoving and pushing past each other to get through doors and onto buses. So Chinese aren't always better or more polite. We wanted you to marry Chinese—"

"*You* wanted your daughters to marry Chinese," Mama Yip interjects.

"Okay, I wanted you to marry Chinese," Papa Yip corrects himself, "because I thought there would be more compatibility. We wanted you to wait to start dating because you make better decisions once your brain is fully mature. When you turned thirty and still had not found a good husband, that's when we started to worry because we thought you'd be stuck with leftovers. It's like finding a job. When you start your job search, you're looking for the seven-figure job. If after some time you haven't landed it, then you might start considering the six-figure job. If you still can't land a job, you might just settle for whatever is available. We didn't want our daughters settling for the leftovers. We wanted you to have the best."

"And now?" I raise an eyebrow.

"You ended up finding a pretty decent leftover," Papa Yip winks and leans into the screen so I can visibly see his cheesy grin. "Our daughters are all in their forties and fifties now. So it's your choice now. As long as your husbands are fully committed to each of you, fully committed to care for you and treat you well, then we're happy."

"Learning to care for each other takes time though," Mama Yip notes. "Marriage, relationships, take time and effort. Even your daddy didn't always know how to care for me." She surveys Papa Yip. "Early in our marriage I got really sick with a high fever. I took the bus to see the doctor by myself. When I got home, I took the medication he prescribed and fell asleep. Your daddy called the apartment and the landlady picked up. She knocked on the door of my room, but I didn't hear it. I was so sick that I fell into a deep sleep. So the landlady thought I wasn't there. Later when I awoke and walked outside, she had a little scare. She squealed, 'You were at home the whole time?'"

Mama Yip chuckles. I laugh alongside her, imagining how freaked out the landlady must've been.

"That's how sick I was," Mama Yip continues. "But your daddy didn't think to go with me to the doctors or come home to care for me. Then months later, when your daddy got sick, I insisted on going with him. It's not safe to ride the bus alone when you're so sick and not thinking straight. After that, he started coming with me to the doctors. And when you girls were growing up, he always insisted on being the one to take you and be by your side."

Papa Yip nods and says, "Even learning how to argue, to cool down, to take ownership of your part in the argument, to call a time-out and talk when you're calm, are things that take time to learn in a marriage. That's why it's important to work hard in a relationship and not default to divorce. Marriage isn't easy."

Ain't that the truth. It's taken a lot of relationship workshops, courses, and practice for Greg and me to learn how to communicate and handle conflict positively. We still fall into our old patterns sometimes, but we're getting better each and every day.

"You remember your wedding day? My speech?" Papa Yip asks.

I nod. I remember the day clearly. It was a warm July evening in Spain.

Papa Yip had a big grin as he stood on the stage next to the swimming pool, mic in hand and wearing white slacks and a cream-colored vest over his white dress shirt. He had met Greg's gaze and smiled, "Gray, welcome to the family. I hand Amy to you to take care of now. Look around. See Amy's mommy? If you don't take care of Amy, her mommy will beat you up." Papa Yip held up a fist to show Greg what he meant. "And you see her two sisters? If you don't take care of Amy, they will beat you up. And you see all of Amy's friends here? If you don't take care of Amy, they will beat you up too. Right?" Papa Yip looked out at all the guests as they all pumped their fists and shouted, "Yes!" Laughter and cheer filled my ears.

"At the end of the day, that's all that matters," Papa Yip asserts. "That our sons-in-law take care of our daughters. If not, we'll beat them up." Papa Yip holds up both fists to indicate he's serious.

Mama Yip and I burst into laughter.

# My Reflections Post-Conversation

Over dinner, Greg and I chatted about the conversation I had with my parents. This led to a discussion about the similarities and differences between our parents' upbringing and what they instilled in us about dating and marriage.

"My dad never talked to me about dating or marriage," Greg explained. "And the only thing my mom mentioned was that I should find someone who's kind and good to children. The latter probably had more to do with the fact that she was a teacher. But neither of my parents ever told me that I had to date or marry someone who worked hard, was ambitious, or had potential for a secure future. Nor did they ever mention their preferences for ethnicity, race, height, or age."

As we chatted, it was interesting to discover how different our parents are. In contrast to my mom, Greg's mom encouraged him to talk to girls, go on dates, and attend his high school dances, but he was a shy kid. In the hope that she could help muster his courage, his mom even bribed him with money to ask a girl to his senior prom. It worked.

Perhaps the variances in Greg's and my upbringing around dating are because of our gender difference. Or maybe there's a cultural factor. My guess is, it's a combination of both.

The conversation with my parents has shifted me from resistance to acceptance. I used to resist my parents' beliefs. I wanted to change them. I thought they were wrong. What has unfolded for me is the acceptance that, while my parents recognize things are different today, they have been shaped by a traditional Chinese value system that has been handed down to them from generations before. Thousands of years have gone into the Chinese teachings of love, marriage, and family. I mean, just look at all the Chinese proverbs about dating and marriage; the expectations of permanency. It's no wonder our parents believe what they believe and that it's hard to let go of. These values are deeply ingrained and embedded into their tissues, their nervous systems, their entire being, making them difficult to unlearn. While I may not agree with my parents' values and beliefs, I can respect their ideas and honor the fact that unlearning something so deep isn't easy.

What I've also come to accept is that despite my dad's expectations being different from my mom's, the end state for both was the same: that I'm in a happy, healthy marriage. Even though I couldn't understand this growing up, now, by understanding the why behind their expectations, I'm able to see this.

I'm able to see that behind my dad's original dating requirements for me, like the guys' college major, success potential, or being Chinese, were his hopes that I could have a "happy ending." I still don't agree with his original requirements, but I do recognize that my own criteria of "Do we have fun together?" while dating guys like "Mickey Mouse" or the "Beast" were probably not the right factors to be focused on either. At that age, I didn't comprehend the importance of communication, kindness, commitment, encouragement, and appreciation in a long-term relationship, let alone a marriage. But I suppose, who really does at that age?

We don't have to agree with our parents, nor do we have to believe that they did all the right things. What's most important is that we are able to see that what our parents want for us is to be happy. And at the end of the day, I'd venture to guess that happiness is also what we want for ourselves.

# A Date with Your Parents

## PRE-CONVERSATION PERSONAL REFLECTION

### Overview

Dating, marriage, and, more broadly, romantic relationships, are challenging enough. But when parents start inserting their expectations and opinions onto us, their "shoulds" and "shouldn'ts" often muddy our awareness of what it is *we* truly want versus what it is *they* want. We lose sight of what matters to us in a romantic relationship versus what matters to them, and we fail to give and receive love and engage in romantic relationships without being hindered by what we learned about giving, receiving, and engaging in love. By understanding which beliefs are our own and which were never ours to begin with, we gain greater clarity about what we want out of relationships and are able to make better decisions about our partnerships.

### Instructions

1.  On a blank piece of paper, draw a horizontal line in the middle of the page. Starting as far back as you can remember, reflect on the highs and lows of your current or most recent romantic relationship. Mark the left end of the horizontal line with the start date of that relationship. Mark the right end of the horizontal line with the end date of that relationship or "present day" if this is a current relationship. Going across this timeline, place X marks above and below the horizontal line to highlight the highs and lows of your relationship.

The scale can be as high and low as you wish to define it. The horizontal line indicates the "neutral" zone. Write a couple of words / descriptions of the peaks and troughs (e.g., first date, big argument, got married, etc.). Consider these questions before you get started:

◈ What are the significant milestones / events in your relationship to date?

◈ What seemingly small event had a big impact on your relationship?

Use a line to connect all the X marks so you can visually see all the highs and lows through the life of your relationship.

2. Reflect on the following questions. Write down anything that comes to mind. There are no wrong answers.

◈ Imagine this relationship line belonged to someone else. How do you feel about that person or their relationship when you look at the relationship line?

◈ What underlying themes or insights emerge when you consider your relationship line?

◈ What beliefs and values do you notice reflected in your relationship?

◈ What do the following mean to you?

✦ Being in a successful relationship

✦ Getting married

✦ Getting divorced

◈ How is your parents' relationship similar to yours? Different from yours?

## THE CONVERSATION

### Conversation Topic

What dating was like for your parents in their youth, how that shaped their beliefs and perspectives about dating and marriage, and how those beliefs have evolved as the world around them has evolved.

### Tips

These conversations can be hard, and potentially triggering. Priority number one is to take care of yourself. Remember to review the Conversation Tip Sheet on page 23 before your conversation.

### Conversation-Specific Suggestions

Memories of romantic relationships can be triggering, especially when there's trauma or unresolved emotions involved. Go slowly and gently as you delve into your parents' past romantic experiences. You may want to have the conversation separately with each parent.

Bring reminders of happy relationship memories as conversation starters. These might be photos of their wedding day, their anniversary celebrations, or memorable moments of them together. You can also bring photos of your or your siblings' wedding days. If you don't have photos, you can bring a list of funny dating or relationship memories that you can laugh at together. For example, I talked to my parents about the first time I brought Greg home and he ate everything, as well as his attempts to speak Chinese and ask my parents for permission to propose to me.

## Questions For Your Parents

### *Lighter Questions*

❖ What was dating like in your day?

❖ How old were you when your parents allowed you to start dating?

❖ When was your first kiss?

❖ Who was your first date? What did you do?

❖ How did you meet my mom / dad?

❖ What was your wedding day like?

❖ How involved were your parents in your dating life? Your marriage? Did you ever feel they were interfering? Did you listen?

❖ What do you remember most about my [or insert name of sibling] wedding day?

❖ What qualities do you believe are most important in a partner? Why do you believe that?

### *Deeper Questions*

❖ When did you know that you wanted to marry mom / dad / [insert name]?

❖ What do you value about the relationship that you share with [insert name] now?

❖ What have you learned about marriage?

❖ When did you know you were in love?

❖ What does being in love mean to you?

- ◈ What are your views on marriage?

- ◈ Do you believe marriage can last forever? Why or why not?

- ◈ What are your beliefs about divorce? What would you think if your kids got a divorce?

- ◈ What are your views on marrying someone of a different cultural upbringing? Different religion?

- ◈ What advice do you have for me to have a successful romantic relationship?

- ◈ What were your hopes, dreams, and expectations of your children for their dating life and marriage as they were growing up? How have these hopes, dreams, and expectations evolved over the years?

## POST-CONVERSATION CONTEMPLATION

After the conversation with your parents, contemplate and journal on the following:

- ◈ What new insights have you gained about

  - ✦ who your parents are;
  - ✦ what their belief systems are around dating, marriage, and romantic relationships more broadly; and
  - ✦ how their upbringing and their own parents' expectations influenced their perspectives?

- ◈ How does what you've learned about your parents impact how you want to view their relationship with each other?

❖ Go back to your relationship line from Step 1 of the Pre-Conversation Personal Reflection. Consider or write down your answer to these questions:

    ✦ What beliefs about relationships and marriage did you inherit from your parents?

    ✦ What beliefs about relationships and marriage are your own?

    ✦ In what ways do you want to change your approach to relationships?

    ✦ What's the most courageous first step you can take towards doing so?

*A great marriage is not when the "perfect couple" comes together.*
*It is when an imperfect couple learns to enjoy their differences.*

~ Dave Meurer ~

# My Parents Must Not Love Me Because They Never Say It to Me

# My Story

## First Grade

"I love you honey! Have a great day at school!" I watched as Jamie, my best friend in first grade, was dropped off at school by her blonde-haired, blue-eyed, White mom, who blew Jamie kisses as Jamie walked towards me.

"Does your mom always say 'I love you' to you?" I asked.

Jamie tilted her head to one side as she gave me a quizzical look. "What do you mean, 'always'?"

"Umm . . ." I purse my lips, pondering how to ask the question without seeming silly or awkward. "I guess, how often does she say it to you?"

"I don't know," Jamie said with a shrug. Then she started counting off on her fingers: "In the morning when I wake up, when she takes me to school, when she picks me up from school, when she puts me to bed, and anytime I hurt myself too." She held up five fingers.

"Oh, okay," I muttered, trying to remember the last time my parents had said those words to me. No memory popped up. My heart flopped and I gulped back a tear as I wondered whether my parents loved me the way Jamie's mom loved her.

Growing up, I witnessed the parents of my Westernized friends, like Jamie, effortlessly saying "I love you" to their children. I would hear "I love you" thrown around on television shows and in movies. But within my household, these words were nonexistent. Instead, my parents would show their love through feeding my stomach. "Are you hungry? Eat!" I'd be told as my favorite dishes were shoved in front of me along with a bowl filled to the brim with rice.

Despite us living in significant scarcity, there was always an abundance of food on our table. My parents would make personal sacrifices to ensure their three daughters had plenty to eat. At the time, I didn't recognize any of this. I so badly wanted to hear "I love you" to confirm for myself that my parents truly loved me. I would often daydream about my parents saying it to me as they showered me with kisses (which also never happened). I could envision what it must feel like—the equivalent of floating on soft clouds in the sky. But in reality, there were no soft clouds. Only a sense of befuddlement. *Why is it so hard to just say three words?* I'd often wonder.

## The First "I Love You"

At the ripe age of fourteen, for no particular reason other than curiosity and a desire to bridge the gap between my Asianness and my Americanness, I decided to be courageous—to dip my toe in the water of this "I love you"-ness and solve this mysterious puzzle of getting my parents to finally express their love for me through these elusive words.

"I love you," I told my mom when she once handed me a plate of diced watermelon.

"Love what? No love. This watermelon is to help you maintain energy to study harder," she said to me in Cantonese as she placed the plate down and walked away.

Wow. Tough love.

As an extremely stubborn and persistent teenager, I refused to give up. For the next four years, I made it my mission to get my parents to say those three little words to me. I would try almost every day, with no luck from either parent. At most, I'd hear the three words, but with a "don't" stuck in the middle: "I don't love you." Their resistance to saying those words, they always explained, was because they felt that words, by themselves, were hollow.

Rejection got tiring and I almost gave up. But my stubbornness finally paid off.

"I love you, Mom."

"I don't love you."

"I love you, Mom."

"You're going to be late for school."

"Whose fault will that be? I'm not leaving until you tell me that you love me. I love you."

She paused, gazed at me, and sighed, "Okay okay okay. I love you. Now get to school."

Success! I felt such immense joy rushing through my body, for I had finally discovered how to hack the "I love you" puzzle with my parents. And it seemed so easy! The key to it was to hold hostage the thing they wanted most for me: to get a good education that would lead to a successful career. Why hadn't I thought of this sooner?

## Finding Leverage

Over the next two decades, I continued to uncover new ways to nudge an "I love you" out of my parents. It wasn't easy and took a lot of courage and persistence on my part.

"You're like a tree, Amy. A young, sixteen-year-old tree. You have to nourish the tree in order for it to grow big and healthy," my dad explained, encouraging me to eat my dinner.

"I'll eat," I started, peering at him with a mischievous smile as big as life itself. "I'll eat after you tell me you love me."

He gave me a once-over, then responded, "Eat your dinner. Nourish your tree."

"Nope. Not until you say you love me," I declared.

With a big sigh and a shake of his head to convince me, or perhaps to convince himself that he wasn't at choice and didn't like what was about to come, my dad finally relented. "Okay okay I love you, okay? Now eat."

This pattern of conversation continued for years. It was a multi-year no-no, a multi-decade initiative.

"Thanks for the burger, Daddy," I began. I glanced around the Marriott hotel bar where my dad worked. It was bustling with customers. I had been on my way to the airport to catch my flight back home to San Francisco, and the Marriott was on the way. I thought I'd stop by to see him since I had time to kill. Of course, as soon as I arrived, he ordered me food to make sure I didn't go hungry during my trip home.

"You're leaving? What time is your flight?" he asked as he poured a beer for a customer.

"Yup, I'm leaving," I said. "Flight's soon." I paused to catch his attention. When he looked up at me, I beamed, "Now give me a kiss and tell me you love me!"

He laughed and a silly grin appeared on his face. "No no no. You're going to be late and miss your flight. That'll be expensive if you miss it. You have to go!"

"Not leaving until you give me a kiss and say you love me!"

He shook his head, familiar with the routine. No longer did he have a straight face on, pretending not to like it. He smiled, kissed me on the cheek, and said, "I love you. Now don't miss your flight."

## My Own Inability to Express Love

Despite how much I craved my parents' outward expression of love for me, the impact of my upbringing was evident in my own inability to express love towards others, especially guys I dated.

"I love you Amy," Gary proclaimed as he stared into my eyes, a soft smile on his face that emphasized his dimple. Gary was my first boyfriend. I was sixteen; he was seventeen. We had just finished watching a Blockbuster movie at my house and I was walking him out the front door.

*We've only been dating for a month*, I thought to myself. *How on earth could he love me?* I fidgeted, feeling my heart pounding as if it were about to jump out of my chest and run out the front door. I glanced down at Gary's feet. *Dammit. He's blocking the door, my escape.*

Thoughts of how to respond shuffled through my mind as I tried to decide what to say next. I studied him, then forced a smile and said, "Umm. Thanks."

He paused. "Don't you have something else you want to say to me?"

I pursed my lips together, deciding whether I should lie or not. "Umm . . . Thank you very much?"

Gary peered at me quietly, then put a smile on his face and murmured, "Oh, okay. Umm . . . You're welcome. I'll see you later." He opened the door and left. As he walked to his car, I closed the door, locked it, then fell to the floor with a sigh. Our relationship didn't last much longer after that.

Gary wasn't the last guy I dated with whom I found it difficult to express my emotions. Into my late thirties, I dated "sweet" guys, including some who wrote poetry dedicated to me, some who surprised me with hand-made photo frames with our picture in it, and some who remembered that I love the Strawberry Passion cake from Cold Stone Creamery and would buy it for my birthday. Yes, they were "sweet," or so I was told by all my girlfriends. At the time, I didn't particularly think any of this was sweet; instead I thought, *He's so cheesy.*

Considering how much I enjoy romance novels and cheesy romantic comedies, it's surprising that I didn't appreciate these gestures of romance and love. Somehow, I couldn't find the courage to live in those romantic love stories myself. My ability to express love felt frozen and numb, as if to protect me like armor from the dangerous elements of life around me. That is, until a special someone named Greg, who eventually became my husband, came along and began chipping away at my protection.

## Love Languages

"What's your love language?" Greg asked me. We were lying in bed in my tiny shoebox of an apartment in Pacific Heights, a posh residential enclave of San Francisco. Greg and I were business school friends who had lost touch. We had recently reconnected and started to date. As a new couple, one of our favorite things to do was ask deep questions to try to get to know each other beyond the surface level.

"Love language?" I asked.

"Yeah. There's a book about it. Basically, people have preferences in how they express love and receive love. What's yours?"

"I don't know," I murmured, noticing a discomfort arising within me as my heartbeat increased and my fingers began to tingle. "What are yours?"

"Physical touch," Greg answered as he scooted over to where I was lying on the bed, wrapped his arm around me, and kissed my forehead.

"Oh. I don't think that's mine," I shared, unable to shake the desire to wriggle away from his hold on me. "What are the other ones?" I wasn't entirely bought into this love language thing. It felt kind of like one of those cheesy things marketed to women. I was surprised Greg would know about it and be interested in such a thing.

Greg rolled over to the nightstand to grab his phone and said, "I forget. Let's look it up."

Whew. I breathed out with a sigh when Greg let go of me to get his phone. Physical touch was definitely not my love language. It made me feel uncomfortable.

"Words of affirmation, acts of service, gifts, and quality time are the other four," Greg shared. He scooted back next to me so we could look at Gary Chapman's Five Love Languages site together.

As we read the descriptions, I couldn't help but analyze the information. "Acts of service" was how my parents expressed their love to me. I pictured my mom in front of the kitchen stove, cooking hot and sour soup. She'd make different batches for each of us: a spicier version for my eldest sister Annie, a sourer version for me, and a balanced version for my middle sister Jenny. I chuckled thinking of Little Red Riding Hood and the three bears. My dad was no different. He'd suffer through the chocolate flavor in the Neapolitan ice cream tub despite it being his least favorite so that I could enjoy my beloved strawberry flavor and my sisters could fight over their treasured vanilla.

Then there were the things I craved from my parents as a child: words of affirmation and gifts. I always wanted to hear that I was good enough, that they were proud of me, that my achievements were sufficient to meet their expectations. I never heard much of that, if any at all. Nor did I receive gifts that showed me my parents had paid any attention to what I wanted or wished for. Birthdays, Christmases, and Lunar New Years would always result in the same present: a lucky red envelope with cash, which would often then be collected to be put into my college savings account.

"So which of these do you think is your primary love language?" Greg asked, pulling me out of my thoughts. "Want to take the quiz?"

The results were surprising, and, at the same time, not surprising.[9] Physical touch was at the bottom of my list, while quality time was at the top.

Quality Time™ — 33%
Acts of Service™ — 27%
Words of Affirmation™ — 23%
Receiving Gifts™ — 13%
Physical Touch™ — 3%

Greg observed my 3 percent physical touch score, then nuzzled his face into my neck as he laughed, "Well, I guess we'll have to work on that, won't we?"

Almost instantly, my shoulders lifted as if they wanted to make space to pull my head in like a turtle does for protection. Something about phys-

---

9    Results of my "5 Love Languages" test from https://5lovelanguages.com/quizzes/love-language.

ical affection felt just as uncomfortable as expressing love through words. I wanted to hide.

## Carrying My Armor

After learning about love languages and our preferences, I couldn't help but shake the constant questions that arose in my mind. Why was it that I so deeply wanted my parents to say "I love you" to me if it wasn't my primary love language and was hard for me to do myself? Why was it that I so deeply wanted my parents' affection and touch towards each other and towards me when it felt uncomfortable for myself?

My thoughts took me to memories of July 24, 2009. I had just landed in San Francisco International Airport along with a few good friends and my parents. There was a buzzing energy in the air. We had all gathered in the Bay Area to celebrate my twenty-eighth birthday with a tour of Napa Valley. I was thrilled to finally get to see the legendary countryside with world-class wine and stunning scenery. It would also be my parents' first experience of wine country and wine tasting. All of that would be for the next day; this day, we were exploring the city.

"Let's go check in to our hotel, then we can grab food!" I shouted to the dozen or so friends gathered around the baggage claim carousel.

The sun was shining, and the weather was cool. We chose Hog Island Oyster Co., a seafood restaurant by the Ferry Building, to enjoy lunch and some white wine. Somehow, I persuaded my parents to have a glass too. They're both extreme lightweights. My dad's cheeks immediately flushed a bright red, and my mom started to laugh a lot. It made my heart sing with warmth to see them enjoy themselves.

After lunch we decided to walk around. As we waited at a crosswalk for the cable car to pass and the signal to change from a hand to a walking figure, I saw my parents gaze at each other and smile. The light changed, the signal indicated we could cross, and as we did so, my dad grabbed my mom's hand. It was the first time I vividly remember seeing them hold hands. My heart opened. My mom met my eyes. In that instant, she must've realized where they were and that I and all my friends were there witnessing their PDA because she immediately said, "Aiya!" and pulled her hand free from my dad's. Her cheeks turned pink as if embarrassed.

"Your dad's drunk and being stupid," she explained to me as if she needed an excuse for their affection towards one another.

Years later, I still remember that moment. It's been permanently imprinted in my memory, and it brings me joy to think about it. It also makes me yearn to have my parents show affection towards one another more often. And yet, I struggled to be affectionate with my own partner. For years I couldn't understand why until, one day, it just made sense: the heavy protective armor I'd been carrying all those years had kept me safe, but it had also prevented me from giving or receiving affection.

## Opening Up to the Many Ways of Expressing Love

I felt my body burning. It hurt to be in this fire. The flames roared a bright red, as bright as the desert sun beating down on the sand and as red as a dark cherry ready to be eaten. I curled up tighter in my fetal position, arms crossed, hugging myself, wishing this would end.

It was the second night of my five-day ayahuasca ceremony in Cusco, Peru. Ayahuasca is a psychoactive tea that originates from the Amazon region. Its name originates from the Quechua language and translates to "vine of the soul." I had come to try to find the answers in my soul, but this burning, painful fire experience wasn't the answer I was looking for. Then again, they do say that ayahuasca gives you what you need, not what you want.

*I don't get it*, I thought to myself. *Why does this hurt so much? Why am I in this fire? Why is my body burning? This is nothing like the ease of my first night.* Tonight felt painful. The visual experiences were powerful. The sensations were intense.

"God, please make this end," I cried. I had thought I was pretty resilient. I had thought I had a high tolerance for pain. But I'd never experienced anything like this before. It was like my entire soul was being burned to embers.

"Babe, it'll be okay." I opened up my eyes to see Greg kneeling next to me. I blinked, confused. He was back in Arizona with his family. He wasn't here in Peru with me.

"Why are you here? How did you get here?" I asked.

Ignoring my question, the image of Greg said, "Time will make it better." He then slowly moved his hand to my back. The pressure and touch comforted me. A part of me didn't want his help, or his affection. I wanted to tell him I was okay on my own. But his touch calmed the pain of the flames. The heat felt less intense.

"You'll be okay. This pain will pass with time," Greg continued as he began to gently rub my back. Lifting me into a sitting position, he sat behind me, and I let myself fall into his open arms. As I did, I felt my body soften and the armor fall away. I closed my eyes and received his love and affection.

It dawned on me that, up until this moment, I had never let anyone care for me, touch me, or hold me like that except for my mama. (For some reason, calling her "Mama" here feels right; she's my mama bear, and I'm her little cub.) Anytime I felt unwell, physically or emotionally, I would curl up in her arms, but I never permitted anybody else to hold me like that. Perhaps it was something I inherently learned from watching my parents or had heard people say about being strong. Needing hugs and physical touch just felt weak to me.

In that moment, through that ayahuasca experience, I realized that it takes more courage to let people in than to keep the armor on. I learned that hugs and affection are powerful, not a sign of weakness. And I recognized just how nice it feels to have physical touch with those you love.

In fact, as a mental fitness coach and mother myself now, I've learned just how critical physical touch is; it's essential for human survival. Babies require touch for physical and psychological development. In the absence of touch, babies can fail to thrive because their growth hormones are inhibited, and they can die as a result. Even into adulthood, the power of touch helps regulate sleep, support digestion, and build the immune system.[10] I was floored when I discovered this. And to think—somewhere I learned I needed to protect myself from touch, when the truth is that touch is actually critical to my life.

That night, my ayahuasca ceremony opened me up to new ways of expressing love. It reawakened the buzzing desire for affection and connection.

Though physical touch is still at the bottom of my love languages (I retook the test), I've discovered that I quite enjoy an affectionate hug, a kiss on my forehead, and cuddle puddles. After all, I'm a human being, and all humans require physical touch and connection. I've also begun to express love towards my parents in all five love languages, especially physical touch, because they're human beings too. Just like the rest of us, they need hugs and kisses, even if they won't admit it.

---

[10]   Shanley Pierce, "Touch Starvation Is a Consequence of COVID-19's Physical Distancing," Texas Medical Center, May 15, 2020, https://www.tmc.edu/news/2020/05/touch-starvation/.

# Mama & Papa Yip's Story

**父母疼囝長流水, 囝想父母樹尾風.**

*fù mǔ téng jiǎn cháng liú shuǐ, jiǎn xiǎng fù mǔ shù wěi fēng.*

The parental love for children is lengthy like the stream, but the children only think of the parents like the wind on the edge of a tree.

# Setting the Scene

It's Saturday morning after Thanksgiving, and my belly is bulging. Not from a Thanksgiving feast, but rather I am seven months pregnant. Greg and I had just moved back to Maryland after having lived nomadically for 557 days and were still settling into our new place. My mom was worried we were too busy getting our home settled and ready for the baby's arrival. So she did what any Chinese mom would do: she cooked bok choy vegetables, steamed fish, and some BBQ roast pork and carefully boxed it up in to-go containers. I had stopped by their house, a close ten minutes from my new apartment.

Of course when I arrived, my mom insisted I eat something first. And so, here I am, sitting in the kitchen as my mom makes scrambled eggs just the way I like them, with a lot of butter. I can smell the creamy melted butter as she cooks. My dad is making coffee. He scoops some instant coffee from a large, Costco-sized plastic container. I see the red label: Nescafé Taster's Choice Instant Coffee, House Blend. Every time I offer to get him a Keurig or a French press (my personal preference), he insists he likes the taste of the instant Nescafé better than any other modality of coffee. My guess is that, more than the taste, it is the convenience, cost, and the ease of cleaning (no grinds) that he truly likes.

With coffee in hand, my dad takes a seat at the corner of the table diagonal from me, where I have placed a photo album of pictures from my and my sister's childhood. My mom continues to putz around the kitchen, cleaning and preparing food as we begin our conversation about love.

# Action over Words

光說不能煮米飯.

*guāng shuō bu néng zhǔ mǐ fàn.*

Talk doesn't cook rice.

"The Asian way to express love, particularly among Chinese people, is about *showing* your love as opposed to *confessing* your love," Papa Yip starts. "I owned my tailor shop in Hong Kong, and I specialized in suits and fancy dresses for foreigners. They loved custom clothing. That was how you could make more money as a tailor. So I had a lot of interactions with foreigners. I still remember how husbands and wives would talk to each other when they came in."

He glances at Mama Yip, who is standing at the stove, then gets up and walks over to her, slowly putting an arm around her waist. I immediately know he's either about to make a joke or demonstrate something. He's only ever intimate with her in front of others if he's joking, trying to prove a point, or tipsy. And he's definitely not tipsy.

Papa Yip continues in a sing-song voice, "'Oh sweetheart' or 'oh honey.' That's what they would say to each other while in my shop." He pretends to give Mama Yip a kiss on her face to emphasize his message before sitting back in his chair. "It would hurt my ears just to listen to that. I wasn't used to it. What was this 'honey' or 'sweetheart' thing? A wife is a wife. A husband is a husband. We're not eating ice cream here."

I start to chuckle uncontrollably as I imagine what his facial expression must've looked like. Mama Yip always says that he's extra conservative and doesn't have a romantic bone in him.

Papa Yip smiles. "It's just not something Chinese people are used to. All this sweet talk. My parents never spoke to each other like that. They never spoke to me like that either. They didn't need to. I knew they loved me because of their *actions*. Both your grandmother and grandfather would always let me eat first. They would save the best things for me. They were also always aware of my likes or dislikes and kept me top of mind."

Papa Yip's words remind me of a story a friend told me about his mother-in-law. When she had asked her father how he learned what love is, he responded, "I learned through the actions of my grandmother. We were poor. She would save me a piece of fruit once a week for the Sabbath." The act of showing love through food spans many cultures, especially when food was scarce.

Papa Yip pauses and gazes away in thought. A smile spreads across his face as he recollects fond memories of my grandfather. He turns back to me and beams as he continues, "I remember this time when I was six. Your grandfather and I were walking home. He saw me longingly eye another street. He knew exactly why. Before I said a word, your grandfather turned down that street, a detour from our route home. I peered at him, and he just smiled at me knowingly. We stopped in front of my favorite food stall. I was so happy that I grinned from ear to ear! I was salivating just taking in all the treats, trying to decide which one to get. That's how your grandfather showed me love. He didn't need to tell me he loved me. He didn't need to sweet talk me. He showed it through actions. I knew he loved me."

Papa Yip pats his chest as he continues, "You place love in the heart, not in the mouth. It's easy to say things without really meaning it. How hard is it to tell everyone you love them? It's harder to actually do things, to show you love someone. Actions speak louder than words."

## It's a Cultural Thing

温故而知新.

*wēn gù ér zhī xīn.*
Studying the past helps to understand the present.

Mama Yip places a plate of scrambled eggs and cut-up pieces of avocado along with a pair of chopsticks in front of me, then takes a seat at the table across from me with her bowl of noodles.

Papa Yip sips his coffee, then slowly puts his mug down and explains, "Our upbringing, and the context of institutional and societal norms in

121

which we grew up, shaped our beliefs around love, including how it should be expressed. You have to remember that China's history is one of extreme poverty. Most people grew up with very little. That shaped societal norms of how you express love. The notion, historically, was that love is shown through money. Money was scarce. At the same time, money could help minimize suffering for those you love. So if you're willing to sacrifice and work hard for money to minimize worries about where the next meal comes from, this provides security and therefore shows your love."

"We didn't have time to say I love you or even think about that," Mama Yip notes in between slurps of her noodles. "The small village I grew up in—"

"Your mommy is a country girl," Papa Yip laughs as he cuts her off. "That's why I chose her!"

"Aiya," Mama Yip says, slapping his hand and shaking her head disapprovingly. She then turns back to me with her jaw set. Her shoulder-length

hair is pulled back behind her ears to avoid getting noodle particles in it. "I grew up in a small village. It was so small that whenever you were told to help on the farm, you *had* to help. If anyone didn't help, that could mean not having enough food for everyone in the village. So we'd all help with cultivating the soil, planting, weeding, and harvesting. Sometimes schools would even close because all the kids were needed on the farm."

Mama Yip sets down her chopsticks and leans back in her chair. "I remember this one night, the weather was really cold. The farmers needed everyone to help harvest before all the crops were lost to the cold. So we were all out there in the fields harvesting in the moonlight. We were there until nearly midnight. I got really sick afterwards with a throat infection and had to skip school. After I recovered from that night, my grandmother refused to let me return to school. The teachers came to our home to talk to my grandmother and try to persuade her to change her mind because I was really smart. They said I had a lot of potential. But my grandmother refused to change her mind: 'I pay for school, but she's always sick or having to work on the farm, so why am I going to waste this money?' And that was that. At age ten, I stopped going to school. I was really good at language skills and math, you know."

Mama Yip finishes proudly. I survey her with admiration and sadness and wonder what would've become of her had she been given the privilege of returning to school. Would she have become the famous clothing designer that she had aspired to be? I wish she could've had the same opportunities that she gifted me.

"That doesn't seem fair," I say aloud.

"Things aren't always fair, Amy," Papa Yip notes. "Many countries in Asia were in similar situations. There was barely enough food to feed all the mouths. Who had time to think about saying I love you or giving hugs and kisses? Everyone was exhausted from thinking about where the next meal would come from. Providing for your family was love."

"That's how we all grew up," Mama Yip explains. "And we were taught that actions are what matter. Not what you say. You *show* love; you don't need to say it out loud."

Mama Yip gathers our dirty dishes and brings them to the sink. Without a word, she begins washing the dishes, not even realizing that she's proving her point by showing her love through the action of cleaning up after us. As she focuses on the task in front of her, she continues, "We're not accustomed to saying I love you or giving hugs and holding hands. So it's hard for our generation to just start doing it."

She pauses before continuing her thoughts. "It isn't just hard for us older folks. It's not just about age or generation. You know our next-door neighbors? They're about your age, late thirties or early forties. They have two kids, maybe middle school or high school age. They came over to the US when they were much younger than your daddy and I when we came. One time, the wife started talking to me about how her daughter gets upset that they don't give her hugs or say I love you. I explained to them that American culture is different from Chinese culture. In America, people say things like that, and people hug and hold hands and kiss in public. I told her how my youngest daughter was born in the US and always forces us to say I love you and always wants to give us kisses."

Mama Yip turns off the faucet to glance back at me. I see the big grin she has on her face. "I shared how hard it was for us to get used to it, but step by step by step, we slowly adjusted to the way things are here. I encouraged her to try just a little because her kids are growing up here and they see this from other parents and families. She said she's trying, but it's hard. Her husband is even more conservative, though, and won't try at all."

"Change is just hard," Papa Yip agrees. "But it's not impossible. Today, if you go to China, the younger kids are more open to saying I love you or showing affection publicly. It might be less than what's normal for American culture though, but it's changing slowly. The old ways of being continue to be passed down from generation to generation, so the societal changes are slow."

I nod. It's not surprising that norms change faster in a country like America, where there is an abundance of cultures melting together and influencing one another, compared to a homogenous country like China, where there's less exposure to other ways of being.

Culture is a funny thing. One culture is not better or more right than another, despite what people might think. I've traveled around the world, and the different perspectives we have about one another's way of being always fascinates me. Traveling to France, I was warned that the French are unfriendly; yet what Americans consider to be friendliness is viewed by the French people as insincere. And while on a business school trip to Israel, I was cautioned that Israelis are straightforward and frank; while Americans see that as rude, it's just a different norm and way of living. I'm starting to see that maybe showing love through words is no better than showing love through actions and vice versa. They're just different expressions of it.

# Showing Our Children Love in Our Own Way

## 不养兒不知父母恩.

*bù yǎng er bu zhī fù mǔ ēn.*

To understand your parents' love, you must raise children yourself.

Mama Yip dries off the last dish and returns to her seat at the kitchen table. "You want some fruit?" I shake my head no. She gets up to prepare some strawberries anyway. As she opens the refrigerator she states, "Your daddy adores you kids so much it could burn a hole."

Shaking his head, Papa Yip responds, "Nope. I don't love any of you." He couldn't help but smile at his joke, and I couldn't resist my eye roll. He has always made unfunny jokes. "We've always loved our kids. We just show it in a different way. Do you remember when you were young, your uncle and auntie wanted to adopt you?"

I nod, remembering the first time meeting my uncle and aunt when I was about seven. My uncle wore a gray sweater vest over a white dress shirt and tie. My aunt had on an argyle pattern sweater and a matching gray, knee-length skirt. I recall feeling wowed by how nicely put together they were compared to my parents who only dressed up on special occasions. Most days, Papa Yip was in his green, collared, polo work shirt that had "Hunan Express" embroidered on the left breast, and Mama Yip would wear our old shirts that she refused to throw out or donate.

"They couldn't have their own kids," he continues. "They also knew we weren't financially well-off. So when you were born, they came to visit and wanted to adopt you. If we really didn't want you, if we really didn't love you, we would've just handed you over to them. We kept you. And we worked even harder to make sure you were taken care of. Love comes through actions, not words."

I vividly remember that visit. My uncle and aunt gave me so much praise and said how adorable I was. My parents had teased me by saying they were going to let my uncle and aunt adopt me. I cried uncontrollably and begged them not to give me away. Thankfully, they never did.

I raise an eyebrow and nod my head towards Papa Yip. "You threatened to throw me into the trash too."

Laughing at the memory, Papa Yip professes, "Words really don't mean much. Chinese people say things like that to their kids when they're being naughty. They say, 'If you don't start being good, I'm going to throw you away.' But they wouldn't really throw their kids away. Just like I wouldn't have really thrown you away. It's just words."

"I think I treated you kids a little differently than Daddy did," Mama Yip chimes in. "Unlike your daddy, I didn't have my parents around for much of my childhood. When I was born, communism had already taken over China. Your grandfather lost his job as a tailor. So when I was five, he left for Hong Kong to work for his uncle. Two years later, your grandmother took my younger sister with her to Hong Kong to reunite with your grandfather, leaving my older brother and me behind. She tried to come back for us a year later, but we had paperwork problems."

"It was your mommy's aunt's fault," Papa Yip cuts in. "She didn't have common sense. She lent this man two yuan, the equivalent of about five US dollars in the 1950s. She then went to him asking for the money back. This was the same man who they needed the help of to do their paperwork. Back in the 1950s, you needed to get approval to leave China. After she asked for the money back, he paid her and then refused to help with the paperwork. It was only two yuan. If you need a favor from someone, why would you ask for it back? She didn't think it through. So your mommy and your uncle couldn't get the approval to leave China."

"We had to wait another three years before we could leave," Mama Yip shares. "I was twelve by then. My uncle, your grandfather's brother, became chief of the district. He was able to sign the paperwork that gave us permission to leave China. So I was separated from your grandfather from age five until twelve, and from your grandmother from age seven until twelve. That's most of my childhood. My older brother and I were left behind and raised by your great-grandmother. When I finally got to Hong Kong, I had new younger brothers and sisters that I had never met before. And as soon as I arrived, I was put to work to help support my family and younger siblings."

I try to imagine myself in Mama Yip's shoes. I would've hated being separated from my parents for so long. I love my grandparents, but their love was different from the love my parents gave me. I can't help but wonder how things could've been different had Mama Yip's aunt not been so cheap. Mama Yip could have reunited with my grandparents sooner. I get frustrated just thinking about it.

Mama Yip continues, "At age twelve, I got an apprenticeship as a bead worker, decorating clothing, making twenty Hong Kong dollars a month, about four US dollars. Legally you weren't allowed to work until age sixteen. So if any inspectors came, we would have to all hide. I remember my first day going to work. I had to walk to the tram station and take a tram to get there. On my way home I got lost. I couldn't remember which road it was that we lived on off the main road. I'd start down a road that looked familiar and walk halfway, then think *This doesn't seem familiar* and turn around to backtrack. I walked back and forth a dozen times. I couldn't ask anybody for directions because I could only speak Shanghainese, not Cantonese, the primary dialect in Hong Kong. I finally found my way home. It was really dark and late. When I got to our building, I saw your grandmother standing outside waiting for me. She was worried sick. Her worry and waiting out there for me was her way of showing she cared about me.

"As much as I appreciated her worry, I didn't get much attention, affection, or love from my parents. We weren't close because they didn't really raise me. That's why I always wanted the opposite with my own kids. So raising you girls, I have always been more attentive, affectionate and told you when you do a good job."

Mama Yip eyes Papa Yip, then continues, "Your daddy was affectionate too when you were really young. It's just when you got a little older that he did it less, but he still showed you he loved you. He showed it in his own way. For example, he would always save the best food for you girls. Even now, he'll

127

buy you those expensive Chinese buns that you like, but for himself, he says it's too expensive. Or just the other day, he was upset by something you said to him, but when we went to the grocery store, he still thought of you and bought the roast duck because you like it. Or all the times you were sick, and he'd worry and immediately take time off to take you to see the doctor."

"No! I don't love you!" Papa Yip says sarcastically as he meets my gaze.

"Right. Sure you don't," Mama Yip smirks.

"You know you love me!" I give Papa Yip a cheesy toothy grin as he shakes his head no.

The six buns he brought me last week dance through my mind. He had refused to eat even one of them, using the excuse that he was full, but apparently he thought they were too expensive for him to eat. I file a note into my memory to go buy him some buns the next time I visit.

As I get up to give Papa Yip a kiss on his cheeks, I whisper, "Thank you for the buns last week, Daddy. They were delicious." His face fills with delight, and he chuckles as he receives the kiss—without pretending to push me away.

Mama Yip beams as she watches our interaction. "Even though your grandparents and I weren't close, I barely grew up with them, they didn't use words or show affection, I knew they cared about me. Your grandmother, worried sick, standing outside waiting for me, was her way of showing this."

"Until your mommy met me, she didn't know how to show affection and sweet talk either," Papa Yip laughs.

"Right. I learned it all because of you. What would the world be without you!" Mama Yip retorts.

I love watching their playfulness unfold. They don't do it often, but when it shows up, my soul fills with warmth and the buzzing of joy.

"Parents express their love in different ways," Papa Yip says, a little more serious now. "We worry for our children. We protect our children. Like there was a time that Jenny got bullied in school. A little girl pulled on her necklace and pushed her right in her chest. Jenny was still recovering from her heart surgery. So we went straight to the school and talked to the teacher. For us, love is about thought, action; taking care of your family with food, shelter, and clothing; providing your family with financial stability and physical safety. That's how we show you love.

"At the end of the day, in order to understand someone, you have to walk in their shoes. Until you've experienced what it's like to be a parent, you may not understand the love and sacrifice that parents go through for their children. Not all parents get it right. Many of them mess up. But most of them love their children. They just show it in different ways."

I gently pat my belly as my baby kicks. I guess I'll understand soon.

## Love Is a Two-Way Street

愛不是 佔有 而是欣賞.

*ài bù shì zhàn yǒu ér shì xīn shǎng.*
Love is not about possession. It's all about appreciation.

Mama Yip plops a bowl of strawberries down and returns to her seat at the table.

"So how do you want your kids to show you they love you?" I inquire.

Papa Yip pushes the bowl of strawberries my way and points to it, indicating I should eat some. "Your mommy and I have been listening to this one Chinese talk show a lot. It's about how us old people can better connect with our children. Let me tell you about this last episode we listened to."

I'm confused about where this is going, but I let him continue.

"It was about a Chinese woman our age. Her son had a baby and asked her to help. She agreed. She did all the cleaning, cooking, and took care of the baby. Her daughter-in-law never helped and would be quite demanding. She'd even say things like, 'I'm hungry. When's food going to be ready?' One day, the mom fell and broke her hip. Even then, the daughter-in-law didn't show any kindness. Instead she made comments about how useless her mother-in-law was that she couldn't even handle a bit of work without falling. The father-in-law got very angry. He said to the son, 'We could be retired now.

Instead we're helping you because you're our son. You don't show any gratitude. You treat your mom like a servant instead of a mom.' He took the mom home, and they stopped helping their son and their grandchild."

I grimace. Mama Yip is planning to come help me the first two months of my baby's life. I can't imagine ever treating her that way.

"You know," Papa Yip continues, "kids these days always expect their parents to understand them. They want their parents to change and show them love, to take care of them, but they don't consider how they can show their parents love and appreciation. How they can take care of their parents. They don't pause to consider how they might try to understand their parents' perspective or how hard change might be for us older folks. Unlearning decades of beliefs and changing our actions is a monumental task.

"True love is a two-way street. Mutual love requires both parties to understand the other side and love without expectation. Why is it that you want your parents to change and show you love through words when that's not how they inherently show love? Why can't the children change and try showing their parents love through actions?"

I nod, absorbing it all and reflecting on my own desires growing up to will my parents into changing and showing me love in the way I wanted, never recognizing how hard it must be for them to change decades of learned behavior. What would it look like for me to show my parents love in their love language, through action?

Papa Yip interrupts my thoughts. "Thoughtfulness and helping is how we show love to our own parents. Your maternal grandparents loved lobsters. So I used to buy lobsters and, after working a sixteen-hour day, I would drive to their home to drop the lobsters off to them. Now think about it. I was already barely sleeping, so I was using my sleeping time to treat your grandparents to lobsters. Not to mention, lobsters were expensive, our income was low, and we had three daughters to support. It wasn't easy to treat them to lobsters. But we knew it would make them happy. This is how we showed our love and appreciation to them."

He pauses and, as if he can read my mind, answers the question I've been pondering: what would children showing love to their parents through action look like?

"If you love your parents, then you need to express appreciation towards them. Let them know how lucky you are to have them in your life. Far too often, parents are taken for granted. It's easy to show appreciation. Call your parents more often. People these days seem to have more time for outsiders than their own family. If something or someone matters enough to you, you make time. So how important are your parents to you? If they matter to you, then make the time to call them. Ask them how their doctor's appointment went. Remember their favorite food and bring it to them."

Papa Yip's words take me back to sitting on the bed with Greg, discussing love languages. What dawns on me is that perhaps the distinction between how those of us who grew up in America express love versus how our parents express love is merely a difference in love languages. I wanted my parents to show me through words, while they preferred expressing love through actions. Similar to Greg and me, they're merely different preferences. Neither is right nor wrong.

"And if you want to hear 'I love you' or get them to be more affectionate, you have to show them how it's done," Mama Yip adds. "If it weren't for you continuously forcing us to say 'I love you,' we wouldn't be doing it now. We used to not be able to utter those words. 'I love you' felt stuck in our throats. After the first time we forced it out, the second time was easier to force out, and it got easier and easier. Now, we're able to say 'I love you' easily. You just have to be patient and practice with your parents.

"Your daddy might respond to you with 'I don't love you' or resist when you try to give him a hug or a kiss, but inside he loves it. He receives it and holds it in his heart."

"Why is that?" I inquire.

"Chinese men can't seem weak by saying they like that kind of thing," Papa Yip explains. "So they can't say that they like hearing 'I love you' or receiving hugs and kisses."

I wonder what my parent's love language *really* is. They say love is expressed through action, but perhaps it's because they've been conditioned to believe that.

"Well do *you* like hearing I love you?" I ask Papa Yip pointedly. "Do *you* like getting hugs and kisses from your daughters?"

"Of course he does!" Mama Yip exclaims.

"You heard your mommy," Papa Yip smiles. "You don't need me to admit it. You heard it already."

I grin, knowing he does like it. I'll just keep showing both of them love in all the ways I can.

# My Reflections Post-Conversation

I love you. Three simple words that can render so much affection, tenderness, and a sense of deep caring. Perhaps that's what makes it so difficult for traditional Asian parents to say these three, seemingly simple words. Verbally expressing feelings is not their strong suit.

To be even more precise, verbally expressing *affectionate* feelings is not their strong suit. This is not for a lack of love for their children. Rather, it's the belief in most Asian cultures that words can often be empty so love should be expressed through action. Though it's easy to cognitively understand this concept, love is an emotion, so processing the Asian way of expressing love is difficult to understand on an emotional level.

On my drive home from my parents' house, I took in their words and their actions. All of it. At some point in my parents' lives, they learned how to show up in the world and that saying "I love you" or showing affection publicly *isn't* acceptable, just as I had learned in America that expressing affection *is* acceptable. That's how all of us develop our worldviews. From a young age, we learn what's right and what's wrong. We develop beliefs and cultural norms that shape how we show up in the world.

As I processed, I was a mix of emotions. Joy and love; sad and speechless. I felt this buzzing in my core as if bees were in there humming and vibrating while in the process of shaking pollen of a flower. Three things bubbled up for me:

1. **My parents love me. Your parents love you. They do. They just show us in their own ways.**

   Sure, there's the occasional parent who can truly be categorized as a "poo-poo bad parent," as I grew up saying, but they're few and far between. The more likely scenario is this: Our parents are human beings. They did their best with what they knew. That means they made mistakes. They aren't perfect (but really, who is?). Their context was different from ours.

The way we like to receive and show love is shaped by our emotional and social experiences. This can include where we grew up; the significant people in our lives; cultural and religious influences; our class, race, and gender experiences; and our current landscapes or surrounding environments. Many of our parents grew up in environments where survival was the primary goal. Perhaps they were in war-torn countries such as Vietnam or poverty-ridden countries such as China. Maybe they were so desperate for a better life that they were willing to leave everything they knew behind to come to a country that mocked and looked down on them.

Putting yourself into the shoes of someone in these circumstances, what would love look like? If you grew up with nothing, what would you most want to give to your children? How would you show your love?

Our parents were shaped by their circumstances. Growing up, my mom would've wanted nothing more than to have her own apple to eat versus having to share a single apple with five other siblings. To her, giving her children their own apple, that's love. And that's how she shows it to her children. Your parents might also be giving you an apple as the symbol of their love.

2. **Even if they can't admit it, parents like to hear "I love you" and receive affection. They really do.**
Just about any human being likes to be hugged. They might not admit it, but they like it.

My dad has told me quite a few times about one of his favorite memories: coming home after work and having his three kids scramble towards the door, each one reaching towards him for a hug and shouting with glee "Daddy!" One daughter would grab one leg, another daughter would grab the other leg, and the youngest (that would be me) would stand in the middle reaching up to be held.

Physical touch is a universal language of love that we have all responded to since birth. Skin-to-skin contact between a baby and its mother is now recognized as a critical building block of infant brain development. Studies have shown that in infancy, physical contact helps improve sleep, reduce fussiness, and improve digestion, among a host of other benefits.[11]

Into adulthood, physical touch is equally beneficial to our health and well-being. In fact, our bodies are designed to respond to touch. We have a network of nerve fibers in our skin that are dedicated to detecting and emotionally responding to the touch of another human being. This helps us affirm relationships and connections to others, and even to ourselves. Through touch, we are able to sense support, love, and compassion. There is plenty of research around this topic.[12]

At the end of the day, we all like to hear and feel love and be cared for. Parents included. We just need to take the courageous step of showing our parents we love and care for them, knowing they might reject our first few attempts.

3. **We can't change our parents, but we can change ourselves.**
As human beings, we're constantly trying to blame and change other people. The truth of the matter is that you cannot control whether someone else changes. Only yourself. Yet we avoid changing ourselves because we know it's hard. So if it's hard for us to change, what makes us think it's easy for our parents to change and do things our way?

Instead of expecting our parents to change *their* ways, how might we start changing *ours*? We can start by thinking about the kind of relation-

11    Julie Greicius, "The Benefits of Touch for Babies, Parents," Stanford Medicine News Center, September 23, 2013, https://med.stanford.edu/news/all-news/2013/09/the-benefits-of-touch-for-babies-parents.html.
12    Nicole K. McNichols, "The Vital Importance of Human Touch," Psychology Today, August 3, 2021, https://www.psychologytoday.com/us/blog/everyone-top/202108/the-vital-importance-human-touch.

ship we'd like to have with them and focus on what we can do differently to help our relationship with them grow. This might look like showing your parents love in their love language rather than your own.

My dad appreciates acts of service and thoughtfulness. He often makes off-handed comments about moments when his kids "forget his requests." A few years ago, his tablet broke and he asked me to help him find a good computer and then teach him how to use it. I forgot for a few months. He knew I was busy, but it made him feel unloved and forgotten. I can see why. I'd feel the same. Once I realized this, I spent hours researching the most user-friendly device for him. Then I helped him set it up and taught him how to use it. My thinking of him more, calling him more, and remembering things he needs and asks for (or even things he doesn't directly ask for) makes him feel loved and strengthens our connection. So today, I serve as his on-demand tech support.

Change is hard. Relationships are hard. Relationships with parents are REALLY hard. Expect to fail at times. Expect to feel angry or hurt (or both) at times. I surely did and still do sometimes.

Working on a loving relationship with my parents has probably been one of the hardest things I've done. It took years of my willingness to get rejected, denied, and lectured. In fact, writing this book and interviewing my parents often triggered anger and hurt in me. I refused to give up though.

I continue to tell my parents I love them, I continue to give them hugs, and I continue to show them love in their own love language as well. By modeling the kind of relationship I'd like to have, I've been rewarded with a more profound connection with my parents. We've truly begun to grow closer.

And my parents were right. I had my first child in the midst of writing this book. Now, walking in the shoes of being a parent, I understand the love a parent has for their child.

# A Date with Your Parents

## PRE-CONVERSATION PERSONAL REFLECTION

### Overview

At some point in our lives, we learned about what love is and how to express it in the world. For many of us in the AAPI community, we've learned to suppress certain ways of expressing love. In particular, we've learned to minimize the value of verbal expressions of love. We've also muted our ability to express love through physical touch and affection, despite the fact that touch is vital for our well-being and is an essential element to human survival. By understanding your own stories and patterns around love and expressions of love, you will have greater choice in how you want to show up in your relationships to give and receive love.

### Instructions

1.  If you don't know your own love language, you can take the same test I took at https://5lovelanguages.com.

2.  Take some time to reflect on these questions and journal your answers to them:

    ◈ What is my fondest memory growing up? What is my most treasured memory as an adult?

    ◈ What roles do love and affection play in my life?

◈ How close and warm is my family? How do we express love towards one another?

◈ When was the last time I told someone "I love you"? Who was it? What was the context? How did I feel about it?

◈ When was the last time I showed someone physical affection? Who was it? What was the context? How did I feel about it?

◈ What are my beliefs about love and the expression of love towards others? Where did I learn these beliefs?

◈ How easy is it for me to communicate to others how I want to receive love and affection? Do I do this often or expect them to figure it out?

◈ How do I express love towards others (family, partner, kids, friends, others)? What feels natural and easy to do? What feels like a learning edge for me?

3.  Review what you've written. What are the benefits of your stories and patterns around love and expressions of love? What are the costs?

## THE CONVERSATION

## Conversation Topic

Where your parents learned about love, and how that has shaped their perspectives about how to express and receive love.

## Tips

These conversations can be hard, and potentially triggering. Priority number one is to take care of yourself. Remember to review the Conversation Tip Sheet on page 23 before your conversation.

## Conversation-Specific Suggestions

Make this Date with Your Parents a special occasion. Create an environment that conjures up fond memories and appreciation for one another. If possible, you might want to bring photos of happy memories when you were younger and start the conversation by talking about those times. Alternatively, you can bring a list of memories that you can talk about verbally without the photos. Share memories with your parents that show what you truly appreciate or admire about them. This helps set the tone for a loving and appreciative conversation about love.

## Questions For Your Parents

### *Lighter Questions*

- ❖ What are your fondest memories growing up?

- ❖ What do you admire most about your parents?

- ❖ How did your father show you love? Affection?

- ❖ How did your mother show you love? Affection?

- ❖ What did you love most about your father? What did you love least about your father? Why?

- ❖ What did you love most about your mother? What did you love least about your mother? Why?

◈ How close was your family? How did you express love towards one another?

◈ What are your fondest memories of me growing up? *OR, you can ask a broader question to encompass all your siblings if you have them, such as,* What are your fondest memories of your children when they were growing up?

## Deeper Questions

◈ Where did you learn about love and how to express love?

✦ What were you taught?
✦ How has that changed as you've gotten older?

◈ What does love mean to you?

◈ If you could've had your parents show you love differently, what would that look like?

◈ How did you show your spouse love early in your relationship? How has that changed as you've been together longer?

◈ How did you show us [your children] love when we were young? How has that changed as we've grown older?

◈ Say, "I love you [Mom, Dad, or what you typically call them]," pause to let them absorb the words, then ask them the following:

✦ How do you feel about me saying it to you?
✦ What makes you feel that way?

◈ Give them a big, long hug or kiss their cheek (give them a virtual hug or kiss if you're not physically together), pause to let them absorb your action, then ask the following:

✦ How did that make you feel?

✦ What do you like about that [hug / kiss]?

## POST-CONVERSATION CONTEMPLATION

After the conversation with your parents, contemplate and journal on the following:

◈ What new insights have you gained about

✦ who your parents are,

✦ their upbringing around expressing love,

✦ their belief systems around love and the expression of love, and

✦ what their love language might be?

◈ How might you show your parents love without any expectations for them to reciprocate that love in the same way?

◈ How do you want to change the way you express love towards those you love, be it your partner, your children, your friends, or others? What's the most courageous first step you can take towards doing so?

◈ How do you want to change the way you receive love from others? What will you do to make the change?

While it might feel uncomfortable to say "I love you" or show affection to your parents, I encourage you to try it. Chances are, you'll be greeted with an awkward silence or an "aiya" in response. I promise you that deep down, they love hearing and receiving it, no matter what their outward response is. After all, they're human too. Just keep trying. Find ways to get leverage, and be annoyingly persistent.

As a Chinese proverb says, 磨杵成針 (*mó chǔ chéng zhēn*): "Persistence can grind an iron beam into a needle."

*The one thing children wear out faster than shoes is parents.*
~ John J. Plomp ~

# I'll Never Be Able To Repay My Parents for Their Sacrifices

# My Story

## My American, Un-Chinese Dream

I held the phone away from my ear, overcome with a mixture of guilt and frustration as my mom, on the other end, rattled on about the lunacy of my plans.

"Why would you do this? Do you know how hard it was for your daddy and I to come to America? We had to leave everyone and everything behind. We had to work laborious jobs so you and your sisters could live a better life. And now you go from a prestigious job to being jobless? Why not just donate money? Why do you have to quit? To be poor? Aiya. You play too much."

I could sense my mom shaking her head in disapproval on the other end, despite the fact that we were on opposite coasts of the US; her in Maryland, me in San Francisco.

It was September 2014. I had just turned thirty-three. My plans, or my dreams rather, entailed quitting my corporate job, volunteering at a nonprofit in Tanzania teaching women business skills, then traveling around the world indefinitely. My goal was to find myself—to finally let go of all the notions about who I "should" or "shouldn't" be, what I "should" or "shouldn't" do, and what "should" or "shouldn't" matter based on others' expectations; to finally follow the American ideology of "finding my passion." But that contradicted the Chinese culture that my parents came from and the mentality they grew up with, which is that you work for money and survival. Work is work; it's not for joy, nor is it a passion. That's why it's called work.

I had anticipated my parents' disapproval. I so badly wanted to avoid my parents' disappointment that I meticulously planned every detail of the story I'd tell them. After all, why endure the lectures if I didn't have to?

"I got a hard-to-get rotation at my job to work overseas for a few years," I'd tell them. The "hard-to-get" part of the story would make them proud! To prevent any unintentional leakage, I'd keep my social media private from any family member or family friend who might mention something to my parents. I shared all the details of my strategy with my sisters, including a FAQ document in case they forgot how to respond to questions that might arise. The one thing I hadn't anticipated was that my middle sister would change her mind on our agreement to secrecy. She broke the news to my parents without giving me any warning.

"You can't keep something so big from them, Amy," she explained over the phone.

"You could've at least let me tell them," I responded as I gritted my teeth and swallowed my frustration.

I knew why she had told them. There was always this unspoken competition among my sisters and I to gain my parents' approval. Jenny had told them about my plans so that they'd disapprove of me. At the end of the day, we all deeply wanted to prove our worth for their acceptance and love—to know that our hard work made all their sacrifices worth it and that they were proud of us.

"Well, I knew you wouldn't do it," Jenny stated matter-of-factly. *God I hate her.*

I ended the conversation with Jenny just moments before my mom had called. Without even a hello, my mom immediately began her tirade about my decision. All I could do was sit frozen in silence thinking about the conversation I just had with Jenny. When I came to, I heard my mom still rattling on about all the reasons she was disappointed in me.

Listening to her on the other end of the phone, my heart sank into the depths of extreme shame and guilt. As a second-generation Asian American, these emotions are all too familiar. My parents had given up everything they had known so I could enjoy the privileges they never got. It was my duty to repay them for their sacrifices, meet their extremely high expectations for what I should do to be successful, and help them "keep face" among their friends and the broader Chinese community.

My sense of obligation to repay my parents for their sacrifices often filled me with guilt. While I badly wanted to live the American philosophy to "pursue your passion," it fundamentally contrasted my parents' expectations. So every time my inner desire would desperately try to claw its way out to see the light of day, I would silence it, push it aside, and continue on my path towards fulfilling my parents' wishes.

But I could only pretend to be happy and fulfilled for so long. The "American" in me had always been waiting to burst out.

## There Has to Be More to Life Than This

"I want to set proper expectations before we go into the meeting with leadership," my manager said to me. "We don't plan to invest money to market the new launch. It just doesn't make sense to do so for such a small product line."

My eyes widened and my jaw dropped. "Wait, so why did you ask me to put together a plan if we're not going to market the launch?" I asked her. I had just pulled an all-nighter to complete the marketing plan for our new lightweight cat litter product launch (yep, I was a brand manager on cat litter once upon a time!).

"The marketing plan is a part of our process. It needs to be checked off that we've done it," she noted as she eyed her watch, avoiding my gaze.

"So I spent all this time on a plan that won't even be considered?"

"Yes."

"And how do you know that we won't spend marketing dollars on this launch?" I dug.

"Because leadership doesn't believe in the product," she revealed. "They're only launching it because Walmart is one of our biggest customers and they want to see it out on the shelf." She waved me towards the meeting room. "Okay they're ready for us. Let's go in."

I was breathless with frustration as I watched her walk into the meeting room where the executives, all older White men, were waiting for our presentation; the presentation that didn't even matter. The meeting was over in a blur. All I could think about was how wrong everything felt.

"What am I doing with my life?" I cried. "I'm a brand manager of cat shit. I'm at a company with leaders who don't believe in honesty and transparency, two of my most important values. Everything is a lie, and nothing I do here even matters." My shoulders slumped. "But I don't even know what I want to do next. I feel so lost." I shook my head feeling completely dejected.

In the depths of despair, I suddenly remembered my long-forgotten dream. It was as if my fairy godmother "Bibbidi-Bobbidi-Boo'd" her magic wand on my head.

"Oh my gosh!" I shouted to myself. "I can finally travel the world with just a backpack! It'll be like an *Eat, Pray, Love* kind of thing!" I closed my eyes and envisioned myself traveling the world and finding my purpose. *Maybe I'll even find the love of my life like Julia Roberts did.* I chuckled. The idea gave me hope for something better than selling cat litter.

And thus began my planning. Planning for not the trip itself, which was the easy part, but for what I would tell my parents. I knew they'd be vehemently opposed to my dream. Unfortunately, my plans didn't unravel the way I had hoped, as evident by my mom criticizing the soul of my being on the other end of the phone.

"I know you and Daddy sacrificed a lot," I mumbled.

"So why would you do what you're doing?!" she shrieked.

The conversation lasted over an hour. I wish I could say that I stood my ground to pursue my "American Dream" and told her how I really felt, but the truth is that I barely uttered a word during the whole hour. After my mom's lecture, I continued to quietly plan my trip, though not without tremendous guilt weighing on my shoulders. The idea of the trip no longer felt joyful. But on the bright side, I was no longer marketing cat shit. No number of lectures could keep me doing that.

# Serendipity

On a cool November morning, two months after my mom blew up at me, I was mindlessly searching for reasonably priced flights to Tanzania, where I had signed up to volunteer with a nonprofit. Just as I was about to hit "Purchase," a new message notification popped up on my screen:

*Hi Amy,*

*I hope this email finds you well!*

*My name is Edmond Abrams, and I am a recruiter here with Google. I came across your profile today and thought your background could be a great fit for the Food Program Marketing and Engagement Manager role I am working on here in Mountain View.*

*Including a link below to the job description.*

*If you are interested in a conversation, can you please send me your availability for a 30-minute conversation?*

*I look forward to speaking with you!*

*Edmond*

Food program? Marketing? That sounds interesting. I clicked the link. It sucked me in. I immediately sent the link to my friend.

"What should I do?" I typed him. "I was about to buy my flight! Prices are going up and flights are disappearing. I've already told my landlord I'm moving out next month, and I've started to sell my things!"

For what felt like an eternity, all I could see were the dots indicating his cursor was in the reply box. I just wanted someone to give me an answer.

DING. "It looks like this job was made for you, Amy. Interview and see what happens."

"Okay, I'll do that," I told him.

What I couldn't admit at the time was that his answer was exactly what I needed to hear so I could give myself permission to opt out of pursuing my dream and choose my parents' approval instead.

Sixteen days after Edmond had originally reached out to me, I received my Google offer. I *had* to take it. I mean, it was Google after all. A food, marketing, *and* a global role that required me to travel? Who wouldn't take the job, right?

## Naming My Truth: I Was Afraid

Let me be real here. The truth of the matter is that I was a little fearful thinking about living my American Dream. Okay, a lot fearful. I mean, who wouldn't be afraid of leaving a stable life and stable income to go into the unknown world with no return date or post-travel plans in place? I was shitting my pants at the idea of all the uncertainty. Plus that guilt. The guilt that sat on my shoulders like a big, heavy anvil further fueled my fears, whispering in my ear every day that I was a bad daughter for wanting something different from "normal."

At the time, I didn't have the awareness or courage to name these fears. So what did I do? I came up with a sound rationale to persuade everyone, myself included, that I was making the best decision.

"It's a job of a lifetime!" I'd say. "If I go on my trip instead of taking the job, it'll be near impossible to find a job like this when I come back. But if I accept the job, I can always choose to travel later. And if I end up not liking the role, I can always quit. I'd be right where I started and just go travel the world."

My mom was ecstatic that I was taking the job. "I prayed every day that something would stop you from going on this trip," she shared with me. "I prayed that you'd either find a really good job that makes you happy or find a man that you're so in love with that you stay. My prayers were answered. You got a new job."

I laughed. I rolled my eyes. And I felt a small tug inside me. Was I caving and giving up on my aspirations to travel? Deep in my belly, the nagging voice of my dreams whispered, "Don't be one of those people who say they have dreams, then say they'll do it later. They wait and wait and wait. Then never do it and regret it their whole lives. Don't be one of them."

"I'm going to stay in this job for a maximum of five years," I told my mom. "Then I'm going to pursue my dreams and travel the world as I had planned."

"What?" she exclaimed. "Aiya! You always want to play. Well now I have to pray that you'll find a husband and start a family in the next five years. Then you won't leave."

Her words fed my inner doubts. *Will I come up with another excuse in five years and let go of my dream completely?* I questioned myself. *I can't let myself down.*

So I shared my five-year plan with everyone, including my new boss. I hoped that voicing it aloud, making a public declaration that I would leave Google by December 2019, would solidify my intentions to pursue my dream of traveling the world. What I didn't anticipate was how much can change in five years. Especially for a woman in her mid-thirties.

## The Pressures of All the "Shoulds"

During my five years at Google, I fell deeply under the pressure of all the "shoulds." One of those shoulds involved everyone around me saying, "Why would you leave Google? Everyone is trying to get in, and you're going to leave? You *should* just stay."

My dad was the biggest proponent of me staying at Google, the "Ivy League" of companies as he would call it. When I started the job, he'd go to town telling everyone that I worked for Google. He wore the Google shirt I got him every chance he could. He even handed out my business cards as if they were free samples at a mall food court.

"Daddy, why did I get an email from Bank of America with your name on it?" I asked my dad over the phone, inquiring about a message I received in my work email.

"The man at the bank asked if I had an email," my dad started. "So I gave him your business card and said to use the email on it. He was very impressed! Said that Google is one of the hardest companies to get into. I told him my daughter got in easily."

I shook my head, partly annoyed, partly chuckling at my dad's incessant desire to "have face," which for the Chinese is about respect and honor. "You have to stop doing that, Daddy. It's my work email. That means it's for work. Not for your banking emails."

Upon finding out that I was planning to quit Google to volunteer and travel the world, my dad shook his head with disapproval and said, "What will I tell people? That my daughter left Google to go make zero dollars volunteering? Aiya. You really *should* stay at Google, Amy."

Another should came along a year and a half into my relationship with Greg. He decided to leave his government job and start his own venture. Though he was originally on board with my dreams to volunteer and travel the world, he was now stressed about leaving his new career behind to go travel. "I just started this, so I feel torn between traveling and focusing on my business," he'd tell me.

He was still supportive of me traveling, but whether he'd join me was now up in the air. I felt the personal pressure to be a "good partner." I felt like I *should* stay with him and support his dreams. That I *should* be the responsible one, our stability. I told myself, *Maybe my dreams can wait.*

The biggest should of all started as I hit my mid-thirties. Everywhere I turned I'd hear things like, "You should start your family. You're getting old and your eggs are rotting." Yep. Someone said that to me. If you're reading this, please don't ever tell a woman her eggs are rotting. It's unkind. In fact, it's one of the worst things you can say to a woman. So let's just stop that. I'll step off my soapbox now.

My mom was the biggest advocate of me settling down. "Amy, time to stop playing and start having children," she would state every time she called me. "I want more grandchildren." Not even a hello to me.

"Sure. Just tell me what race you would like your grandchild to be. Half Asian, half White? Half Asian, half Black? Or maybe full Asian, but a blend of Chinese with something else? I'll go find a man to impregnate me once you tell me what kind of grandchild you want."

"Aiya! Don't say that!"

"What? You asked for a grandchild, and a grandchild I shall give you." That stopped her requests for a grandchild, but she continued to insist I stop playing.

All the shoulds from parents, managers, and society ate away at me. I struggled with what to do. I continued to say aloud that I was committed to leaving Google, but internally I was questioning myself, especially as December 2019 approached.

## Breaking Down

The day before my wedding, I unexpectedly broke down in tears as my mom and I were chatting on her bed. Tears streamed down my face.

Reaching out to bring me into her arms, my mom asked, "What's wrong?"

As I bawled into her shoulder, I expressed the pain I felt, the sense of guilt, the shame that I *should* be thankful for everything I have instead of wanting something else, and how much I didn't want to disappoint them or have them lose face.

"I know you don't want me to travel the world. I know you want me to stay and just work and start a family. I know you want to have more grandkids. I know you want me to marry a good Chinese boy, and here I am marrying a White guy! You and Daddy gave up everything for us. You hoped I'd be a boy and I turned out to be a girl. I don't want to disappoint you and Daddy anymore. But I also want to be happy. I want to do things that make me happy. And I just want you to understand and love me anyway."

The words poured out of me between my tears. All the words that had sat heavy in my heart for much of my adulthood came out like water bursting from a broken pipe.

"You know, Amy," my mom started, "I'll never understand you or your dreams. Nobody will understand except for you. And that's okay. I do want you to be successful because I worry that you'll have to work the way your daddy and I did. That you'll have to live penny to penny, uncertain of whether you'll have enough to feed your family or how you'll ever pay for your kids to go to school. But more than that, I just want to see you happy. And if going to volunteer and travel makes you happy, then do it. I'll worry about you, but I will always love you and be proud of you."

My mom wiped away my tears and looked into my eyes with pure motherly love. As I stared back into her eyes, it finally dawned on me that there was no monetary amount that could ever make up for her or my dad's sacrifices.

## Sacrifices Can Never Be Repaid

They had given up everything. They left all they knew. They left their lives, their families, and their two daughters in Hong Kong and landed in the US with only $1,700 in their pockets to establish themselves in a foreign country. They did all this so that I could have a better life and their future lineage didn't have to grow up in a communist country.

Growing up, I watched my parents always making sacrifices for their children, day in and day out: waking at 5 a.m. and not getting home until 11 p.m., working two jobs nearly every day, and dedicating their single day off a week to take us to the zoo or an amusement park or chauffeur us from one activity to another. I witnessed how they helped their parents and siblings immigrate to the US, then house and feed them with the little spare money they had. They were always selfless. They always put their family first.

I always believed that I needed to repay their sacrifices. I thought I needed to work hard like they did, make money, be successful, and make them proud in order to make their sacrifices worthwhile. Otherwise, it was all wasted effort on their part.

Looking into my mom's eyes at that moment, seeing her love for me, I finally understood what truly mattered to them. I could work hard for the rest of my life and continue to make incrementally more money, but it would never be enough. At the end of the day, all my parents wanted was for their kids to be truly happy and pursue their dreams, a privilege they never had.

My wedding day was one of the most joyous days of my life. I married the man of my dreams, surrounded by some of our closest friends and family in beautiful Malaga, Spain. But even more importantly, a weight had been lifted off my shoulders. I finally felt like I understood my parents a little more and that I had their love and support for marrying Greg, a White guy, and pursuing my dreams to travel.

## Pursuing My Dream

Six months later, in January 2020, my husband and I sold all our belongings in our little New York City apartment and took a one-way flight to Ghana, where we would volunteer at a breast cancer nonprofit with plans to travel the world after.

As things would have it, a pandemic hit the world by surprise shortly after starting our travels abroad. Borders in Ghana closed, and we ended up stuck there for over seven months. Oftentimes, when people hear this, they say things like, "That must've sucked to be stuck there!" To be honest, it was exactly what I needed. I had a moment to slow down and enjoy the simplicity of life. Stuck together in a small room, Greg and I deepened our relationship. And even my parents were grateful that I had left New York before the pandemic hit the city hard.

When the borders of Ghana finally reopened, most of the world remained closed to American citizens. Though we couldn't travel the original route we had planned, Greg and I did get to live nomadically in countries we never considered before, including an empty Dubrovnik, Croatia, a city that's typically overrun by tourists. It was like having a private tour of the most popular tourist attractions.

Despite much uncertainty in the world at that time, there was one thing that I was and continue to be 100 percent certain of: the only way to repay my parents' sacrifices was to continue to be happy with what I had and continue to pursue my dreams, even if the world had other plans for all of us.

The greatest gift of all? While living abroad, Greg and I decided to start trying for a baby. And not because of anyone else's shoulds, but because we were ready on our own terms. Two months into trying, I got pregnant naturally. How ironic that my fear of getting too old and not being able to have a healthy baby was one of the biggest shoulds that almost held me back from my dreams, and what brought me back home was a pregnancy with a healthy baby boy.

No longer do I carry around a sense of guilt that I've let my parents down. I recognize that I have more experience, education, and privilege than my parents ever did, and for that I'm forever grateful. My parents did the best they could with what they had; the best thing I can do in return is to accept myself for who I really am and recognize that what I'm doing is enough.

At the end of the day, each person has a choice in their life. My parents made theirs, now I have to make mine.

# Mama & Papa Yip's Story

**不當家, 不知柴米贵.**

*bù dāng jiā, bù zhī chái mǐ guì.*

Not the head of the house, don't know the cost of fuel and rice.

## Setting the Scene

It's a Wednesday afternoon. My mom had called me in the morning to tell me that chicken was on sale and asked if I wanted to come over for dinner. I agreed and decided to arrive two hours before dinner so that we'd have time to chat. The kitchen is warm and smells of minced garlic cooking in the wok. My mom stands by the sink washing some Chinese broccoli. From my seat at the kitchen table, I watch her move back and forth from sink to stove as I wait for my dad to return.

I just spent the last hour setting up his new Chromebook and showing him how to use it. It wasn't an easy feat, considering he never remembers his usernames or passwords for any of his accounts—not his email, not his Facebook, not any app that he uses. I had to do a lot of password resets. As I watch my mom float around the kitchen wondering how she's able to so easily "throw things together" with whatever ingredients happen to be on sale, my dad returns. He settles into his typical seat diagonal from me, and we begin our conversation about the sacrifices they made for their children.

# The First Settlers

前人栽樹, 后人乘凉.

*qián rén zāi shù, hòu rén chéng liáng.*

The predecessors plant the tree, the descendants cool off in the shade.

"Parents are like the first settlers," Papa Yip starts. "Pioneers. When you're the first settler and you find barren land, you have to build a home, tend to the land, grow crops, raise animals. You start with nothing and build something. Your children, grandchildren, great-grandchildren, and all the future generations get to benefit from your hard work. It's just how things work when you're the original settler who is putting down the foundations for your family. You do it because that's what you have to do. Your grandparents did that. We did that. All for our family."

My thoughts travel to my favorite game in elementary school, The Oregon Trail. Your mission, as the leader guiding a party of settlers, was to successfully navigate your party from Independence, Missouri, to Oregon's Willamette Valley, in good health. I always thought being the leader of new settlers was a challenging task.

Papa Yip pulls me out of my memories of childhood computer games as he continues, "My father was a successful businessman. That all changed when communism took over China. He was no longer permitted to own a business, and his fortune slowly dwindled. Your grandfather realized that he could no longer support our family living and working in China. So in 1956, he escaped to Hong Kong with hopes and dreams of building a new foundation for his family. He arrived in Hong Kong unable to speak the dialect, unfamiliar with the culture, but he did what he had to do for his family's stability and future."

I study Papa Yip with a mix of emotions. I wonder what it was like for him, at the young age of nine, to have my grandfather leave him behind. Did he understand? Did he feel abandoned?

"How did you reunite?" I ask.

"We were separated for nearly five years," Papa Yip sighed. "It was a long, thirty-eight-hour journey for me to get from China to Hong Kong. From train to boat to clamoring up a steep mountain in the dark and a lot of waiting in between, your grandmother and I finally made our way to your grandfather. When we arrived, I discovered that he had been renting a twin-sized bed in a dormitory to save money for us. Our first week, the three of us all shared that bed. I slept with your grandfather on the bed, and your grandmother slept on a wooden plank that she pulled out and set up as an extension to the twin bed after others in the dormitory fell asleep."

"A twin bed for all three of you?" I nearly shriek.

I can't imagine two adults and a thirteen-year-old sharing a twin bed. How uncomfortable they must've been. My husband and I recently upgraded to a king-sized bed because we felt our queen wasn't roomy enough. Boy, I feel privileged now.

"You did what you had to do," Mama Yip utters with her back still to us. She turns off the faucet and walks to the stove with a plastic colander of freshly washed Chinese broccoli.

Papa Yip nods. "Your grandfather eventually secured a forty-square-foot apartment for us." He looks around and motions at the kitchen we're sitting in. "Smaller than this kitchen."

"Forty?" I shout. "Four–zero; forty?"

"Yes, four–zero, Amy," Papa Yip confirms. "It was just a room for the bed. We had shared bathrooms and a shared kitchen."

I squeeze my eyes and purse my lips. It's hard to fathom the things they went through. A feeling of guilt for my privileges and the easy life I have rushes through my body like a river.

As if reading my mind, Papa Yip cuts into my thoughts. "It's what parents do. Your grandfather sacrificed for me too. Rather than send me to work, he sent me to school. He preferred working harder himself so that I could attain an education. He even paid extra to send me to an English language school. You see, I didn't learn English in China, but in Hong Kong, English was one of our main classes. Other kids were already speaking English fluently, and here I was; I couldn't even say the ABCs!"

He glances out the window and smiles before continuing, "I got made fun of by the other kids, and it was hard to adapt to life in Hong Kong, but none of that mattered. Those first few months in Hong Kong were the happiest days of my childhood. Your grandfather made sure of that."

Papa Yip's grin widens as he returns his gaze to me. "Every evening after dinner I'd go to my English language school. Your grandfather would give me money to buy ten buns on my way home. The buns were supposed to be for my breakfast the next day." Papa Yip giggles like a mischievous child who has just gotten their hands in the cookie jar. "Guess what happened to those buns?" Before I can answer, he tells me, "I ate most of them while walking home from class. When I got home, your grandmother would ask how many were left. I told her two. She yelled at me, 'Why would you do that? What will you eat tomorrow morning?' But your grandfather would just give me more money so I could have breakfast the next day. Your grandmother didn't like that."

Both Mama Yip and I crack up. She turns around and points to Papa Yip's bulging belly, and with a twinkle in her eye says, "Your daddy has always had a big appetite, especially for buns. But now he's an old man, and buns are bad for his health and physique, as you can see. So I don't let him eat them anymore."

Papa Yip winks at me. I nod knowingly. Papa Yip is prediabetic, probably as a result of his love for sweets. When I was young, he'd chop a large watermelon in half and we'd sit there watching WWF on television, scooping out bites of watermelon with a spoon as though the half-rind were a bowl. His love for sweets hasn't diminished. When Mama Yip isn't paying attention, he'll still sneakily gobble down a sweet bun.

"You said the first few months in Hong Kong were your happiest," I begin. "What about after?"

Papa Yip sighs. "Your grandfather wanted me to be happy. He wanted me to get an education and have a better life than he did. That's why he made sacrifices. Unfortunately his health declined, and he passed away just a few months after I arrived in Hong Kong, so attending school was short-lived." Papa Yip's eyes glisten. He looks away and avoids my eyes before continuing, "Your grandfather was the first settler in Hong Kong for our family. He worked hard so that his future lineage could have a better life. That means me. That means you. That means your kids, your grandkids, and beyond."

Papa Yip gets up and walks over to his metal thermos that forever holds boiling hot water in it. As he pours a cup of hot water, I see him swipe at his eyes. My heart fills with sadness. I know how much he loves my grandfather and how much he misses him.

Mama Yip glances back at me from the stove and says, "And that's what your daddy and I did too. We wanted to give our kids a chance at a better life. So when we first came to America, we left everything behind, including your sisters, so we could establish our family's foundation here. It's what the first settlers *have* to do."

## Sacrifices for a Chance at a Better Life

千里之行, 始于足下.

*qiān lǐ zhī xíng, shǐ yú zú xià.*
A journey of a thousand miles begins with a single step.

Papa Yip sits down with his red Chinese ceramic tea mug and takes a sip. "We arrived in the US with just a thousand seven hundred dollars in our pockets. We didn't know what things cost here, how long our money would last us, or how much we had to save to support our family. On top of that, we had promised to send money back to your grandparents in Hong Kong for taking care of your sisters while we got our lives settled in the US. Our financial struggles and not speaking English when we arrived in the US made surviving here extremely hard."

Lines appear between Papa Yip's brows before he continues. "But the hardest thing for us wasn't the money or speaking the language here. The hardest, most painful part was leaving our two young daughters back in Hong Kong; it was not knowing when we'd be able to see them again."

Papa Yip gazes over at Mama Yip. As if she felt him, Mama Yip stops cooking and glances back at us.

"Every day I would wonder how they were doing," Mama Yip murmurs. "I would wonder whether they were sleeping, whether they were eating, whether they were happy."

"Your mommy shed a lot of tears," Papa Yip notes. "Her eyes were always red."

"What about you?" I question as I take in the sight of him.

"I did not cry like your mommy," Papa Yip proclaims. For a moment, he is lifted out of his sad memories. He grins as he flexes both biceps to show off his strength. "I had to be the strong man and comfort her!"

I see Mama Yip, her back to us, shaking her head as she continues to cook. I imagine she's probably also rolling her eyes.

"Okay seriously, Daddy. How did you feel about leaving your daughters behind?"

"Well of course I missed your sisters," Papa Yip exclaims. "Who wouldn't? But we knew what we had to do. Our short-term sacrifices would benefit our entire family in the long term. For your sister, our sacrifices meant life or death. She was born with a hole in her heart. The doctors in Hong Kong couldn't do anything for her. If we didn't come to America to get her medical care here, she might not be with us anymore."

Papa Yip shuts his eyes as he travels down memory lane. With a deep sigh, he shares, "I still remember when your sister was five. She said, 'DiDi! DiDi! Do you want me to dance for you?' Of course I said yes. So she danced. But after just a few short minutes she stopped. She looked up at me and said to me, 'DiDi, I'm sorry. I'm too tired to dance any longer. I need to rest.' That broke my heart. Kids at five have a lot of energy. They don't stop moving, even when you try to get them to stop. And here she was, five years old and tired after dancing for a few minutes. Your mommy and I knew that we needed to make it here. There was no other option. That's what gave us strength and courage to do what we needed to do; to take the hardest step, the first step."

I peer at Mama Yip's back, moving with ease in front of the stove and not pausing for a moment. Shifting my gaze to Papa Yip, I see the wrinkles on his face, the cracks in his hands, and the love that they represent. My heart fills with gratitude and admiration for my parents' courage and strength.

# Appreciate the People Who Gave You What You Have

## 飲水思源.

### *yǐn shuǐ sī yuán.*

When you drink the water, remember the spring as the source of the water.

"This isn't a loan," Papa Yip begins after I ask him how children can repay their parents for their sacrifices. "You can't ever repay your parents. The best thing you can possibly do for your parents is to value them while they're still here."

"If you're lucky enough to have your parents still here, then appreciate them," Mama Yip chimes in as she sets down the Cantonese poached chicken and Chinese broccoli she just cooked. Her tiny figure hovering over me, she meets my gaze. "Appreciate even their nagging. Because one day when you want to hear their nagging, you won't be able to hear it anymore. These days it seems like everyone is always too busy for their parents. But then when their parents pass away, they're sad. Instead of being sad when they're gone, show them love and care while your parents are still here. That's how you can show your parents you appreciate what they've sacrificed for you."

I open my mouth to defend myself, but no words come out. Oof. I am guilty, as charged, of always being too busy for my parents. Oftentimes, when Mama Yip calls me to tell me about the latest grocery sales, I tune out and get irritated that she's wasting my time. Without another word, Mama Yip turns around to get the garlic sauce she's prepared for the chicken.

Papa Yip leans in and studies me. "Amy, most parents made these sacrifices willingly. Not all parents, but maybe—" He pauses as he ponders what the right number is. "Maybe 90 percent; 90 percent of parents willingly made the sacrifices they did for their children."

Where did my dad get that number from? I'm sure he pulled it out of thin air, but I go with it and don't argue or question. I stay open to what he's sharing.

"Us baby boomers who grew up in Asia know what it's like to have nothing," he shares. "We know what it's like to be uncertain where your next meal is coming from. To barely survive. No parent wants to pass that suffering onto their children. So our number one priority has always been to give our children, our grandchildren, our future lineage, a better life than we could've ever had.

"You can't repay us by working as hard as we did or suffering like we did. That would be silly and contradict why we worked so hard to begin with. We didn't have a choice. When we arrived in the US, we had to take any job that would pay because we didn't speak English, we didn't know anybody, and we had very little in our pockets. But we made that choice so you could live differently. So you could actually start enjoying your life before you're too old to enjoy things."

Papa Yip points to Mama Yip who has joined us at the table. "Look at your mommy. She has teeth missing. Look at me. My knees are always in pain. We have financial security now, but we're too old to enjoy life. We made sacrifices so that future generations in our lineage can have things a little easier. A little easier to make money, a little easier to stay healthy. And we don't expect any of you to repay us," Papa Yip finishes.

Mama Yip picks up a drumstick with her chopsticks and sets it onto my rice bowl. "You know Amy, we tried to give you everything we could."

"Yeah, I know," I mumble, biting into my food.

"Every time you remind us of all the things we didn't do for you, it hurts your daddy," Mama Yip shares. "Like the Christmas tree or the trip to Hawaii."

Papa Yip had promised me many things as a child. He thought I'd just forget about it once he said yes and nudged me away. What he didn't realize is how good of a memory I have. Every December, I'd ask if this was finally the year we'd get the Christmas tree he had promised. Every July, I'd ask if this was finally the year we'd take a trip to Hawaii as he had promised. He'd always respond with, "Next year! Not this year." I made him promise, and even pinky swear to me, that "next year" would actually be the year. This went on year after year until my hopes fell and I began to resent broken promises. I had mentioned to Papa Yip that, now as an adult, I abhorred it when people couldn't keep their word and that I had traced this back to his broken promises. I never realized that telling him that would hurt him.

I desperately want to explain myself—that that's not what I meant and that I had a right to feel the emotions I felt. It's my go-to reaction when I feel I've been wronged or misunderstood. But this time, I let that urge to protect myself go. I zip my lips and just listen. I give my parents airtime to share and be heard, something I don't do often enough.

"Both of us did everything we could," Mama Yip explains. "We had to make tough decisions. We didn't take you on big vacations or buy Christmas trees because we needed to save that money for our family's financial stability, ensuring there was a roof over our heads, food to feed your bellies, and clothes to keep you warm. We only made a few dollars an hour, Amy. We wish we could've afforded things like vacations. We couldn't. And your daddy is hurt that you don't see that. You only mention the things we didn't do."

Mama Yip gazes at Papa Yip. He glares at me while shaking his head in disapproval, but he can't hide the lopsided grin creeping up on his face as he pretends to be upset.

"I'm sorry," I breathe. I genuinely am sorry that I never shared my gratitude and appreciation for all their sacrifices. I was always so focused on what was wrong rather than what was right.

"We wish we could've spent more time with you girls," Papa Yip shares. His jaw sets, and he glances up towards the ceiling as he ponders how to phrase his thoughts. "One of my biggest regrets," he sighs, "is working so much. I was always worried about money. I didn't think about how fast time would fly by or how quickly you girls would grow up. I didn't realize I wouldn't have that time with you anymore."

My heart wells up. My throat chokes. I wish we could go back in time. I would've loved to have my parents around more growing up.

Mama Yip smiles lovingly at me and says, "It's easy to always point out what your parents have done wrong. We all make mistakes. We're all human.

And at our age, it's hard to admit or even recognize the ways we've failed as a parent. Just know that your parents' love is undying. There's no need to ever repay a parents' sacrifices. It's impossible to do so. But you can forgive them for shortcomings. You can show them that they matter to you."

Papa Yip chimes in, "Call them. Visit them. Ask them how they are. Remember their birthdays. Drop off their favorite foods. Parents will never ask for anything. They know you're busy. They don't want to bother you. All they want is a phone call or a visit from you. They want to be remembered and cared for. They want to be respected and appreciated. We all want that. Who wouldn't? That's all you can do to repay them. Help them feel cared for."

## Unfulfilled Dreams

老骥伏枥, 志在千里.

*lǎo jì fú lì, zhì zài qiān lǐ.*

An old warhorse in the stable, still longs to gallop a thousand miles.

Papa Yip puts down his chopsticks, leans back in his chair, and says, "I remember just before your grandmother passed away, she told me that her dream has always been to stay in a hotel. I never knew about this. Both your mom and I worked at a hotel. We could've easily made her dream come true, but we never thought to ask her. By the time she told us, it was too late. She was ill in the hospital . . . A lot of parents have unfulfilled dreams. Children can easily ask their parents what their unfulfilled dreams are, then try to help their parents reach these dreams."

"What are your unfulfilled dreams?" I inquire curiously.

"As a kid I dreamt of being a worldwide ping pong champion," Papa Yip laughs. "I was really good. I won a lot of competitions and was our school captain." He flexes his bicep muscles as if it were proof that he was a talented ping pong player.

"Aiya," Mama Yip yelps. "That's not what she means, old man."

"What else did you dream of?" I ask.

"Well, when we first got married, I promised your mommy three things," Papa Yip says before giving Mama Yip a once-over. "The first promise was to buy her a house with a garden and pool. We have this house, which has a small front yard and backyard." He points out the kitchen window towards the community swimming pool behind their house and chuckles, "And we even have a big swimming pool in our backyard!"

I shake my head and smile at his attempts to be funny. Mama Yip rolls her eyes.

"The second promise I made to your mommy," Papa Yip holds up two fingers, "was to buy her a yacht. I've done that too!"

I furrow my eyebrows. "You don't own a yacht."

The corners of his mouth turn up. "I've done better than a small yacht, Amy. I've taken your mommy on cruises! Big cruise ships!"

Mama Yip snorts, "Oh yeah. You sure got me the biggest boat there is."

Papa Yip winks at her, then turns back to me and continues. "The third promise I made was to ensure all our kids get to graduate college. All of them have. So all my promises, all our dreams, have been fulfilled. For this last part of our lives, we just want to live peacefully and go peacefully. We're already preparing to leave. We've bought our graveyard space, and we've sewn our Chinese departure pillows and blankets that's part of our Chinese Buddhist tradition. Being able to leave knowing that our three daughters are doing well, that they are happy, get along with each other, and are healthy, gives us peace of mind."

My heart tightens and I choke back a tear. The thought of my parents departing this world hurts me. A part of me wishes that I had had these conversations years ago and that I showed them appreciation and love over the last few decades. I feel a sense of regret for not having spent more time with them when I was younger. I'm appreciative that they're still here with me now, that I haven't let this moment go by, and that I still have a chance to show them my appreciation and love.

Not wanting to leave any rocks unturned, I question, "So how do you want to live this last part of your life?"

"We like cruises," Papa Yip answers. "So before we leave this world, we just want to go on more cruises. Doesn't really matter where we go. We just like to relax and hang out. Cruises are great for that. When we're tired we can rest, sit on the top deck, and get some fresh air. When we're hungry, there are plenty of places to eat."

"My friend just went on a six-month, round-the-world cruise," I mention.

"Oh no, that's too long!" Mama Yip squeals. "I think a few two-week trips every year is a good amount."

"I agree," Papa Yip smiles at the thought of this. "That's a nice way to relax after all those years of working."

I'm not a huge cruise person. I much prefer the freedom of exploring different countries by land to being stuck on a boat. But if it meant spending time with my parents and helping them fulfill their dreams, I could learn to enjoy a cruise here and there.

Papa Yip knowingly cuts into my thoughts, "Amy, your mommy and I can go on cruises by ourselves. Don't think that you have to come on a cruise with us as some sort of repayment. All we want is for you to live a good life while you still have the energy and time, not making the mistakes we did by working so hard that you forget to enjoy life. That will make our hard work worth it. That is repayment enough."

I smile and get up to give him a kiss on his cheek. Then I walk over to Mama Yip, who is now in front of the sink washing dishes, and give her a hug and kiss as well.

# My Reflections Post-Conversation

Throughout the rest of the evening and the days and months that followed, I contemplated all that my parents had shared about their journey to the US and the sacrifices they made. Three themes have continued to surface for me (I like the number three; in fact, three is my favorite number!):

1. **A parent's love is truly unconditional.**

   There is truth in a Chinese saying about parents holding their children close at heart, while children only think about their parents in passing, like a breeze on the tip of a leaf. Reflecting on much of my childhood and into my twenties, I didn't understand my parents' context and why they were the way they were. And to be honest, I was an asshole kid. I even threatened to call the police on them if they used that feather duster again. (If you don't know about the feather duster, just Google "Chinese parent feather duster.")

   I told my parents that I hated them more often than I'd like to admit. But they never stopped loving me no matter what I did, what I said, or how much my words and actions hurt them. When I was sick, they were there for me at a moment's notice. When I was craving something, my mom made it for me to eat. Though my parents might not have shown love in the same way as Western cultures do, they showed it in their own love language. And now that I'm a bit older and have spent more time learning about who they are as human beings, I recognize how unconditional their love for their children is. As a mother myself now, I carry this same love into this new role. I always tell my kiddo that I'll mess up sometimes, that he'll probably piss me off sometimes, but that no matter what, I will always love him. After all, real love isn't based on conditions needing to be met. It's unconditional.

2. **Nothing can ever be done to repay my, your, or any parents' sacrifices.**
   Immigrant parents made sacrifices. These sacrifices were choices. And they were choices our parents made as an act of unconditional love they have for their children. All they wanted was a better life for their children. They understood suffering and were willing to do anything for their children to not have to experience that same suffering. So what makes us believe that we could ever repay them for that? What makes us believe that our suffering, our working hard, our burnout, could ever right the wrongs our parents experienced? They can't.

   Certainly there are parents who say things like, "I did XYZ, so you owe me." In my opinion, that's like forcing a gift onto someone then asking for something else in return. What our parents did for us wasn't actually a gift to begin with. Even if it had been, we could never repay them.

   The best thing we can do is make our parents' sacrifices worth it. "Worth it" means something different in each family: it might equate to us (the children, grandchildren, and future lineage) having more financial freedom, better health, and more happiness and joy—all the things they couldn't. "Worth it" might also equate to us letting go of the guilt we've been holding for the sacrifices they made.

   Appreciate them. Then pay it forward.

3. **Parents are human. They want the same thing that we (and any human being) want: to love and be loved, to care and be cared for, to belong and be remembered.**
   No matter what your parents say, no matter what your parents (don't) ask for, they just want to be appreciated. Theirs is one of unconditional love, and I can imagine how it must feel when those you love unconditionally don't have time for you at all.

   As a new mom, I look at my infant and know that whatever he does, even if he's an asshole to me, I'll still love him. I know it'll hurt when he's off living his life and doesn't have any time to call and say hello or stop by for a visit. But I also know that when he does, it'll brighten my day. Reflecting on my parents' lives, our parents' lives, I now understand what means the most to them: a simple call or visit—a reminder that we remember them, appreciate them, love them, and care for them.

For some reason, many of us have come to believe that by working all the time, achieving successes like titles and promotions, and not having any time left to spend with our parents are the keys to repaying them. How bizarre does that sound? The truth is that the most valuable thing we can give our parents to repay their sacrifices is our time.

# A Date with Your Parents

## PRE-CONVERSATION PERSONAL REFLECTION

### Overview

If you carry the belief that you need to repay your parents' sacrifices, you might struggle to feel that who you are and what you do is enough. There's a blanket of guilt that weighs you down. By loving yourself and giving yourself credit for all the amazing things you've done in life, you'll be taking a first step towards recognizing that you're making your parents' sacrifices worth it.

### Instructions

1. Write yourself a love letter. Celebrating yourself positively impacts your well-being, from your physical health to your ability to handle stress. It also gives you a sense of how amazing you truly are.

   ◈ Use the template below.

   ◈ Set a timer for five minutes.

   ◈ Write as if your life depended on writing as much as possible. Don't put your pen down! Fill the page! Here's some inspiration for things you can celebrate if you're feeling stuck on where to begin:

      ✦ Having courageous conversations with your parents
      ✦ Moving to a new city alone

- Being able to deal with a bully from seventh grade
- Overcoming a job loss
- Loving your kids regardless of what kinds of shit they pull
- Traveling alone
- Running a marathon

---

**TEMPLATE**

Dear _____,

    I am your confidence. The part of you that has and will always be innately within you and will never give up. I am telling you that you freaking rock because . . .

With Love,
Your Confidence

---

2. Read your letter aloud. Imagine this love letter belongs to someone else. How do you feel about that person when you look at the letter? If you were this person's parent, what would you be proud of?

3. Now write your parents a love letter to uncover what you appreciate about them. You can write either a single letter to both or individual letters to each.

    ◈ Use the template below.

    ◈ Set a timer for five minutes.

◈ Write as if your life depended on writing as much as possible. Don't put your pen down! Fill the page! Here's some inspiration if you're feeling stuck on where to begin:

✦ Always cutting me fresh fruit to eat
✦ Moving to a new country so I could have a better life
✦ Helping me take care of my kids
✦ Working tough jobs all those years
✦ Saving me the best parts of every meal
✦ Making food for me, even after I became an adult
✦ Sending me news articles because you worry about me

---

**TEMPLATE**

Dear _____,

    I appreciate you. I am telling you that you freaking rock because
. . .




With Love,

_____

---

## THE CONVERSATION

### Conversation Topic

What sacrifices your parents made, how they feel about those sacrifices, and what would make those sacrifices worthwhile.

## Tips

These conversations can be hard, and potentially triggering. Priority number one is to take care of yourself. Remember to review the Conversation Tip Sheet on page 23 before your conversation.

## Conversation-Specific Suggestions

Some of your parents' experiences around their sacrifices might be hard for them to share and might trigger difficult emotions and stored trauma. Take the conversation slow. If necessary, consider engaging a therapist in these conversations.

Bring the love letter you wrote to your parents and share it with them on this date. Read it aloud if that feels comfortable. Alternatively, hand the written letter to them so they can read it themselves. The sense of feeling appreciated may warm them up to this conversation. Remember that Google Translate might be useful if your parents can't understand English very well.

Tailor the questions to your specific circumstance. For example, if your parents are second-generation or beyond, you might ask them what they think about their ancestors coming to the US. Or, if your parents didn't immigrate but sent you to a new country to live with a relative or attend boarding school, you might ask about what the experience was like from their perspective.

## Questions For Your Parents

### *Lighter Questions*

- ◈ What was your childhood like? What are your favorite memories? What are your least favorite memories?

- ◈ What were your dreams growing up? What happened?

◆ How did your parents show you they were proud of you?

◆ What are your fondest memories of your parents?

◆ What was your experience of leaving [insert your parents' country of origin] like? What motivated you to leave? How did you feel about leaving? *OR*, What was your experience of sending me to [insert country] like? What motivated you to send me? How did you feel about me leaving?

◆ What was it like when you arrived in [insert country]? *OR*, How do you feel about our ancestors immigrating to [insert country]? What stories can you share about that?

## Deeper Questions

◆ What was the hardest part about being an immigrant in a new country? *OR*, What was the hardest part about sending me to live away from you?

◆ How did you feel about raising your children outside of your home country? How did you approach parenting in this circumstance? What were some of your core values or belief systems about what mattered most?

◆ What have I done that makes you proud? *OR*, *ask a broader question to encompass all your siblings if you have them, such as,* What have each of your kids done that makes you proud?

◆ Looking back, how do you feel about immigrating? How do you feel about the sacrifices you made? What, if any, regrets do you have about the sacrifices you made?

◆ In your mind, what would make the sacrifices that you made worth it? How could your kids repay you for those sacrifices?

◈ Do you have any unfulfilled dreams? What are your dreams for the remainder of your life?

## POST-CONVERSATION CONTEMPLATION

After the conversation with your parents, contemplate and journal on the following:

◈ What new insights have you gained about

✦ who your parents are,
✦ why they made the sacrifices that they did,
✦ how they feel about needing to repay them for their sacrifices, and
✦ what would make your parents' sacrifices "worth it"?

◈ What do you most appreciate about your parents now? About the sacrifices they made?

◈ What is one thing you can do more regularly to show them your appreciation?

◈ What beliefs about repaying your parents do you want to keep?

◈ What beliefs about repaying your parents do you want to let go of?

Using the above insights, go back to the love letter you wrote to your parents and see if there's anything you want to add to it.

**BONUS:** Remember that all our parents are human beings who have dreams—perhaps unfulfilled dreams and, quite possibly, dreams they never got a chance to pursue because they were too busy sacrificing for their children. How might you help them fulfill their dreams for how they wish to spend the remainder of their lives?

*They may never say it, but your parents really are proud of you when you follow your heart and chase your dreams.*

~ Robert Cheeke ~

# I Don't Belong Anywhere

*My Story*

## My First Encounter with Racism

"Go back to your own country," a Black woman yelled at my sisters and me.

I looked up from my crouched position where I had, just moments ago, been busily focused on observing the little ants crawling in and out of their little dirt tunnels. As my eyes met hers, her eyebrows furrowed. With her hands on her hips, she glared at us with aggression, like a panther about to pounce on its prey. At the time, being just three years old, I couldn't put my finger on what her expression exuded. I now recognize it as disgust.

My body froze like prey being hunted. I was overcome by a mixture of confusion and hurt. Her expression reminded me of the way my mom looked when she was extremely angry with something I had done. I just couldn't figure out what that something was. My two older sisters and I had come to the playground to enjoy the beautiful Sunday weather. What could we have possibly done to upset this woman?

"Why is she saying that?" I whispered to my sisters. As a second-generation Chinese American, born in Maryland, my first language always having been English, I couldn't comprehend the notion of "go back to your own country." America *was* my country.

My eldest sister Annie, who was thirteen at the time, tugged my hands and muttered, "Doesn't matter. Let's go home."

"She's not being nice though!" I argued as I dug my heels into the dirt, accidentally crushing those ant tunnels I'd been admiring just moments before.

My mom had always taught me to be kind to others, and this lady was not being kind. Though I didn't understand the meaning behind her words nor comprehend the notion of race and that we were of different races, I could tell by her tone and body language that she didn't like us.

Annie shook her head, grabbed my hand, and began to drag my middle sister Jenny and I home.

I stared at Annie with complete confusion, searching for an answer. "But Mommy always said we have to be nice!" I exclaimed.

Annie refused to meet my gaze. She kept her focus on the sidewalk in front of her as she took one big step after the next, moving forward with determination.

Heat quickly rose from my belly into my throat as if something wanted to be launched out of me. In a flash, I pulled my arm out of Annie's grasp and twisted around to face the woman, who was now glaring at us with a smirk. I cupped my mouth and shrieked as loud as my little voice could muster, "Don't be mean you . . . you . . . you chocolate lady!"

Before I had a chance to witness the lady's response, Annie grabbed my hand back into hers and hissed, "Let's go!" With Jenny in one hand and me in the other, she half dragged, half ran towards home.

Upon entering our two-bedroom apartment, we were immediately welcomed by the scent of freshly pan-fried scallion pancakes, Chinese doughnut sticks, an assortment of steamed buns, and hand-squeezed soy milk. I closed my eyes and sniffed the air. There was nothing like my mom's cooking, especially on Sundays when she'd go to town making some of my favorite things. I quickly forgot what had happened at the park that day. And I never told my parents about the incident.

Though I didn't realize it at the time, this was my first encounter with racial hatred. It was the first time I experienced someone trying to tell me that I didn't belong because of the color of my skin. Unfortunately, it wouldn't be the last.

# First Grade: The Sweatshirt

*I wonder what Grandma got me! I bet it's something nice*, I thought to myself with anticipation.

I waited patiently for my turn as my grandma passed out gifts to my parents and my sisters from her big, blue suitcase. She had just returned from a trip to Hong Kong, and her suitcase was brimming with gifts for us.

Because I was the youngest of three girls, the only gifts I ever got were money in red envelopes or decades-old hand-me-downs that had been passed from my eldest sister to my middle sister, then to me. By the time I received these out-of-style, faded clothes, they often had patched-up holes in them. So, as you can imagine, I was eager with anticipation to find out which of the gifts was for me.

I stood on my tiptoes to peer over my grandma's head and into the suitcase, hoping to catch a glimpse of what was in there. Without a word, my mom narrowed her eyes at me and shook her head. I understood that look and immediately took a step back.

My grandma dove into the suitcase for the next package, raised it up over her head as if she'd just won a trophy in a competition, and turned to me. "This is for you, Amy."

I lunged forward, quickly forgetting my mom's look and nearly knocking my grandma over with glee. "Can I open it?" I shouted.

"Of course," my grandma smiled.

I tore the wrapping off as quickly as my little fingers could go. My eyes widened as I unraveled my new treasure.

"A new sweatshirt! My very own NEW sweatshirt! And it's in my favorite color. Hot pink! Oh Grandma, thank you! I love it!"

I felt like the luckiest kid alive. *All the kids will think I'm cool with this new sweatshirt*, I thought. Unfortunately, I was wrong about that. Very wrong.

"Ching Chong, where did you get that Ching Chong shirt from?" a fellow first grader taunted during recess as he pulled the edges of his eyes outward to make slanty eyes.

Another boy joined in, shouting, "What kind of English is that on your shirt? Chinglish?" Laughter erupted.

I looked down at the words on my sweatshirt, mortified at what I read. They were right. The words made no sense. Why hadn't I noticed that before? I looked up and scanned the faces staring at me. As I glanced from face to face, it felt like time had slowed. They were all pointing at me, laughing as they pulled their eyes into slits.

My face turned bright red. My body tensed. My heart pounded like a drum in my chest, faster and faster as if it were a racehorse closing in on the finish line. I felt like I was on fire, like someone had set a slow, steady match deep in the pit of my belly and I might combust at any moment. And then I did.

"MY NAME IS AMY!" I shouted, choking back tears of hurt and rage. I ran into the girl's bathroom, blinded with anger.

The rest of the school day felt like a haze. After the final bell rang, I ran home and tore the sweatshirt off. I never wore it again.

Thus began what I call the "shame phase" of my childhood, which lasted throughout my elementary and middle school years. I abhorred being Chinese. I wished I could have blonde hair, blue eyes, and parents who spoke perfect English. I just wanted to fit in.

## Fifth Grade: Accents and Lunches

Through the wet droplets that had landed on my dark brown eyelashes, I saw a familiar car pull up next to me. It was an '89 gold Honda Accord with a tan interior. As the car slowed down in front of me, the window rolled down to reveal my mom, who was inside warm and dry.

"Get in. The rain is coming down hard. You're getting all wet!" she shouted out to me in Cantonese.

As if the powers that be had perfectly timed things just to torment me, a few kids from school walked by at that exact moment. "Ching chong ling long," I heard behind me. Out of the corner of my eye, I could see three boys laughing at my mom. Or maybe they were laughing at me. Or maybe they were laughing at both of us. I wasn't sure. Nor did I care to be sure.

I froze. That familiar anger roared through my body. I desperately wanted to get out of the cold, wet rain that was drenching me. I hate rain. But more than my dislike for rain, I disliked being seen as Chinese. I was ashamed of it, and I was ashamed of my parents. At that moment, all I wanted was to have my mom leave the scene.

"It's okay. I'd rather walk," I whispered to my mom, praying that nobody would hear me speaking Cantonese. I waved her off, too embarrassed to get in the car and be seen with her.

Furrowing her eyebrows and scrutinizing me with confusion, she opened her mouth to say something, but then she noticed the boys. Her face fell. She didn't say a word and drove off. I could tell she understood and was hurt. My heart sank, yet I couldn't help but also feel relief.

Throughout elementary and middle school, this was a typical encounter with my parents. Kids would make fun of my parents' accents and say things like, "Why are your parents so weird?" I felt so embarrassed about my parents that I never wanted them to show up for any of my school activities. Not to PTA meetings, not to pick me up from school, and especially not to bring home-baked goods for class Valentine's Days or Halloween parties. Who knows what my mom would conjure up! As much as I loved red-bean buns, I refused to let my classmates see me eat them. They'd be disgusted by the poop color and pasty texture, and I didn't need them making fun of yet another thing I ate. Lunchtime was horrific enough.

"Ewwwww what is that you're eating?" a classmate said as she peered into my plastic Chinese restaurant takeout container that my mom had repurposed into my lunch container.

"Rice . . . with mapo tofu and seaweed," I mumbled, staring at my food.

"That looks disgusting! Like someone threw up! You're eating someone's throwup!" Other kids joined in, sing-songing, "You're eating throwup!"

My cheeks flushed. I felt paralyzed. I just stared at the lunch sitting in front of me, wishing I could disappear. It was as if every pair of eyes in the lunchroom was laughing at me and the "throwup" in front of me.

I don't know how long I sat there. It felt like an eternity. When the bell rang, my body shook as if I had awoken from a coma. I slowly got up and threw out my lunch. Mapo tofu was one of my favorite things, but I couldn't eat it in front of my classmates anymore.

"Why can't Mommy just make me a normal lunch? A peanut butter and jelly sandwich would be nice," I mumbled to myself as I looked around at all the half-eaten sandwiches and potato chip bags being thrown out by other kids. "I just want to be normal."

My mom could never understand what was wrong with eating mapo tofu at school, nor why I would want to trade it for a boring peanut butter and jelly sandwich. She couldn't comprehend that all I wanted was to not stand out.

## High School: Asian Pride

"Amy, you should run for Historian of AAC, the Asian American Club," Anna beamed. Anna was a well-liked, popular junior, with a bubbling personality.

I turned to her, sitting at the desk to my right, and gawked. My mind raced. *AAC? I've been trying to avoid being seen as Asian my whole life. Why would I join the AAC, much less run for a leadership position? And there's no way, as a freshman, I could win. These elections for school clubs are merely popularity contests.*

"Me?" I questioned, more to myself than to her. "Um. I don't think so."

"Why not?" she implored.

"I don't know . . ." I trailed off, "I'm just not a leader type. I don't really like the limelight. I'm not really loud. You know, those things leaders should be good at." I paused, pondering all the times my parents had reminded me what it meant to be a good Chinese girl.

"Amy, you need to listen to authority, to your elders, your teachers. Don't talk back. Keep your head down, work hard, and avoid getting into trouble," they constantly reminded me. I was sure they wouldn't want me in a leadership role of any sort in a school club, especially speaking out for a group of students. My parents just wanted me to focus on going to class, studying, and getting good grades. They were always afraid that extracurricular activities would distract me from the real work: doing well in school. I had to argue with them just to play on the volleyball team. It wasn't until their educated, well-off friend told them that playing sports would show that I'm well-rounded and help me get into college that they finally relented.

Anna shook her head at me and replied, "You don't have to be in the limelight. As historian, you'd be helping us remember the year, taking photos, tracking things we do."

I bit my lip. "I'm only a freshman. I don't know anything about being a club officer."

Anna grinned. "You learn by doing. I've never been the president of a student club and I'm running. I'd love for you to run for historian. It's only a school club. Not like we're running the country. We'll figure it out." She paused, then added very matter-of-factly, "Plus, being a leader of a school club will look great for your college admissions."

The bell rang, indicating the start of second period.

"I'll think about it," I replied.

Throughout class I kept going back and forth on the pros and cons. Anna was probably right. Doing more activities, and in a leadership role at that, would probably help with my college admissions one day. I was sure my parents wouldn't argue with me if they knew it would help with college. And what's the worst that could happen? I'd be responsible for taking photos and making an end-of-year scrapbook. Not exactly a critical assignment.

By the time the bell rang to end second period, I had my mind made up. I turned to Anna and exclaimed, "Okay, I'm in!"

So as a freshman, I ran for Historian of AAC at my high school. I won. This moment triggered my pendulum to swing the other way, from shame to pride. I felt a sense of belonging among my community of Asian peers. Rather than feeling shame for being Asian, I suddenly became proud of being Asian. Or as we used to say in high school, "Azn Pryde." We even had bumper stickers with that saying.

Looking back now, I should probably find Anna and let her know the impact she had on my life. That nudge from her transformed me. For one, it marked the start of me embracing my natural leadership skills; historian was the first, but certainly not the last leadership role I took on in high school and into college and corporate life. For another, it shifted me from my shame phase to becoming proud of being Asian American. I found myself hanging out with more Asian American kids, and I dedicated my time to the Asian community by volunteering to teach English at Chinese elderly homes and Chinese to three-year-olds at a Chinese school. I also became involved in advocacy work to give greater visibility to the AAPI community.

This sense of pride and belonging lasted for nearly two decades. But I guess a pendulum must swing back the other way at some point. For me, that point was when I started my role on the Food Team at Google.

## My Mid-30s: Life at Google

I cringed as I walked into the Googleplex café to grab dinner. There were hordes of families there—not just the partners and children of Google employees, but parents, grandparents, and more. Kids were running around with familiarity as if they frequented the café, while their parents sat with platefuls of food in front of them. Next to those plates of food sat four, five, six, sometimes eight to-go boxes stacked up high, filled with tomorrow's lunch and dinner. As I scanned from table to table, I saw that most were Asian families. By the sounds of their languages, I could tell they were primarily Indian and Chinese. I lowered my head as I walked past the tables towards the dinner line.

"I hope nobody thinks I'm like them," I mumbled. "I hope nobody thinks I'll be taking advantage of this free food and feeding my whole family off of it."

Here's the thing: Google offers free meals to their employees. At least they did while I was employed. Employees could bring an occasional guest for a meal. Note the word "occasional." "Occasional" does not equate to bringing guests every day, nor does it mean visitors should be taking home stacks of to-go boxes filled with food. The to-go boxes were meant for employees who needed to grab a bite between meetings, not for guests to take home meals for the days to come.

The food program at Google originated to bring employees together over a meal, just like a family does. But as the company grew, abuse of the program also grew. This abuse was an issue and frustration for both the company and many employees. Internally, there were many discussion threads and groups talking about the issue and the proper etiquette. At times, the Chinese and Indian families that frequented the cafés were called out.

As a global leader on the food team, I became uncomfortable with these conversations, especially when "my people" were being called out as part of the problem. I was ashamed of being Chinese again, part of the "cheap Chinese taking all the free food." Unconsciously, I started to lean away from my roots. For the first time in two decades, I started avoiding anything that would connect me to my Asian background. I refused to join the Asian Employee Resource Group at work, I never referred to my ethnicity, I no longer participated in any AAPI organizations or events outside of work, and I stopped advocating for and mentoring the younger AAPI generations.

It seemed as if the last two decades of being a proud Asian had suddenly dissipated like smoke in the wind. And the funny—or maybe not-so-funny—thing is, I wasn't even consciously aware of what I was doing. It didn't occur to me that the pendulum had swung again and that I had slid back into my shame phase.

# Not Belonging Anywhere

Over the coming years, I made myself smaller as I heard comments ridiculing my country of origin:

"This is all communism's fault."

"The Chinese are so corrupt. They're horrible people."

"China's cheap labor is stealing all American jobs. Look at Apple, Nike, or any of the other big companies who are outsourcing to China!"

"Made in China. Cheap shit."

I remained unconscious of the fog of shame that surrounded me, hiding me from my own reality. I just shrank myself. I didn't want to be seen or heard. I didn't want to rock the boat. But the shaming only got worse. Perhaps I started noticing it more, or perhaps it was showing up with more regularity. One thing for sure is that I felt like an outcast in the US. Yet I didn't belong in China either.

"Your Chinese is not bad for an American!" a waitress at the noodle shop in Shanghai said to me as I ordered my meal from her. "Where did you learn?"

I had taken a trip to China for work and decided to extend the visit into a vacation. "I speak at home with my parents," I said to her in Chinese.

"Oh, not bad, not bad. You have an American accent, but not bad!" She gave me a once-over, then added, "You look very American though. Not Chinese. Chinese don't have funny dots like that." She pointed at the freckles on my face. Before I had a chance to respond, she walked away to place my order of noodles.

This wasn't the only time on my trip to China when locals made unsolicited comments about my "Americanism," nor was it the only time the "funny dots" on my face were pointed out. Though I enjoyed my time in China, exploring the Great Wall, the Forbidden City in Beijing, and the Terracotta Army in Xi'an, I was also reminded that I didn't belong. The "funny dots" on my face were a reminder of that.

The waitress's comments about my "funny dots" took me back to when I was four. That's when the first few dots appeared on my cheeks. My dad noticed them first and worriedly yelped, "What are those? They look like a skin disease. We must fix it. We must get it off!"

I was immediately taken to see a dermatologist.

"It's freckles," the dermatologist calmly explained. "You can't remove them. They come out because of sun exposure."

"No. Chinese people don't have freckles!" my dad proclaimed as he wagged his forefinger.

"Can you bleach it off? Lighten the spots?" my mom inquired.

I shrank back onto the medical examination table, embarrassed at my "weirdness," as my parents and the dermatologist went back and forth about the dots on my face. In the end, the doctor conceded and prescribed some skin-whitening medication, but not before warning my parents that if I went in the sun, the freckles would return.

Reflecting now, I know my parents meant well. They were worried. Perhaps they had never encountered freckles and didn't know what to make of them. But it didn't make their comments sting any less. I started believing that I was weird, not a real Chinese person. Returning to China, sitting in this noodle shop, I was reminded that I don't belong in China. When I'm in the US, I'm constantly reminded that I don't belong in America. I don't really belong anywhere.

## The Trump Era

My eyes widened, my jaw dropped, and my heart sank. "Trump won? But how?" I blurted out to nobody in particular.

I had just awoken and was lying in bed with my phone in hand, scrolling the news. Every headline was about the election and Trump's victory. I never cared much for politics, but in the moment that Trump won, I knew I needed to care. My intuition said that something in the world was massively shifting.

My intuition was right.

After Trump's election, researchers found compelling evidence to support the "Trump effect" hypothesis: a surge in hate crimes across the US.[13] For a while, I had distanced myself from my race, and now, for the first time, I was afraid because of my race.

Living in San Francisco didn't make me feel any safer, despite the large AAPI population. Stories spread like wildfire on all social media outlets. There were incidents of hate on the Bay Area Rapid Transit, including an angry man who shoved an Asian woman and told her to go back to her "chink" country. There was news of a car of White men who drove by a group of Asian students on the Berkeley campus and yelled, "You don't belong here!"

Jabin Botsford @
@jabinbotsford

Close up of President @realDonaldTrump notes is seen where he crossed out "Corona" and replaced it with "Chinese" Virus as he speaks with his coronavirus task force today at the White House. #trump #trumpnotes

11:06 AM · Mar 19, 2020 · Twitter Web App

It felt like a never-ending stream of news about hatred targeting anyone who looked or sounded remotely Chinese.

Little did I know this was just the beginning of a rise in hate crimes targeting Asians. And this would be nothing compared to what was coming our way with the coronavirus.

"China Virus! It's the f-ing China Virus! You f-ing Chink. Take your damn virus back home with you!" a Black woman with ripped pants and a dirty T-shirt shouted angrily at me as she waved her umbrella with the end pointed at me.

---

13  Benjamin Newman et al., "The Trump Effect: An Experimental Investigation of the Emboldening Effect of Racially Inflammatory Elite Communication," *British Journal of Political Science* 51, no. 3 (February 17, 2021): 1138–1159, https://doi.org/10.1017/S0007123419000590.

Well shit. It felt like life had come full circle. I was brought back to my childhood when that woman had bitterly shouted the same sentiment.

As I glanced at the woman, who was still waving her umbrella my way, people kept walking by, ignoring us as they passed. My mind raced to the recent news footage I had seen: images of innocent people from the AAPI community getting kicked, having their heads stomped on, and being beaten for no reason other than their race.

Clearly, nobody else was going to step in or say anything. I kept my head down and quickly scuttered away from this woman and her umbrella, not wanting to attract any more attention to myself. I was scared for my safety.

More than my own safety, I was scared for my parents' safety. Many of the innocent Asians who were being beaten in the streets were my parents' age. My parents worked hard and gave their all to this country, yet there was still hate towards them just because of what they looked like and where they came from. The thought of anything happening to them triggered anger to flow through me like lava.

I'm glad (or maybe not) people think that I hold the power to unleash a virus onto the world or steal the jobs of Americans, but really? Enough is enough.

## March 16, 2021
## Atlanta Shootings—An Awakening

"8 Dead in Atlanta Spa Shootings, With Fears of Anti-Asian Bias."[14]

I cried as I read the headlines. My heart ached for these women I didn't even know, for their families, and for the AAPI community. I felt so damn tired of all the hate in the US towards Asians; of people telling us we didn't belong. As tears streamed down my face, it was as if years of hurt and sup-

---

[14] "8 Dead in Atlanta Spa Shootings, with Fears of Anti-Asian Bias," *New York Times*, last modified March 26, 2021, https://www.nytimes.com/live/2021/03/17/us/shooting-atlanta-acworth.

pressed pain were finally given permission to exist. Something reignited in me. I no longer felt the dark numbness that had been sitting inside me over the last five years. Suddenly, I felt heat and passion come alive.

"I will no longer stand for this," I found myself saying aloud to Greg. "I was born in this country. My parents have lived here for decades. They've contributed to this country to make it a better place. My sisters and I have contributed to making it a better place. We all belong here." There was again a deep-seated passion and fire in my words.

We were in Albania during a portion of our nomadic life, driving around the country.

"You do belong," he said softly, turning his head away from the road to smile at me with love twinkling in his eyes.

"I do belong," I said quietly.

Over the coming weeks I hibernated. I went into my own shell. I needed to process. I don't know how long I stayed there, but I eventually emerged like a caterpillar emerging from a cocoon as a butterfly. I emerged with clarity.

"I'm shifting my coaching focus," I announced to Greg one morning. He was in the kitchen of our Airbnb, making us coffee in a neon-green French press. He looked up at me curiously, waiting for me to say more. "I'm going to focus on working with the AAPI community. Especially AAPI women. I want to empower AAPI women to be seen, to be heard, and to fucking rock that damn boat because I'm tired of the bullshit!"

As I made this proclamation, I could feel the solidity of the ground beneath me—an unwavering sense of who I was and what mattered to me.

Announcing my renewed focus on working with AAPI women was a monumental decision for me, like a moment of reckoning with the skeletons in my closet. You see, when I first started coaching, a part of me knew that I wanted to work with AAPI women. I knew what it felt like to be stuck beneath all the "shoulds" of parents, teachers, managers, and society at large. I knew how heavy it felt to carry armor and hide who I was to fit in with the world's expectations of me.

But I was too chickenshit to declare what I longed for. And I say that about myself in the most loving way.

When I started my coaching practice, I recognized the challenges of focusing my practice on AAPI women. First, many of us grew up being told not to air our dirty laundry; that we needed to save face. We've become amazing at hiding our feelings and emotions and not sharing or asking for help when things aren't going well. So for an AAPI woman to admit that things aren't going well and reach out to a coach for help is a significant barrier. Second, many of us AAPI women have been taught to prioritize others first; to put others' needs ahead of ourselves and that our needs don't matter as much. The end result? We don't invest in ourselves because it feels selfish to do so. Coaching requires a significant investment in both time and money; it requires someone to prioritize themself.

These were barriers in my own growth and initial hesitancy in seeking out a coach, so it scared me to declare that I would be laser-focused on AAPI women. As much as I wanted to help the community, I also needed to make a living to support my family.

So I chickened out.

Instead, I broadened my scope to working with high-achieving, ambitious, professional women who have a desire to let go of shoulds, strengthen their mental fitness, and be the author of their own stories. My business thrived. I believed that I had made the right choice with my focus.

Then the Atlanta incident happened.

Something deep within me awoke. I knew it was time to lead with my heart and intuition rather than my rational brain. It didn't matter how hard this renewed focus would be. It's what mattered to me.

I was angry that, despite the increased hate crimes and racism, people in the AAPI community were still saying we needed to just stay quiet, keep our heads down, and not rock the boat. I disagree. It is time for change. It is time to be seen, to be heard, and to fucking rock the boat. Because we do belong.

And thus began my journey back to being proud of my history, my ancestry, and my lineage. And I do believe I've come home to myself and am here to stay. The pendulum is no longer swinging; it has found its balanced place, its grounded place. I'm proud to be Asian and proud to be American.

Greg grinned a wide grin at me as he poured a cup of coffee for me and said, "I like that."

As we went for a walk, I held his hand lightly and walked beside him, proud of who I am, all of me.

# Mama & Papa Yip's Story

**化干戈為玉帛.**
*huà gān gē wéi yù bó.*
Replace weapons with jade and silk.

## Setting the Scene

After finishing my last coaching session for the day, I waddle out of my home office to join my parents in my kitchen. They came over to our apartment to help us prepare for the big day, Lunar New Year, and the other big day, the arrival of my baby, which could be any day now. As I walk into the kitchen, I see my mom staring at the microwave above her head trying to figure out which button to hit so she can warm up a pork bun for my dad. My dad is sweeping my floor with a yellow broom in one hand and a dustpan in the other. I'm not sure what exactly he's sweeping up since I had just cleaned the floor, but he somehow always notices dirt and dust that needs to be swept up.

Seeing that I'm done with work for the day, my mom opens the microwave door and plops two more buns on a white plate before putting it back into the microwave. I walk over and hit the "One Minute Express Cook" button, then sit down at the kitchen table and invite them to join me. A pizza box with my dad's favorite thick-crust pepperoni pizza is on the table. My husband had picked it up for us. Once the floor feels sufficiently dirt- and dust-free, my dad joins me at the kitchen table in the chair next to me. My mom sits diagonally from me as she places pork buns down on the table, and we begin to talk about belonging.

# Everything Is a Choice

入鄉隨俗.

*rù xiāng suí sú.*
When entering a village, follow its customs.

"We belong in America," Papa Yip states without hesitancy. "There's no question about it. The foundation of this country was built on welcoming all. I am part of that 'all.' When we landed on US soil in 1978, this became our home. Nobody has the right to tell us that we don't belong. *We* get to decide that."

My chin hits the ground and I blink a few times. I'm taken aback by what he shares. I always thought my parents were proud of being Chinese. As far back as I can remember, they've taught me to honor my elders, to learn about my Chinese history, and to never lose touch with my lineage. That's why they insisted I go to Chinese school every Sunday, which I did for over a decade of my childhood. I never thought my parents saw themselves as Americans or that they viewed the US as their home. I'm at a loss for words as I slowly chew my pork bun.

Not noticing my shock, Papa Yip continues, "We came to America for the same reasons many immigrants came to America: opportunity. This is the land where dreams are possible. Our dream was to give our children a chance at a better life; an opportunity for better health, better education, and better work."

He gazes at the floor, lost in memories. I lean forward, elbows on the table, chin resting on my hands, waiting for him to continue.

"The choice to come to America meant the difference between life or death for your sister Jenny," Papa Yip whispers. "She had a hole in her heart. Medical proficiency wasn't as good in Hong Kong compared to the US. Had we chosen to stay in Hong Kong, she would have likely died.

"The choice to come to America also meant different opportunities for you girls. Opportunities we never got because we didn't make it beyond elementary school. In Hong Kong, there are only two universities. So getting admitted is hard. Getting a scholarship is nearly impossible. And in Hong Kong, during the 1970s, there wasn't such a thing as educational loans. So even if you girls got into one of the two universities, there was no way your mommy and I could afford the tuition for even one of you. So we had to make a choice."

Mama Yip sighs, "We knew what we needed to do, but it didn't make it any easier. Coming to America meant we had to leave your sisters behind while we established ourselves here. Your sisters were only seven and two."

"Before leaving Hong Kong, we tried to mentally prepare for what was ahead," Papa Yip explains. "Leaving all that we knew for a land halfway around the world where we knew nobody and nothing. But no amount of preparation can ease the challenge of leaving your children at such a young age, knowing you'll miss pivotal years in their life and not knowing when you'll get to see them again. On our flight to the US your mommy couldn't stop crying. She would keep saying, 'I wonder how they're doing,' 'I wonder if they're sleeping okay,' 'I wonder if they've eaten.'"

Papa Yip's eyes glisten and he swipes at his face. I glance at Mama Yip. Her shoulders are slumped, her eyes pressed shut. My heart fills with pain and love for them, a mixture of warmth and heaviness.

Mama Yip opens her eyes to meet my gaze, a single tear swimming in her eye. "The most painful part was not knowing if your sister would survive during the years ahead. Would she make it until we were able to bring her to the US for heart surgery? What if something happened to her and we never saw her again? We didn't know what would happen. And that hurt beyond words."

"But we made a choice," Papa Yip says as he turns to me. "And when we landed here in America in 1978, we chose this country to be our new home."

I realize I've been holding my breath as my parents shared. I feel dizzy and disoriented. As I breathe in the choices my parents were faced with at the mere ages of twenty-eight and thirty, my heart flutters. In my late twenties, the biggest decisions I had to make revolved around which MBA program to apply for and what career move I wanted to make. I can't imagine the heaviness of their decision; the pressure of your child losing their life if you don't succeed. I bite my tongue and swallow back a tear that I feel arising. I don't want to cry in front of them. Papa Yip would worry and ask a lot of questions, shifting the attention to me. I want to stay focused on their story.

"Nobody can tell us we don't belong," Papa Yip asserts with strength in his voice. "Just look at history. Who truly belongs to the US? Not White Americans, nor Black Americans, nor Asian Americans. It's the Native Americans who truly belong on this land. Most people are here because at some point, their ancestors immigrated here. So nobody has a right to decide for us or for you if you belong. You have to make the choice: do I belong here or not?"

Papa Yip sits up straight and wags his finger, as if he's a professor giving students a lecture. "If the answer is yes, you belong here, then you need to truly believe that you belong. If you don't, then why would anybody else believe it? You need to wholeheartedly invest in putting America first, whether by voting or contributing back to the country. It has to be like a faithful marriage, the type of marriage that you're in for the long haul. Not the ones you get into, then assume you'll divorce right away. You can't have one foot in and one foot out. Commit fully if you're going to choose to belong to this country."

"And if the answer is no you don't belong?" I wonder aloud.

"If you feel like you don't belong, you also have choices to make," Papa Yip asserts. "Do I leave this country? Can I leave this country? Do I stay? How can I fight to show that I care and belong? Where do I need to learn to adapt?

"Stepping into America was like stepping into a whole new world for us," Papa Yip shares about their arrival in America. "But we made the choice to stay. We made the choice to belong. So we had to learn to adapt to this new world."

Mama Yip pushes the box of pizza towards Papa Yip, urging him to eat it before it gets colder.

"Like having to learn to eat pizza!" he exclaims as he folds a slice in half and, with three bites, consumes the whole piece.

"Maybe you should adapt to eating slower," Mama Yip jabs.

He smiles at her with a mouthful of pizza as he reaches for another slice. "Some things were easy to adapt to. Like how much open land and fresh air there is here. Or the size of homes, and the fact that many of them have more than one bathroom!"

My eyebrows raise.

"In Hong Kong, we only had one toilet shared among all of us, like at the tailor shop I worked at. If you really have to go and someone is in the bathroom, you'd be standing outside, banging the door, yelling at the person inside to hurry. You have to squeeze your legs together like this." Papa Yip scoots his chair out from the table to demonstrate. "You squeeze and hold, desperately hoping you can keep it in until the person comes out." Papa Yip gently slaps his knee as he laughs at the memory.

My huge grin spreads from cheek to cheek as I imagine Papa Yip standing in front of a door yelling that he needs to go. I suppose now I understand why he's always loved his quiet time alone in his bathroom. He could be in there for hours reading the newspaper and enjoying the peace and quiet, not having to worry about someone else needing to use it because we had two other bathrooms in the house.

"Adapting isn't always as easy as getting used to having your own bath-room though," Mama Yip puts forth. "We had to learn a new language, a new culture. Here, your daddy had to work for someone else, work more hours, and make less money. We missed our community in Hong Kong. We had to constantly remind ourselves why we were in the US: a better future for our kids, grandkids, and great-grandkids. That's what gave us the courage and strength to keep going, keep going through all the tough times in our new life in this country because we made the choice to belong here."

Mama Yip gathers up the empty plates. "You always have a choice."

# The Power to Change Things Is in Your Hands

## 風向轉變時, 有人築牆, 有人造風車.

*fēng xiàng zhuǎn biàn shí, yǒu rén zhú qiáng, yǒu rén zào fēng chē.*

When the winds of change blow, some build walls, others build windmills.

I silently study Mama Yip, who is standing at the sink, drying clean dishes. She's a tiny woman: five foot, three inches; quite possibly five foot, two inches or even shorter now. As she's aged, she's gotten shorter. She's a resilient woman, but tiny. Barely a hundred pounds. Papa Yip always worries about her not weighing enough. Unfortunately, her love of vegetables makes it hard for her to gain weight. Seeing her standing there, I can't help but wonder, *What if she had been one of those elderly Asian women who was beaten for no reason while just walking the streets?* It scares me. It pains me.

Turning my gaze to Papa Yip, I ask, "I get the importance of adapting, but how can you adapt to all this hate towards Asians these days? All the beatings of innocent people and crimes?"

He studies my face for what feels like an eternity, then leans back in his chair and says, "You know, Amy, nothing is ever 100 percent fair. Life is not fair. People like to complain about things being unfair, but complaining won't ever change anything. Staying quiet won't change anything either."

I give Papa Yip a sideways look. "But you taught us to keep our heads down and avoid trouble. Not to make situations bigger and bigger. So what do you mean 'staying quiet won't change things'?"

Papa Yip nods, "You are right. We have always believed that if you can avoid conflict that's a good thing. Follow the rules. It was taught to us growing up. And we passed our learnings on to you. When we first arrived in the US, we were seen as outsiders. So we thought it would be smart to avoid trouble and conflict. But things in America are different, especially now. So you can't just take our old Chinese teachings and apply it to your life here. What we taught you might not be right for that."

My forehead creases as I piece together in my head what he's saying. For much of my life, I thought that my parents wanted me to choose the Chinese way of being. They always said I was becoming "too American" anytime I spoke my mind or anytime I did something for myself instead of thinking about everyone else first. Even when I embraced activities such as backpacking or running marathons, I was becoming "too American." I had always felt like they didn't understand me at all; that they couldn't comprehend the challenges of trying to adapt and fit into American life while trying to meet the Chinese expectations they set at home.

I lean in towards Papa Yip, furrowing my brows. "You mean you might've been wrong?"

He smiles at me. "Not wrong."

"Your daddy is never wrong," Mama Yip teases.

"That is correct," Papa Yip wags his forefinger. "I'm never wrong. What I taught you just might not be right for the world today. That's why it's your job to discern: Does what I've been taught help me or harm me in my current circumstance?

"There's a Chinese saying, 'The wise adapt themselves to circumstances, as water molds itself to the pitcher.' So you need to adapt to how things are now. Use your voice. Your voice matters. Not to just complain, but to change things. If there are small issues, you have to make them big issues. With the big issues, like the hate crimes, you have to make them even bigger issues.

"The beauty of this country is that no matter who you are, where you came from, what color your skin is, what your gender identity is, by law, you are not to be discriminated against. That's a starting point that many countries haven't even reached yet. There are many countries where it's still legal to discriminate; it's legal to censor speech. In those countries, if you speak up against the government or say something they don't like, they lock you up. In the US, you can speak up if you don't approve of the president or the government. You have basic human rights to use your voice. It certainly isn't implemented perfectly, but the starting point of this country is further ahead than many places. Use that to your advantage.

"Work hard, move up the ranks, be successful, gain power. Power helps you gain leverage to drive the type of change you want to see. Get into politics and do things for the betterment of all people."

Do I know this man? Is this the same man who told me not to talk back to my teacher? The same man who told me to listen to my managers? I squeeze my eyes shut and rest my forehead into my palms as I absorb what Papa Yip has just advised.

"And if you're truly scared of the hate crimes against Asians, then learn kung fu!" Papa Yip suggests.

Walking back to the kitchen table as she dries her hands with a white dish towel, Mama Yip scrutinizes Papa Yip. "You want your daughter to learn kung fu now?"

"Well, it doesn't hurt," he laughs. "In the grand scheme of things, I do believe that the percentage of people who hate and act out to show their animosity is a small number. Most people don't have hateful intentions. Most people are good people. But if you're afraid of the violence then, yeah, learn kung fu." He peers at my thirty-nine-week-large belly. "Or maybe for now just be more vigilant and aware of your surroundings."

I chuckle. Papa Yip's beliefs have changed tremendously since I was a young girl. I like this new version; this version that's politely letting me know that it's time for the next generations to rock that damn boat and make some noise—for him, for Mama Yip, and for all the generations of AAPI that call the US home.

## Love Can Overcome Hate; Community Can Overcome Separation

人無完人, 金無足赤.

*rén wú wán rén, jīn wú zú chì.*
No man is a perfect man, no gold is sufficiently bare.

"The lady said what to you?" Mama Yip yells angrily, like a bear protecting her cub. I had finally shared my experience as a three-year-old at the park getting told to go back to my own country. I left out the part about my playing with ants. She would've cringed hearing about that. "How could she say that to little kids? And why didn't you tell me?"

"You should've told us, Amy," Papa Yip agrees. He shakes his head. "But you know, hate and separation is nothing new for us. It happens everywhere in the world. If it's not race, it's something else. In China, people from Shanghai, where I grew up, thought they were higher class than those who came from the countryside, where your mommy grew up. Shanghainese thought those from the countryside were too old-fashioned; that they were uneducated. Right, country girl?" Papa Yip taunts, leaning towards Mama Yip with a smile so big you can see all his teeth.

"Yeah. I'm a dumb country girl. I don't know anything," Mama Yip bristles as she rolls her eyes.

Papa Yip turns back to me and continues. "In China, us Shanghainese made fun of people from the countryside. But when I went to Hong Kong, people in Hong Kong would make fun of me for being from Shanghai. They'd ridicule how we spoke and dressed and tell us we didn't belong in Hong Kong. We eventually adapted. Coming to America, the same thing happened. People tried to tell us we didn't belong."

"It wasn't just other racial groups or ethnicities that told us we didn't belong in the US," Mama Yip asserts. "Other Chinese made fun of us too. When we arrived in the US, most of the Chinese here were from Tai Shan. They immigrated to the US decades before others in China. So the Tai Shan Americans would say to us, 'You aren't the real Chinese. People from Tai Shan are the real Chinese.' They would treat us as inferior and look down on us. But you know what happened? Most of the Chinese who immigrated to the US over the last few decades were quite wealthy. They'd tell the Tai Shan Americans, 'You came on boats. We came on 747s.' This showed their wealth and progress while indicating that the Tai Shan Americans were outdated."

"It's human nature to find reasons to separate and create tiers of status," Papa Yip remarks. "There will always be people that don't accept you and try to make you feel as if your existence is wrong; that you don't belong. There will also be people who are always trying to help you. People who will stand up for you. I believe that those who separate are a small minority of humanity. More people are kind and willing to help."

Papa Yip leans forward and shares, "Let me tell you a story. There was this one snowy night when I was driving home from work and my car broke down. A Black man pulled over to help me. He tried to push my car towards the gas station. He kept pushing and pushing. But my car was on an uphill slope, and it was freezing cold. I told him I would call Triple A. He waited with me until they arrived just in case it took too long. He didn't want me waiting in the cold alone. It's not just about race. People can be kind. People can be unkind." Papa Yip meets my gaze. "If people hate you, if people treat you badly, you need to love them more, be more kind to them. I know that's hard. It's easier to retaliate and hate them back. But more hate won't overcome hate. It will only cause more separation. People who hate others need more love. Only love can overcome hate and bring people together."

"That's a Buddhist belief," Mama Yip explains, "loving kindness. I was working in the kitchen of a big chain supermarket, and two male colleagues would always make fun of my name and my accent. Even after a decade of living here, English didn't get any easier for me. So they would say to me, 'Your English isn't good English. It's Chinglish. Chinese English!' Even though they made fun of me, I was still kind to them. I helped them when they struggled with making a dish. I would teach them how to be more efficient. I even cooked things like fried rice, shrimp, all kinds of deli salads, and BBQ ribs and shared with them. Everyone would gather in the dining room to eat together when I made food. All my coworkers appreciated my kindness, and we all ended up getting along quite well. Even the two guys who initially made fun of me."

As my parents share their experiences of kindness, it takes me through my own life experiences. Sure, there were many experiences of people making me feel like I didn't belong, but there were also many instances of loving kindness. I remember the little girl who held out her hand and asked me to play after other kids made fun of my eyes, the man who pulled over on the highway to help me with my flat tire, and the woman who offered to switch seats with me so my husband and I could sit together on the bus. Kindness is out there if you look for it, just as hostility is out there if that's all you look for.

"This is our home and the home for our grandchildren, our future generations," Papa Yip announces. "So our hope for America is that it will thrive, and everyone here can live happier, more inclusive lives together, not be split by gender, race, ethnicity, education levels, or something else. For that to happen, people need to come together. All people. Not just the Asian community. You can't solve issues and make things more equitable and fair if you're only thinking of one group. If we only think about what we can do for the Asian community and push for changes that help the Asian community, it'll lead to inequalities towards other groups. So to move our country and world towards a more positive place, we have to think beyond the Asian community towards what we can do for everyone. It's not about being White or Black, Hispanic or Asian. It's about acceptance with love. That's how a country can thrive.

"When we first moved to Hong Kong, the Cantonese and Shanghainese disliked each other. They'd look down at one another. They're both Chinese, but they felt they were different and separate. Over time, we eventually melted together and stopped talking about who's better or who's from where. We were all living together in Hong Kong. And for Hong Kong to do well, we all needed to come together."

Papa Yip straightens in his seat and raises his arms up. "The future of America also relies on all of us coming together. And I do think it'll happen over time as we all melt together. Just look at all our grandchildren. They're the beginning of this coming together. We have two grandchildren who are a quarter White, a quarter Black, and half Chinese; two who are half Korean and half Chinese; and one grandchild on the way who is half White, half Chinese." Papa Yip points at my belly. "This is the beginning of the future."

Mama Yip nods. "We just need to be friendlier and kinder to each other, like our neighbors. Just last week, our next-door neighbors, who are Chinese, were working in their yard. The man two houses down, who is Mexican, saw them and went over to help. Then the White family across the way came by to lend them some shovels. That's what we need more of. Loving kindness. Caring for each other regardless of where you were originally from."

"That's what we hope for for the future of *our* country: America," Papa Yip finishes.

# My Reflections Post-Conversation

Throughout my childhood, all I wanted was for my parents to understand me. I wanted them to understand how their expectations contradicted who I thought I needed to be in order to fit into the American lifestyle. What I'm realizing now is that although they might not fully comprehend my experiences, they get them. They get what it feels like to not belong. They get what it feels like to try to adapt. They also get that while their way of adapting worked for them, times are different, and what worked for them may not work anymore.

As I closed my eyes, I could feel my baby kicking my belly. I couldn't help but wonder what kind of a world my child will grow up in being half White, half Chinese. I wondered where my child would belong and how he would feel about his place in this world. I have friends who are of mixed race, and they frequently talk about feeling out of place as they were growing up. They never felt they belonged to one group or another, and that made them feel like an outcast.

Just like my parents didn't fully understand what I experienced trying to straddle the cultural line between Chinese and American, I won't ever fully understand my child's journey straddling the racial line between White and Asian. And that's okay. I don't need to understand the specific circumstance; I understand what it feels like to be excluded, to not belong. And I also know how to address the issue if it arises. I know what I can do to help my child recognize his place of belonging no matter what. I recognize the importance of teaching him to love more and hate less, especially towards himself.

Though separation and comparisons are unavoidable, if we want to change how the world works, that's what we all need to do: move from fear to love. We need to, as my parents said, love more—love the people we care about, love even those who hate us. The ones we don't want to love are the ones we need to love the most. It's the only thing that will overcome the separation that exists. If we fuel the flames of separation with more separation, the flames will only get bigger.

The image that comes to mind is a kid who's growing up and wants to escape their parents' cuddles and kisses because they're "too cool" for that now. Those parents just need to keep grabbing them and hugging them with love. That's what I'll be doing with my own kid.

What I want to keep reminding myself of and teach to my child is to love more and hate less; that's how we create a sense of belonging.

We're also always in choice and have two obvious options:

1. **We can choose where we belong. Our sense of identity must come from within.**

   A lack of self-identity is what leads to confusion about where we belong. We end up looking to others for answers. The truth is, nobody can tell us where we belong (or don't belong). Nobody can tell us who we are or aren't. There will always be people who make us feel excluded, but there will also be those who make us feel included.

   For me, I've had to decide for myself how I choose to fit into America and what I want my role here to be. For my kiddo, he might need to uncover his sense of identity around being White, Asian, or something in between. Or perhaps he might decide that it's not even an important part of his identity.

   At the end of the day, it doesn't matter what others say or do. You get to choose, and so do I. Nobody else can do that for us. I choose to be American with a Chinese lineage. I want to teach my son that he has a choice about who he is and where he belongs based on his own internal compass, not on what others say or how they make him feel. And I will teach him that I will love him no matter what his choice is. As Aristotle told us, knowing ourselves is the beginning of all wisdom.[15]

---

[15] This quote is a common adaptation of Aristotle's discussion on intellectual virtues: Aristotle, *The Nicomachean Ethics*, trans. J. A. K. Thomson (London: Penguin Classics, 2004), book VI.

2. **If we're not happy with the way things are, then we can do something to change it.**

Things won't ever be perfect. Life isn't perfect. But we always have a choice to change things and make them better. It might feel like we're not in a place of power or that we can't make a difference, but a look at history shows us that change often happens when the underdog or those who aren't in power fight for what they believe in. So let's do something about it. Yes, it'll take time. It might not happen while we're alive. But if we believe something needs to change, then we must act.

And on that note, I'm going to take action and go finish writing this book now in the hope that more people will love more and hate less, especially in their relationship with their parents.

# A Date with Your Parents

## PRE-CONVERSATION PERSONAL REFLECTION

### Overview

When we embody a connection to ourselves, we are able to be in reciprocal connection to those we love, those in our community, those all over the planet, and even the planet itself. By having a sense of our own selves, we learn to hold our own dignity and the dignity of others through love and conflict, how to partner with the world around us, and how to shift from disconnection to healing connection. We are able to build stronger relationships with ourselves and with others, truly living from a place of belonging. It starts with you knowing who you are and choosing which parts of your identity are most important to you.

### Instructions

1. Take some time to reflect on these questions and journal your answers to them:

   ◈ What factors have shaped your identity?

   ◈ Consider the different parts of your identity.

      ✦ Which parts did you choose for yourself?

      ✦ Which parts were determined for you by other people or by society?

✦ Which parts are you most proud of?

✦ Which parts did you struggle the most with growing up?

✦ Which is the most important to you?

✦ Which is least important to you?

2. Sit with what you've written. Review and absorb it. Perhaps take some time away to let it sink in as you ponder the following:

◈ What patterns are you noticing?

◈ Who are you when you give yourself full permission?

◈ What stories about your identity no longer serve you?

Pretend I'm sitting next to you (or it can be a friend, a manager, or a potential employer) and I ask, "Tell me who you are without telling me what you do. No titles or roles." Based on what you've uncovered, how do you respond? Say it aloud. Let it flow. There's no right answer. Record what you say (a computer or phone works just fine) so you can go back and listen to it.

## THE CONVERSATION

### Conversation Topic

What your parents' experiences of belonging were like and where your parents feel they belong today.

### Tips

These conversations can be hard, and potentially triggering. Priority number one is to take care of yourself. Remember to review the Conversation Tip Sheet on page 23 before your conversation.

## Conversation-Specific Suggestions

Create an atmosphere that can represent a blend of your parents' country or countries of origin and their current one(s). That might include where your parents immigrated to and from, or, if they sent you to a new country to live with a relative or go to boarding school, it might be where you were born and where you were sent.

Perhaps order food to enjoy together that's representative of both places (e.g., we ate pork buns and pizza), or bring a map so they can point out where they grew up and show you their journey from then to now. Photos that show their early life or yours right after immigrating also work well. You can do this even if you don't live near each other by using food delivery services to send them food or bringing a map or photos that you can show them over video.

Start the conversation with curiosity about what it was like to leave one life behind and start anew. You can use the food, map, or photos to start the conversation. For example, "How did you feel about pizza when you first arrived in the US?"

Tailor the questions to your specific circumstance. For example, if your parents are second-generation or beyond, you might ask them what they think about having been in this country for X generations. Or, if your parents didn't immigrate but sent you to a new country on your own, you might ask about their perspectives on that experience.

## Questions For Your Parents

### *Lighter Questions*

◈ What were you most pleasantly surprised by when you immigrated to [insert country]? What were some unpleasant surprises?

✦ **OR,** What were you most surprised by after sending me to [insert country]?

✦ **OR,** What continues to surprise you about living in [insert country], despite our family having been here for X generations?

◈ When you first arrived, what did you miss most about [insert country of ancestral origin]? What do you miss about [insert country of ancestral origin] now? Do you long to go back? Why or why not?

✦ **OR,** What did you miss most about having me away? How do you feel now?

◈ How did you have to adapt to life in [insert country]? How did you feel about having to adapt? What was most exciting? What was most scary?

◈ How did / does it feel to be in a land with people who are different from you? *You can state examples such as speaking different languages, experiencing different cultures, or looking different.* What stories can you share about those experiences?

◈ What do you love most about the country you live in?

◈ What do you love most about the city or town you live in?

## Deeper Questions

◈ Where do you feel you belong? Why? Tell me more about it.

◈ What factors shape your identity? What part of your identity is the most important to you? What part of your identity is least important to you?

◈ Tell me who you are without telling me titles or roles. How has your sense of identity changed over time?

◈ How do you feel about children of immigrant parents having to adapt to two different cultures and belief systems? What advice would you give them? *To give context, you can share some of your experiences of having to adapt. For example, I shared the notion of speaking up versus staying quiet and its impact on my career.*

◈ How do you feel about all the hate crimes, biases, and racism happening against the Asian community? What should the current generations do about it?

◈ What have you always wanted to ask me?

## POST-CONVERSATION CONTEMPLATION

After the conversation with your parents, contemplate and journal on the following:

◈ What new insights have you gained about

✦ who your parents are,

✦ what it was like for them to adapt to change, and

✦ what their beliefs are around belonging and identity?

◈ How could you help your parents feel a greater sense of belonging?

◈ How does what you've learned about your parents shift the way you think about your own identity and where you belong?

◈ Listen to the recording you made about who you are from the Pre-Conversation Personal Reflection. What parts of this do you want to keep? What parts of this do you want to let go of? What else do you want to add to it?

*To be lost is as legitimate a part of your process as being found.*
~ Alex Ebert ~

## MYTH 6

# I Must Be Mentally Tough and Never Ask for Help

# My Story

## I Want to Be a Psychologist

"I'm going to study psychology," Jenny announced during her senior year of high school.

"You're what?" my mom said, eyebrows furrowed, staring at my sister. "Why would you want to work with crazy people? You'll become crazy too!"

*Crazy is contagious?* I wondered. I was only twelve, so my exposure to anything related to mental health encompassed only the white-walled psychiatric wards I witnessed on TV shows and movies and what I heard from my parents, none of which painted a pretty light on the subject.

"What will we tell people? That our daughter works with psychotic people? We will lose face," my dad thundered.

*Oh here we go again. Back to the whole "saving face" thing.* My dad always seemed worried about losing respect from others and avoiding family embarrassment.

Jenny clenched her fists. She wasn't going to back down. She's always been the rebel, the fighter, the typical middle child.

I left the scene quickly, not wanting to witness what happened next.

I never did find out how the conversation turned out. At some point, my parents relented. Perhaps they realized that my sister would have the prestigious doctor title. Or maybe they learned about the breadth of psychology fields that exist. Quite possibly it was a mix of both. When my sister finally started school, and especially upon graduating with her doctorate, my parents moved from disapproval to pride in their daughter's achievements.

Despite this shift, we still never talked much about mental well-being. On occasion, Jenny would bring up what she was learning about obsessive compulsive disorders, her area of expertise. Outside of that, my knowledge and insight into mental health was relegated to how the topic was portrayed on TV shows or in movies. The narratives would depict either a psychotic murderer or a homeless lunatic in the streets who was laughing at nothing, yelling for no reason, and showcasing what was described as "abnormal behavior." The storylines would often be something like this: the person was "normal," then a trigger event such as a cheating spouse, bankruptcy, or job loss would occur that led to the downward spiral of the individual's mental capacity, resulting in lunacy.

*That's not me and won't be me*, I always thought. *I'm tough. I can eat bitterness and get through anything on my own. Just like my parents.*

Growing up, I witnessed my parents always doing what they needed to do no matter how hard it was physically, emotionally, or mentally. Never a complaint and never a whimper, they were always taking care of others and making shit happen. I rarely spent much time with them. But I didn't expect to. Take my mom, for example. She worked two full-time jobs. On her days off she grocery shopped, prepped food for the week, cleaned the house, did laundry, drove her kids to and from where they needed to be, and barely slept a wink. It would've been selfish for me to expect more time with her. Then there was my dad. Even after long hours at multiple jobs, he would deliver groceries to my grandma's house. Despite making very little himself and having a family of five to support, he continued to send money to his brothers in Hong Kong and China.

Watching my parents, I learned about eating bitterness; that if things are hard, just tough it out. Suppress the need to complain. Don't ask for help. You just have to be physically, emotionally, and mentally tough. And I thought I was.

# Mishap in Tank 4

It was Sunday, March 11, 2018, 7:01 a.m. I was lying in my queen bed scrolling through my phone when a new email notification popup caught my eye. Subject line: "Important Confidential Message." From: the fertility center I had used when I lived in San Francisco.

*It's probably an email about a data breach or some privacy changes*, I thought to myself.

As I read the email, my heart stopped and my mind began to race.

"Greg!" I called out. "Can you come here?"

"What's up?" Greg asked, poking his head into our tiny bedroom in New York City. Honestly, it was more like a coffin than a bedroom. Two sides of the bed were up against the walls with about a two-foot clearance on a third side. When the door shut, it closed right at the foot of the bed.

"Read this and tell me what it means," I said, handing him my phone.

As he read the email, I anxiously scanned his face for an answer, some comfort.

"Unfortunate incident in the lab," he mumbled aloud. "Equipment lost liquid nitrogen for a brief period of time. Your tissue was stored in the affected Tank 4; it may have been impacted."

He glanced at me. "Well, I know it sounds bad, but let's not worry yet. It says to call the number. Let's do that."

What we discovered was that, along with over two hundred other households, our tissues were in a tank that had failed to maintain its temperature. They couldn't tell us the viability of our embryos unless we planned on using them.

Greg and I had frozen our embryos because we wanted children, but we also wanted to wait to have children. We had dreams of volunteering overseas and traveling the world before settling down.

So now what? After my first experience with the in vitro fertilization process, I had said to myself, *I never want to do this ever again.* My body didn't do well with shooting myself up full of hormones.

After the Tank 4 incident, I felt like I needed to do it again. After all, I was already thirty-six, soon-to-be thirty-seven. Age wasn't on my side. So I tried again. Every evening for two weeks, I diligently injected needles filled with hormones into my stomach. "Be sure to find a new spot for each injection," my fertility doctor had warned me. And so I did. My belly was covered in little polka dots where I had already injected on previous nights.

The hormones were rough. I could feel them coursing throughout my body almost immediately. I felt bloated like a big round helium balloon that's been overinflated. The cramping was relentless. More than anything, the toughest part about the process was not feeling like myself—for two straight weeks. Emotions felt a hundred times stronger. The tiniest things would upset me. I was thrilled when the two weeks were over and it was time for my egg retrieval. Fifteen were retrieved.

We waited as the labs fertilized my eggs and provided me with daily updates. Out of the fifteen eggs, only one was a "good quality" embryo, versus the three we had lost in Tank 4.

My fertility doctor explained, "The likelihood of a live birth rate with a good-quality embryo is 64 percent." According to statistics, I needed at least three good-quality embryos for a chance at pregnancy. But I couldn't physically or emotionally go through in vitro again.

I sank into a deep sadness. I felt lost in a dark, cavernous hole. But I couldn't possibly say anything to anyone. I had a great job working at Google, I was dating the love of my life, and I had loving friends and family. To everyone around me, my life was a dream.

*I should be grateful for my life,* I'd often remind myself. *Some of the people who were impacted by Tank 4 can never have kids because of cancer. At least I'm still healthy and fairly young. I have a good job and people who love me. What more do I need? How could I possibly want more? I'm being selfish.*

Yet the nagging feeling of not being okay kept resurfacing. A part of me said I should settle down and start a family; that the embryo incident was a sign for me to do the "normal" thing. Another part of me resisted; it told me to pursue my dreams of world travel. I didn't know what to do. More importantly, I felt a heaviness that I had never experienced before. It weighed me down like a ton of bricks.

But I couldn't possibly seek help or guidance from others. I couldn't air my dirty laundry. I would lose face. I would shame my family.

I was taught that if I worked hard enough and was smart and tough enough, I should be able to figure things out on my own. So what did I do? I started my self-help journey by quietly reading self-help books. I spent eight months reading book after book for an answer to my questions. From Brené Brown to Malcolm Gladwell, I read them all.

Eight months came and went, and I got no closer to an answer. *Do I have babies, or do I pursue my dream to travel?* I felt pathetic. I felt my time running out. I was losing hope.

## Asking Mother Ayahuasca for Help

"You know there's this thing called ayahuasca you should check out," a good friend, one of few who knew what was really going on with me, suggested. "It's supposed to give you clarity."

"Clarity?" I exclaimed. My eyes widened and I felt a surge of energy filling my heart with hope. "That's exactly what I need! I need clarity!"

I immediately started researching ayahuasca. The more I discovered, the more I felt a pull to it. *I need to meet with Mother Ayahuasca herself to find answers*, I thought to myself. *Finding clarity through ayahuasca doesn't mean I'm weak or wrong*, I convinced myself. *I'm merely searching within myself. And I wouldn't be airing my dirty laundry.* So off to Peru I went for a five-day ceremony.

In the simplest terms, ayahuasca is a psychoactive and entheogenic brewed drink traditionally used as a ceremonial or shamanic spiritual medicine among the indigenous peoples of the Amazon basin. The brew is made from a vine called ayahuasca and a leaf from the chavruta plant that contain a psychoactive molecule called dimethyltryptamine. Indigenous tribes have been using ayahuasca for thousands of years in ceremonial settings for healing at every level—physically, emotionally, mentally, and spiritually. There has been an increasing amount of interest in ayahuasca from both Western societies and scientific communities. Studies have shown that it may potentially clear the body of parasites, reduce depression, and cure drug addiction, and it can be used as a cancer therapeutic.[16] For many though, ayahuasca is a source of answers, used on their journeys of self-healing and spiritual awakening.

The answers I received over the course of the five days were not what I expected.

## Ceremony 1: I'm Not in Control

I entered the spacious teepee and looked around. There were already two other participants who were settling in. The shaman was standing in the center of the room, dressed in all white, a woven, red poncho with embroidered patterns over his attire. A colorful headdress of feathers and other decorations adorned his head. Next to him stood a nurse, a doctor, and several other support staff. They all smiled at us as we entered and waited patiently for everyone to settle in. It was a small group of six participants. An intimate ceremony. Finding a perfect spot for myself, I grabbed blankets and cushions and created a comfortable space for myself.

Once everyone got comfortable, a young woman, the coordinator, spoke about what to expect for the night. We even practiced the right way to purge to avoid choking on our own barf. I shuddered. I hate barfing. I looked around at the faces of others. Nobody else seemed to mind the thought of regurgitating.

*Stay strong, Amy! You got this*, I pumped myself up.

The shaman led us in a song and opening ceremony ritual. Each participant was handed a small shot-glass-sized cup filled with a black tar-like substance. We all drank it together.

---

16   Jonathan Hamill et al., "Ayahuasca: Psychological and Physiologic Effects, Pharmacology and Potential Uses in Addiction and Mental Illness," *Current Neuropharmacology* 17, no. 2 (February 2019): 108–128, https://www.ncbi.nlm.nih.gov/pmc/articles/PMC6343205/.

As the bitter, earthy concoction hit my taste buds, I involuntarily gagged. I quickly swallowed the rest of it and chugged from my water bottle to wash it down. Then I lay down to let the magic do its work.

Almost immediately, I heard someone throwing up. I cringed and curled up into a fetal position. One by one, others joined in the vomiting. Then I heard someone laughing. Someone else started wailing loudly. My mind raced. I felt uncomfortable. And not just from the earth medicine I had just ingested, but from the idea that I might soon lose control over what emotions bubbled up out of me.

*What if I laugh crazily like that guy? What if I start bawling my eyes out for no reason in front of these strangers? No. I can't let that happen. I must stay strong. I must stay tough.*

And so I tried to control the situation. The more other participants let go and surrendered to Mother Ayahuasca, the more I held tightly, refusing to succumb. By the end of the night I was mentally and physically exhausted. I did purge, but that was it. I was no closer to the answer I was seeking.

"How was last night for you?" the staff psychologist asked me the next morning as we debriefed the previous evening.

"I felt the substance. I threw up. But nothing else really came up for me."

"Tell me more," he dug in.

"Maybe it just doesn't work for me. Maybe my mind is too strong for it to work."

"I see," he noted. "Tell me, Amy, how easy is it for you to let go of control? To fully surrender to something?"

I eyed him cautiously. "Surrender?"

"Yes."

"I don't ever surrender. I'm a fighter. I fight. I win."

"I see," he paused and studied me. "Why are you here?"

My mouth tightened as I refused to answer the question. He noticed.

"Look Amy," he started, "Mother Ayahuasca is powerful. And you have to surrender to her. The more you try to control and fight, the more you'll just tire yourself out. What would it take for you to try to let go of control just a little for this evening's ceremony?"

I paused. All my life I've always held onto control intensely. I try to plan, predict, and prevent things that I cannot really plan, predict, or prevent, whether it's the weather on a trip or the punctuality of a friend I'm meeting for dinner.

As we continued our conversation, I realized my need for control was rooted in fear. Fear that if I wasn't in control then I would be controlled; that everything would go wrong and not according to my expectations or the way I wanted.

That night, for the second ceremony, I made up my mind to let go and fully surrender to and welcome what is with open arms. It was then that I fell into a deep sense of peace and calm. I put my ego away and opened up to the possibilities, and I found more joy, insights, and freedom. I let go of control because I don't really have control. I never did. I never will.

## Ceremony 2: It Takes Courage to Ask for Help

Night two was drastically different from night one. I let go. I felt my body falling the way I do when I've hit my bed after a long day and quickly drift off to sleep. I hit something soft. A bed? Perhaps. A cushion? Maybe. I'm not sure what it was. My attention was on the roaring, bright-red flames that were blazing high like mountain ridges and encapsulating me in the center. As the flames slowly inched closer and closer to me, my heart beat fast, like prey running from its predator. I curled up into a ball, shrinking myself to evade the flames for as long as I could.

But the flames eventually reached me. I couldn't escape them. And I felt my body burning. I hurt. A loud wail escaped my mouth.

I wished for my mom—the only person I've ever allowed to take care of me; the only person I've willingly, with open arms, asked for help. I wished for her to just hold me.

I opened my eyes. Instead of my mom, Greg was kneeling there next to me. His hazel eyes met mine. I didn't want him to see me like this: weak. I didn't want to have to ask him for help. My mind raced to a conversation we had recently had.

"I want you to *need* me," he voiced.

"I don't *need* you. I don't need anybody. I'm an independent, self-sustaining woman. I'm fine on my own. But I *choose* you. Isn't that better than me being with you only because I need you?" I questioned. I never asked him for help with anything. I thought that was a good thing.

"You don't get it," he responded.

I didn't get it back then. But now, as our eyes met, I got it. Greg reached out to hold me, and I let him. I didn't try to fight him off to prove that I didn't need his help.

"Time will make it better," he whispered into my ear as he held me. I nodded and smiled, then pointed to my forehead. He gently kissed it.

As Greg held me, the pain slowly dissipated.

Mother Ayahuasca humbled me that night. She beat me down physically, emotionally, and mentally. She showed me that I am fragile and weak and that that's okay. I realized that a willingness to show weakness is actually a strength. It's harder to be vulnerable and ask others for help than it is to hide in the solitude of what I've always believed is strength. True strength is actually the awareness that strength and weakness are one. There can't be one without the other. My willingness to be vulnerable means that I am merely human. My openness to relying on others creates the connections, bonds, and relationships that are truly meaningful and filled with depth.

## Ceremony 3: Together Is Better than Alone

I held hands with Mother Ayahuasca as she led me through the beautiful forest. The sky was a luminescent blue, vibrant and shining. The trees in the forest were a multitude of shades of shimmering, translucent green. I looked around in awe of the beauty. I had never seen anything like it.

"I wish Greg were here with me to share in this experience," I exclaimed to Mother Ayahuasca. "He would love it. Especially the green of the trees. Green's his favorite color."

"Are you sure?" She gazed down to meet my eyes.

I paused. The scene of us sitting on our sofa, discussing plans for our worldwide trip, danced across my mind.

Before Greg came into my life, I had already been planning this adventure for myself. I got so close to going that I even quit my job at Clorox, started selling my things, and gave my landlord my one-month notice. Serendipitously, a Google recruiter contacted me out of the blue for a dream job. So I stayed. But I was still committed to going on this trip.

Then Greg entered my life. He was on board with leaving everything behind and traveling the world for a bit, but he had different ideas about the itinerary. Incorporating his ideas would mean I would have to shift my original plans and modify the route that I had painstakingly mapped out years ago.

"I get that you had a route that you really wanted to follow," Greg had noted, "but now that you have someone joining you, how does that change things?"

I dug my heels into the ground. My eyes narrowed. "Nothing. Nothing changes. It's still *my* trip. You're just joining me on the trip now. I'd go with or without you."

Greg sighed. I felt bad, but I refused to give up on my dreams and let anyone change them.

A blue glimmer took me out of my thoughts. I looked up at Mother Ayahuasca and said, "Yes. I want Greg here with me. I want to share this experience with him. I wouldn't want it any other way."

She nodded. POOF. Greg's head appeared out of nowhere. Just his head, bopping in the soft, white clouds like a bobblehead.

"Hey babe!" He smiled at me.

"Hi!" I beamed, gazing up at him, excited he was here with me. "Look at how pretty everything is! The sky is so blue. The trees are so green! I thought you'd love the colors."

His head bopped right and left as he scanned the scene. "Oh wow! You're right! It's gorgeous! I love it."

Greg's eyes met mine. His grin made my heart sing. I was grateful he was here with me. In this moment, I realized that the stunning scenery wasn't the most important thing. The most important thing was being able to share the beautiful scenery with my partner in crime.

That night, I learned that together is better than alone. I used to value independence and freedom; I wanted to prove myself and do things on my own. I didn't want to be dependent on anyone else, not even my partner. But now I realize that being with someone is better than going at it solo. And perhaps depending on my partner isn't such a bad thing.

## Returning Home from Ayahuasca

Though I learned a lot from my time in Peru, I didn't get any closer to an answer to my question: Do I have babies, or do I pursue my dream to travel?

That's the thing with ayahuasca; it gives you what you need, not necessarily what you want. We often jump straight to what we want and forget the foundational things we need first. Mother Ayahuasca will work on what you need first, whether it's healing your physical ailments or helping you discover things in your unconscious mind that you need to address before working on anything else. It might be painful, it might not be something you want to face, but it'll be what you need. The plant "knows" you better than you know yourself.

Ayahuasca is like a coach that guides you towards finding the truths you already know. While we all might believe that our decisions and emotions are based on conscious choices, the unconscious mind is the real controlling force in our lives. It leads us to the decisions we make, the emotions we feel, and the actions we take. It's where our inner souls and truths live.

Unfortunately, the unconscious mind is usually inaccessible. Ayahuasca enables the conscious and unconscious minds to connect. It drags up the contents of the unconscious mind and holds a mirror up to them so a person can access the truths that are already within them and begin to heal.

The real work begins *after* the ayahuasca ceremony is over. Ayahuasca merely serves as an amplifier to healing and spiritual journeys. It helps gain insight, vision, understanding, and awakening to deep inner joys and pains. What is done next determines the extent to which someone will turn this experience into something that will serve them for the rest of their life.

Ayahuasca shows us the door, but we have to decide to walk through it. I chose to walk through that door.

## Coaching

"I'm getting my coaching certification," a coworker shared with me as we were settling in for a team meeting.

It was a few weeks after I had returned home from Peru. A lot had begun to shift for me. I started asking Greg for help with things I wouldn't have before my ayahuasca experience, such as carrying the grocery bags. We even began planning *our* trip together, though I still had one foot in and one foot out, so to speak. There was a constant battle between my heart and my head. I felt pulled in two directions: have babies, or pursue my dreams to travel? The last bits of sand were slowly running down the hourglass. I needed an answer soon.

"Coaching?" I asked my coworker. The only coaching I was familiar with was sports coaching.

"Yeah. Coaching helps people change in the way they wish and move in the direction they want to go," he explained.

"What if they don't know where they want to go?" I questioned.

"A coach can help with that too."

"Oh," I muttered just as the meeting started and our conversation was cut short.

How could someone else help me figure out what I want, especially if they don't know me? My parents raised me to believe that I'm smart enough to figure it out on my own; to use my own head to find the answers. But my head was failing me, and that darn clock was ticking away in my ear.

I was curious. I was open. I was committed to taking that next step forward; qualities I had opened up to from my ayahuasca experience. Maybe a coach could help me find the answers. And honestly, what did I have to lose?

So I did my research, scheduled initial discovery calls with several coaches, and selected one that I connected with.

"What are your choices?" my coach asked me during one of our first coaching sessions.

"I stay and have babies or leave to pursue my dreams," I stated matter-of-factly.

"What's at risk if you choose to pursue your dreams?"

"I'll get older while I'm away, and when I return back to the US I'll be too old to get pregnant. Maybe I won't be able to have kids because of my age."

"Hmm," she murmurs. "What makes you believe you won't be able to have kids if you're older?"

"All the doctors say it becomes harder," I answer. "I'm slightly younger now than I'll be after traveling. If I stay, I can have kids now. I'm healthier, and the babies will be healthier. Fewer complications."

"And what makes you believe that if you stay, you'll be able to have kids?"

The air caught in my throat. I pursed my lips and cupped my chin with my hands. During my ayahuasca experience, I had learned that I'm not in control of much. I suppose that includes my ability to have children. Many of my friends have been going through years upon years of fertility treatments, unsuccessfully. Quite a few have become so hyper-focused on having a baby that they're miserable and have lost the joy I used to see in them. And these friends are younger than me. Who's to say I can have kids even right now?

"Well," I started. "I guess I'm not in control of that. I mean, look at what happened to my embryos. Who could've ever guessed something like that would happen? And I know a lot of people even younger than me are struggling to get pregnant. So even if I stay, I'm still not guaranteed children."

For the next three months, we continued our coaching work together, exploring my fears through courageous conversations I needed to have, and started developing a plan for what all this meant.

I made two decisions during our work together.

First, I decided to pursue my dreams of volunteering and traveling the world. I would regret it if I didn't. And at the end of the day, I wasn't in control of whether I could have kids if I chose to stay.

Second, I decided that I wanted to be a coach and help others the way my coach helped me. It sucked to feel like I had to be mentally tough all the time, carry heavy armor everywhere I turned, and not ask others for help. I wanted to be the person who would help others break down those myths and beliefs, the way my coach helped me to do.

## September 2021: Panic Attacks

My chest tightened. I started gasping for air. I felt like a Marvel character in the middle of shape shifting. I pressed my hands to my chest as my body started trembling uncontrollably.

"Oh my god, what's going on? Breathe. Breathe," Greg whispered in my ear.

I heard his voice. It sounded like it was far away, as if I were drifting deep into the depths of water and his voice was coming from the surface. I could hear only a soft murmur from him, telling me to breathe.

As quickly as whatever this was appeared, it disappeared, and my senses returned. "What happened?" Greg asked me.

"I . . . I . . . I don't know. I think I blacked out. I couldn't breathe. I don't remember."

It was my first panic attack. I just didn't realize at the time that that's what it was.

During a catch-up with my best friend, I mentioned the "weird thing" that had happened to me. She explained, "You had a panic attack. You know that, right?"

"I did? What's a panic attack?" I questioned.

"It's sudden intense anxiety. Rapid heart rate, shaking, shortness of breath, tightness in the chest, a host of different types of symptoms. Usually high-stress situations like the one you're in can trigger it."

"Holy shit," I said. The experience felt scary. I felt out of control. And despite the work I'd done on letting go of control, I still hated not feeling in control.

The thing is, I've always dealt with stress quite well. At least in the "Amy way" of handling stress, which typically entails burying myself in work and getting all the shit done before giving myself permission to have fun. I've always been able to handle the most challenging situations and come out alive. But at this point in my life, my world was falling apart. Or at least it felt that way.

I was nearly five months pregnant and had just returned to the US after a period of living and working nomadically around the world. Ironically, what originally held me back from leaving the US was my fear of getting old and not being able to have children when I returned, and what brought me back to the US was pregnancy.

Greg and I had sold everything before we left, so upon returning to the US we had a lot of big decisions we needed to make in a short amount of time. The baby wasn't going to wait for us. Who knows! It might even decide to arrive early. In the four months we had left before the baby's arrival, we not only had to decide where we were going to settle down, we also had to find a home, furnish it, and buy a car, all while planning for the baby's arrival. And this was amid all that COVID-19 had brought with it, including illness, housing crises, furniture delays, the need for everyone to stay indoors, and a shortage of cars.

On top of that, my husband was without a steady income. I was the breadwinner in our relationship for the few years prior, but now I needed our roles to swap. As an entrepreneur, I didn't have the luxury of maternity leave, so the weeks and months I chose not to work once the baby arrived meant no household income.

The pressure was tremendous, and I felt crushed beneath it. When the pressure came, I succumbed to my conditioned ways of being. I tried to control everything. That's what led to my panic attacks.

Despite everything I knew, everything I had learned, I didn't get help. It's not that I wasn't willing to find a therapist. I had moved past that obstacle. But another one lay in my path: I was so busy setting up my family's future that I put finding a therapist on the backburner. I had my blinders on and couldn't see what I couldn't see—that getting help would've helped me move through this challenging phase with greater ease.

Months came and went. We decided to live close to my family, a short ten minutes from my parents. Greg accepted a job offer a week before our baby's arrival. My mom came to stay with us for two months to care for both the baby and me. But my emotions were still riding a roller coaster. I became easily irritable, my anger would flare in bursts, and I would cry for no reason. Having a newborn was not easy.

"You need to find a therapist," my mom started with a frown on her face. "You really need one. It'll help you."

I looked up from the bowl of chicken soup sitting in front of me that she had made for me. She stood, surveying me from the kitchen sink where she was washing some vegetables. At first I was floored that she proposed I see a therapist. After all, this was the same woman who didn't want my sister to study psychology for fear that she'd "catch the crazies." My surprise quickly turned to hurt when I thought, *She's saying that something's wrong with me.*

My face must've been a dead giveaway to my emotions because my mom walked over and sat in the empty chair next to me. As she put a hand on my shoulder, she softly said, "Amy, this isn't healthy for you or the baby. Something is going on with you. You've been through a lot. I don't want you to always be upset or crying."

Tears started streaming down my face. She pulled me in as I nodded.

After I finished my soup, I got to work on finding myself a postpartum therapist. I ultimately landed with Meg, a therapist who specializes in pregnant women and new mothers.

"What do you think happens after death?" Meg asked me in one of our sessions.

I closed my eyes, thinking of the same recurring experience nearly every night. The moment I would lie down in bed, the fear of loss would grip me. My breath would stop without me realizing it. I'd immediately gasp for air, and my eyes would fly wide open. I'd reach next to me to feel for Greg, feel the rising and falling of his back as he slept peacefully. I kept my hand on him, afraid that I would lose him the moment my eyes closed. This fear started to take over my life. I'd cry thinking of losing those I loved. I struggled to sleep. The insomnia only made the thoughts of death more frequent and powerful.

My eyes fluttered open. "I don't know," I responded. "That's why death feels scary."

"It's quite common during postpartum to have intrusive thoughts, Amy, especially around death and dying. It's the unknown and uncertainty that fuels the fear." Meg observed me. "Are you religious? What do you believe in?"

"My family is Buddhist, and I was raised Buddhist, but I really don't believe in any religion anymore," I muttered.

I then shared with Meg how I had lost my faith when I witnessed religion separating groups of people rather than bringing them together in loving kindness. It was a warm summer night. I was twelve years old. A few of my girlfriends and I had decided to spend our evening at the local county fair. After we stopped at the face-painting booth that a local church was running, I picked out a pretty pink butterfly and sat down to have my face painted.

"So what's your religion?" the face painter asked me.

"Well, my parents are Buddhist, so they raised me Buddhist," I answered.

"Oh—" the face painter responded. "Well you know, your parents raised you wrong then. God is our savior, and only Christians will go to Heaven."

I felt something within me burst like a firecracker. I stood up abruptly and hissed, "Do not say my parents raised me wrong. My parents did not raise me wrong!" then stalked off with half a butterfly on my face.

From that moment forward, I held a bitterness towards religion and people who claimed they were deeply religious. For decades after this incident, I stopped praying. I refused to be associated with any religion and became somewhat of an atheist. The next time my best friend mentioned praying for me, I responded with, "Don't worry. I'll be in Heaven."

"How? If I don't pray for you, how will you go to Heaven?" she asked.

"Because I'm going to Hell. I'll befriend the devil. And together, we'll raid Heaven."

She gasped. "Don't say that!"

"Then stop saying you're going to pray for me. I don't need it," I retorted.

After that, she stopped badgering me about becoming Christian. Surprisingly our friendship survived and, even to this day, we're the best of friends. But I never did have a strong spiritual belief again.

"You need something to believe in, Amy," Meg spoke gently, taking me out of my thoughts. "It doesn't matter if it's a religion or something else. If you believe in something, then death won't feel so scary."

Over the coming weeks and months, we explored the notions of spirit, hope, and prayer, as well as the mysteries of life. Meg helped me process my anger, hurt, frustrations, and fears. Most importantly, she helped me find myself again. I wish I had started working with her sooner. I wish I would've had the nudge sooner to prioritize my well-being. But better late than never, right?

Throughout my journey, from reading books to imbibing ayahuasca, and from working with my coach to working with my therapist, I have learned, and continue to learn, that I am not in control of most things. Especially not death. I *am* in control of the choices I make and how I respond to life while I'm still living it, though. I've also been reminded over and over again that asking for help is not a weakness. It takes courage and strength to do so. So I choose to be courageous.

# Mama & Papa Yip's Story

**逆来顺受.**

*nì lái shùn shòu.*

When adversity comes, receive it favorably.

## Setting the Scene

I'm twelve weeks postpartum. Three weeks ago, my mom "retired," as she calls it, from helping us care for our newborn, Logan. Her health hasn't been the best the last few years. So every day while she was staying with us, she prayed to Guanyin Pu Sa, the bodhisattva of compassion. She prayed for the energy to care for us. She prayed for the strength to carry Logan without falling. Her prayers were answered the entire eight weeks she was with us. Ironically, a week after returning home, she slipped and fell, badly bruising her tailbone. Of course, she never told me she fell. Even when she called to ask how Logan was doing, whether he was eating well and how much he was sleeping, she didn't mention her fall. It was only after I insisted on visiting them with Logan (because I knew she missed him tremendously even though she wouldn't directly admit it) that my dad told me about her fall. He figured I'd find out anyway during my visit.

So here I am, sitting at the kitchen table, watching my mom standing in front of the stove cooking despite a bruised tailbone. In one hand she holds a cane to support her tiny body, and in the other hand she holds a spatula for stirring the onion in her wok. She's making onion pork chops. I wait patiently for my dad to join me. Logan is sleeping soundly in the living room. My parents and I haven't had a deep conversation since before Logan was born. I'm excited and nervous. Ever since my mom suggested that I see a therapist, I've become even more curious about their perspectives on mental toughness and resilience. My dad walks into the kitchen, sets down a blue Vita Coco drink and an orange in front of me, and joins me at the kitchen table.

# You Don't Know What You Don't Know, Until You Know

知之為知之, 不知為不知, 是知也.

*zhī zhī wéi zhī zhī, bù zhī wéi bù zhī, shì zhī yě.*

To know that you know, and what you don't know, that is true knowledge.

"Someone who runs around the streets madly yelling at everyone they pass, someone who pulls out a knife and stabs random people for no reason at all, or someone who dances wildly in the streets with no sense of the circumstance. Their head isn't on right, and you don't know when they might attack you. Those are the types of people who need to see a therapist. At least that's what we were taught growing up in China," Papa Yip explains.

Without turning around, Mama Yip adds, "At some point in our lives, we were warned to be careful of people who needed help from a therapist. By the time someone needs to see a therapist, they've already completely lost it."

I chuckle at the thought of all the years I lived in San Francisco. My friends and I would get costumed up and dance wildly in the street any chance we got, from the "Hunky Jesus" contest during Easter to SantaCon over Christmas. Or my favorite, Bay to Breakers, a 12K fun run in May. Though to be honest, it was more about the fun than running. One year, a group of friends and I costumed up as a sperm bank for the event. Our tallest friend dressed up as an egg, and others were dressed as medical staff or sperm, donning white swim caps. We held up "Sperm Bank" signs and distributed clear jello shots in little plastic containers as we thanked people for their donation. Had we done this in Hong Kong or China in the 1950s, I'm sure they would've thought we were a little loony.

Papa Yip interrupts my thoughts. "In the 1950s and 1960s, psychiatric hospitals were built in China and Hong Kong to maintain social stability and security. During these times, therapists only worked in the psychiatric wards. Their job was to help treat people with psychosis and prevent relapse. Truthfully, us commoners didn't believe treatment was possible. We thought that once you went to the psychiatric ward, you could never fully recover from whatever issues you had. Sure, you might get a little better, but a few years would pass and it'd come back. I don't know where that idea came from. I suppose it's just passed from generation to generation. Growing up, we were warned to avoid people who seemed atypical for our own safety. We were told that they're dangerous and could turn on you at any moment."

Mama Yip hobbles over, cane in one hand, plate of pork chops in the other, and sets the food down. Her eyebrows are furrowed, and her forehead is creased, as she takes a seat next to Papa Yip and asks, "You know what the problem is with Chinese people?" She doesn't wait for an answer and bellows, "They care too much about face. They judge each other too much. If one person in your family appears to be 'crazy' then word spreads. People assume it must be because of hereditary issues or poor parental upbringing. So families tried to hide any clue that their family members might have mental health problems. They're too ashamed to get help."

Mama Yip's anger dissipates into pain as her eyes begin to water. Her voice quivers as she goes on. "It's why your grandparents were always so embarrassed about your uncle. They called him stupid and an embarrassment. He brought them shame. And I always felt so bad for him. When we were growing up, kids would pick on him. The teachers never did anything. His own parents never did anything. I always had to stand up for him. Even now, he's still mistreated by others. It's not his fault."

I nod in understanding. My uncle came to live with us when I was young. I'll admit, he was different. He once peed in the street on his way back from work. When the cops tried to stop him, he freaked out and ran. You can imagine what happened next. They chased him down, tackled him, and took him to jail. It shook him for weeks. I think he suffers from mental illness, but he's never been diagnosed or received treatment. At the same time, he was very kind. The way people spoke to and about him broke my heart. My paternal grandmother, who also lived with us at the time, would often warn me to be careful around him, especially because I was a young lady, and one "never knew what a man who wasn't right in his head would do."

"If someone in your family is mentally ill, other families would not want to associate with your family," Papa Yip explains. "People were afraid because you never know if and when they'll snap and come after you. So if you owned a business, people would stop buying from you. If you worked for someone, they'd fire you. Nobody would want to marry into your family because then it would dirty their family lines. Admitting that someone in your family has a mental health problem could be the end of your financial status, social status, even the end of your family lineage because there might not be any marriage prospects. So people hide it. Mental health, therapy, all of that was just not understood back then."

It irritates me just thinking about how that ignorance and lack of knowledge must've caused great pain. I can only surmise that this likely led to an increase in mental health issues. It reminds me of the Salem witch trials. People are afraid of what they don't understand. And fear leads us to act irrationally and mistreat other human beings.

## Changing of Perspectives

隔靴搔癢.

*gé xuē sāo yǎng.*
Scratching an itch from outside of the shoe.

Mama Yip pushes the plate of pork chops my way. "Eat it before it gets cold."

I obey and pick up a piece with my chopsticks, serving Papa Yip first before picking another piece for myself. As I bite into the tender meat, the flavors explode in my mouth. Mama Yip has always been an amazing cook. "So what changed for you then?" I ask between bites, my gaze on her. "If mental illness is so taboo and brings shame to the family, how come you wanted me to find a therapist?"

Mama Yip meets my eyes. "You know me. I'm not like your daddy. I've never cared as much about face. Who cares what other people think about you? As long as you know in your heart that you're a good person, that's all that matters."

"Then why didn't you want Jenny to study psychology?" I ask.

Mama Yip sighs. "Amy, I was concerned. Like your daddy said, we thought therapists only worked in psychiatric wards. We were worried about her safety. But your sister is stubborn and was adamant about studying psychology. So I asked a good friend of mine for his opinion. He's educated unlike us. He opened up our minds about the breadth of the field. There's marriage therapy, postpartum therapy, and even therapy for burnout. None of that existed when we were growing up. Once your sister started studying psychology, we learned even more."

Mama Yip nods towards Papa Yip and grins. "Your sister even diagnosed your daddy with OCD. Now we understand his constant need to check if doors are locked and whether the gas is off."

Papa Yip throws up his hands, "That's just me trying to keep us safe!"

Mama Yip smirks, then returns her gaze to me. "Now that we understand more, our perspectives have changed. That's why I encouraged you to see a postpartum therapist. I noticed things were off with you. You were cranky and moody; always worrying, thinking too much, stressed, and anxious. I didn't like seeing you like that. That's why I encouraged you to get help. Who cares about face and what people think anyway? My daughters' well-being and happiness matters more to me."

My body fills with warmth and love. I reach over and kiss Mama Yip on the cheek. "I listened to you and started seeing a therapist," I whisper.

"Good," she smiles.

# On Vulnerability, Asking for Help, and Friendship

孤掌難鳴.

*gū zhǎng nán míng.*

It's hard to clap with only one hand.

I chew my food, deep in thought. Mama Yip has always been more open to asking for help. Papa Yip is a different story.

Growing up, we were eligible for food stamps, but Papa Yip refused it. He always said, "I don't need food stamps. I don't need that kind of help. I can support my own family," and Mama Yip always said, "Your daddy cares too much about face and what others would think if we were on food stamps."

I gaze at Papa Yip and carefully choose my words. "What do you consider are times when things are hard enough that it's okay to ask for help?"

He sets down his chopsticks and stares out the window as he ponders my question. Peering back at me, he remarks, "After communism arrived in China, your grandfather was no longer permitted to have his own businesses. Everything was government owned. So his wealth slowly disappeared. In 1956, he left for Hong Kong to try to reestablish himself. It wasn't until five years later, 1961, that I reunited with him.

"When I first arrived in Hong Kong, your grandfather was very sick. He didn't have a job. So we didn't have any money. But your grandfather didn't want me to work. I was only thirteen. He wanted me to get an education instead. My brother was even younger than me, eight. Your grandmother didn't speak Cantonese, the dialect in Hong Kong. It would've been hard for her to find a job that paid enough money to support our entire family.

"It's situations like this where you need to be able to ask for help. Your grandfather reached out to his friends. They all pooled money for us. At that time, when money is lent, you come to an agreement on when the money will be returned. But his friends didn't specify a date, nor did they charge interest. They knew your grandfather might not make it, and in Chinese culture your

247

family members carry your debt if you pass. That meant me, a thirteen-year-old kid, and your grandmother, a woman who didn't speak the local dialect, would have to carry the debt once your grandfather passed. Who knew when we'd be able to pay them back!" Papa Yip exclaims, shaking his head. "They still lent us money."

"What happened?" I lean in towards Papa Yip with curiosity.

"Your grandfather passed away shortly after I turned fourteen. On his deathbed, he wrote down the name of every person and the amount he owed. He handed it to me so I knew who to pay back. Back then, lending and borrowing money depended on integrity and trust. There were no contracts or laws that held you accountable. People trusted your grandfather because he had integrity, and he taught me to be the same way."

"So you quit school then?" I ask.

"Yes. After he passed, I got a tailoring apprenticeship making forty Hong Kong dollars a month. In the evenings I would go take English classes. It was hard work. Fifteen-hour days, seven days a week. We only got seven holidays the entire year. I ended up having to quit my English classes because I could never make it. After five years, I finally paid your grandfather's debts off. I am forever grateful for his friends. We would've been on the streets without their compassion."

I notice Papa Yip's eyes glisten. My heart fills with warmth. I wish I could've met my grandfather.

"What about a time when you had to ask for help?" I inquire.

"The Changs," Mama Yip chimes in as she gets up to gather the plates with one hand, cane in the other. I stand up and indicate that I'll help her, but she shoos me back into my seat. Clearly, things aren't "hard enough" for her right now to warrant receiving help. I shake my head as I sit back down.

Carrying the dirty dishes to the sink, Mama Yip continues. "We met them when we first arrived in the US. They've helped us tremendously. We were living in a tiny room and not making very much money. They knew we needed to save money faster to bring your two sisters from Hong Kong to America. The Changs rented their entire basement to us, refusing to accept more than our previous rent. They also helped your daddy find a tailoring job making three times his original salary!"

Papa Yip shares, "I remember that job. The owner was Portuguese. His English was like mine, not so good. He'd always say, 'Mr. Yip! What's up! What's up!'" Papa Yip shrugs and tilts his head in a look of confusion. "I didn't understand what 'What's up' meant. I'd respond, 'Nothing going up. Everything going down!'"

Mama Yip and I burst into laughter. Papa Yip is a stellar storyteller with great humor and facial expressions.

"We could barely speak English," Mama Yip states without turning around from the sink where she's washing away. "Couldn't fill out complex forms. So we asked the Changs to help us when we wanted to sponsor your sisters, and later your grandparents, to come to the US. Later, when we needed to learn how to drive a car, they taught us. They even took us car shopping and negotiated for us."

Papa Yip looks around the kitchen walls and adds, "We might not have had this home without them. They helped us apply for the loan, did all the paperwork, and translated for us. A week before our closing date, the bank hadn't approved our loan yet. I was worried. I didn't have an extra twenty thousand dollars just lying around. What would I do if I didn't get the approval in time? My family was relying on me to get this house.

"I called Mr. Chang for help and guidance. He said to me, 'Don't worry. If the bank doesn't approve the loan before your closing date, we'll help you. You'll get the house.' In the end, the loan was approved just in time. We didn't have to borrow money from them. But I'll never forget all they've done for me, your mommy, and our whole family."

I nod in agreement. I remember the Changs throughout my childhood. They always helped my family without expectation. To this day, they still do. When Greg and I first moved back to Maryland, they knew we didn't have any furniture and that our baby was arriving soon. They offered us some of their furniture and their grandchild's baby things. I'm forever grateful for their kindness.

"It's not easy to ask for help, but sometimes, you have to," Papa Yip concludes. "That's why having real friendships like your girlfriends are important. They're always there for you at a moment's notice. You help them; they help you."

My mouth curves into a smile thinking about my six closest girlfriends, whom Papa Yip is referring to. We've called ourselves the "Chicky Babies" since our friendship began in elementary school. If you meet us, you'd think we're completely different. You might even wonder how on earth we're friends. Yet, no matter how far we physically are from each other, our friendship is deep and has lasted over three decades. "Yeah, they're pretty fabulous," I nod.

# It's a Different World

小洞不補, 大洞吃苦.

*xiǎo dòng bù bǔ, dà dòng chī kǔ.*

If small holes aren't fixed, then big holes will bring hardship.

"So you're supportive that I'm seeing a therapist?" I ask Papa Yip.

He studies me before answering, "Amy, the world is different today, even for kids. When we were growing up, things were simple and carefree. Today, the stressors are vastly different from decades ago. Information is flowing out at an overwhelming pace with all these sophisticated gadgets. Kids are on tight schedules from the moment they're born. They can't even just be kids. When I was young, going outside to play was our form of therapy."

The word "play" makes me glance over at Mama Yip, who is standing at the sink. Sadness envelopes me. Papa Yip knows how to be silly, to have fun, to play. I see how he interacts with my kiddo every day. He laughs and giggles with my son. One time, when Papa Yip visited me at Google, he immediately hopped on a scooter and went as fast as he could up and down the hallway. He's also done that with a Google bike. Mama Yip, on the other hand, seems to have forgotten how to play. She only knows how to work hard and serve others. I make a mental note to try to find ways to instill more play into Mama Yip's life.

"These days, therapy for kids requires more than play," Papa Yip continues. "Just look at your sister Jenny. She works with families and children with OCD. It's not surprising there's a tremendous need for therapy considering the complexity of our world today and the stress and anxiety it brings. Even for me!"

Papa Yip points to his phone. "I get overwhelmed and anxious with all this email and on-the-line stuff. Just the other day I got a Facebook message from someone who knew my name. I didn't know who it was. It got me scared about what information they have of mine. When I don't understand things, I have to use a Chinese–English dictionary to translate every word and try to figure out what it's saying. Can you imagine how much time and stress that causes me every day? I can't imagine how you kids deal with all the information coming your way! I'd go out of my mind."

"You just worry too much, old man," Mama Yip yelps.

I laugh. Papa Yip often calls me about emails he needs me to read because he can't tell whether there's a problem. He's always been a worrier. Mama Yip is right. He definitely worries more than she does, especially about saving face and what others will think.

"So you're supportive that I'm seeing a therapist?" I ask again, surveying Papa Yip.

"It's becoming more normalized to see a therapist now," he responds. "Even in China, there is more research about mental health; more people are seeing therapists. People are starting to realize that sometimes, when things are really hard, you just need the extra help."

I'll take that as an indirect, "Yes, I'm supportive. "

# My Reflections Post-Conversation

Reflecting on my own breakdowns and these conversations with my parents, I began to realize that there's a place for being mentally tough, and there's a place for being mentally sensitive. Mental toughness is the ability to tune out distractions and relentlessly push through obstacles, while mental sensitivity refers to the capacity for self-awareness—self-awareness about who I am, what my emotions are signaling to me, and why I think about things and make choices the way I do.

My parents, and I presume many of our immigrant parents, were in survival mode. I later asked my parents whether they would've sought therapy if they had access to it. My mom responded, "We didn't need therapy, nor did we have time. Our biggest pressure was money. As blue-collar workers, every hour we didn't work was money lost. There wasn't time to think about stress, much less go to therapy for it."

They had no choice but to be mentally tough.

My life is different from theirs. I'm not in constant survival mode. I don't need to rely on mental toughness as my single tool in the toolbox. Sure, mental toughness got me through some tough situations such as in that labor room delivering Logan, but I can choose other tools outside of that delivery room. I don't *always* have to be mentally tough. I can choose mental sensitivity to make decisions based on the core of who I am and what I want rather than what I think I "should" want. I can choose mental sensitivity to be more human, to have the capacity to feel a wide range of emotions and the courage to connect with others, and even to ask for help.

Ayahuasca, coaching, and therapy all nudged me towards this place where I can embrace both mental toughness and mental sensitivity. But for the longest time, there was still one handcuff holding me to my automatic

252

default of mental toughness: my parents' permission. By hearing my parents' story, I received that permission. The handcuff has now been released. Their openness and encouragement that I seek help and heal myself has given me full permission to let go of always being mentally tough.

My parents say their perspective has changed about therapy. I believe the full truth is that their perspective has changed about *other* people receiving therapy, not themselves. They've told me that others, like me, can benefit from it, but they don't believe it could help them. Though my parents may never get help for the trauma and hardships they had to endure, I can offer them a listening ear and unconditional love.

And the best thing I can do is accept their encouragement to do what they felt they couldn't: ask for the help I need.

# A Date with Your Parents

## PRE-CONVERSATION PERSONAL REFLECTION

### Overview

Our bodies are intelligent and have a natural way of releasing stress. Every mammal has a way of doing so. (Check out the YouTube video "Impala Escapes Death & Shakes off Stress" for an example.) Stress, anxiety, and PTSD are completely normal reactions to stressful life circumstances and trauma. But if we don't release it, the energy from these emotions will continue to be stored in our bodies and trapped in our nervous systems.

Many in the AAPI community don't allow what has entered to exit. Instead, we stay quiet about our problems, push our emotions down, and even numb ourselves to avoid feeling. The exercise below will start the process of helping you tune in to what's happening. By understanding your own emotions, you can start to recognize when to ask for help. Change starts with awareness.

### Instructions

*Note: I am not a licensed therapist. The prompts and exercises below are not a substitute for counseling, psychotherapy, psychoanalysis, mental health care, or substance abuse treatment and should not be used in place of any form of diagnosis, treatment, or therapy.*

1. Pick at least two prompts from List A and two prompts from List B, then reflect and journal on them.

   **List A**

   ◈ List eight things that made you smile today.

   ◈ Write a paragraph about what you love about your life right now.

   ◈ Write a paragraph about what made you happy today.

   ◈ List ten things that make you happy.

   ◈ Identify an important person in your life who you're grateful for. Write a paragraph about why this person is important and what you're most grateful for about them.

   ◈ What is something that's going right in your life right now?

   **List B**

   ◈ List three to five things that trigger feelings of anxiety.

   ◈ List three to five things you're currently stressed about.

   ◈ What situations make you the most fearful?

   ◈ What experience made you feel sad in the past? What meaning can you make from that experience?

   ◈ List three to five things you tend to dwell or ruminate on that increase your stress or anxiety.

   ◈ What are some habitual thoughts you have that tend to make you feel worse?

2. Take a look at what you've written. Reflect and journal on at least five of the prompts below that you most resonate with.

◈ What is a self-care strategy that you've been curious about trying?

◈ List ten things that *you* have the ability to change to make things better.

◈ What have you done for your well-being over the last seven days?

◈ List people who are part of your support system.

◈ Who in your life understands and can relate to your stress, anxiety, and fears?

◈ List three things you can do to reduce your stress.

◈ What ways can you improve your mental health?

◈ Write a list of coping strategies that you've developed over the years (e.g., working out, scrolling social media, talking to friends). On a scale of 1 to 10, with 1 meaning "doesn't work well" and 10 meaning "works very well," assign a number to each coping strategy for how well each one calms you down and supports you in handling emotionally distressing circumstances. Evaluate which ones should stay and which ones should be retired.

◈ If a close friend were going through what you're going through, what advice would you give them?

◈ When times get tough, what is something you need to remind yourself of? Write yourself a message for those bad days.

3. Take a look at what you've written in Step 2. What are one or two things you *want* to try in the next hour? In the next day? Over the next week? Which things *will* you try?

4. What are you discovering about your own emotional needs? Your ability to ask for help?

## THE CONVERSATION

### Conversation Topic

What your parents' beliefs and perspectives are and where they learned about mental toughness, asking for help, and going to therapy.

### Tips

These conversations can be hard, and potentially triggering. Priority number one is to take care of yourself. Remember to review the Conversation Tip Sheet on page 23 before your conversation.

### Conversation-Specific Suggestions

Consider getting professional help such as therapy or coaching as you embark on this conversation. Therapy and coaching are different methods of support. They have overlapping characteristics but also some key distinctions. One big one is that while therapy has well-established and stringent licensure requirements to practice, professional coaching has some credentialing institutions, such as the International Coaching Federation, but lacks a governing board. My experience as a coach, as well as being a recipient of both coaching and therapy, is that therapy focuses on treating mental illnesses while coaching focuses on building mental fitness. Therapy tends to focus on the past, whereas coaching is future-oriented. Both have a place in supporting you as you embark on doing further inner work beyond the personal reflection prompts in this book. Some therapists and coaches also offer services to facilitate difficult conversations like these.

Be sure both you and your parents are in a positive mental and emotional state for this conversation. That means you don't have any significant burdens or stressors happening in your lives right now. Also, consider that your parents might have unaddressed trauma(s) that could benefit from additional support.

Older generations grew up without the privilege of having access to the knowledge and education related to mental and emotional health the way that current generations do. You may want to find research, news articles, or other related evidence about well-being and send these to your parents to read ahead of this conversation. If your parents' primary language isn't English, find something in their native tongue. If they're not literate and can't read, find podcasts or videos instead. Help expand their knowledge base before you enter into this conversation.

## Questions For Your Parents

### *Lighter Questions*

◈ What do you think about [insert name of article, podcast, or whatever else you sent to your parents]?

◈ How is the world different from when you were a child? Has it stayed the same, become worse, or gotten better? Why do you believe that?

◈ What makes you happiest?

◈ What do you love most about your life?

◈ What makes you smile?

◈ What advice would you give to someone going through a tough time?

◈ What do you believe about asking other people for help? Is it shameful to do so? Good to do so?

◈ What advice would you give your younger self about going through hardships?

◈ What did you discover in the last decade or two that you wish you discovered sooner?

◈ What are your current worldviews about mental health? What or who has influenced these views?

◈ How have your views about mental health shifted from when you were younger? What caused the shift?

◈ What are your beliefs about emotions? Where did you learn these beliefs? *Examples: Are certain emotions "good" or "bad"? Are emotions "controllable" or "uncontrollable"?*

◈ When are emotions a problem?

### Deeper Questions

◈ What qualities and characteristics make a true friend?

◈ What kind of friend are you to others?

◈ How would you describe the friendships you have?

◈ What are your biggest fears?

◈ What gives you the most amount of stress?

◈ What do you worry most about?

◈ What were some of your biggest hardships in your life? What helped you get through them?

◈ What was the saddest time of your life?

◈ Did you ever ask others for help when you had to face a problem? Tell me about it.

◈ Which emotions are most familiar to you? Which do you tend to resist or are numb to (don't feel)? How do you typically handle these emotions?

◈ Do you find it easy to explain your emotions to another person? If not, why is it difficult?

◈ What have you always wanted to tell me but haven't had the courage to?

## POST-CONVERSATION CONTEMPLATION

After the conversation with your parents, contemplate and journal on the following:

◈ What new insights have you gained about

✦ who your parents are;
✦ what their beliefs and stories are around mental toughness, mental and emotional well-being, and asking for help; and
✦ what they did to get through tough circumstances?

◈ What are two or three things you could do to help your parents improve their mental and emotional well-being?

◈ How does what you've learned about your parents shift the way you view mental and emotional well-being? About asking for help?

❖ What beliefs and stories about mental and emotional well-being or asking for help do you want to keep? What beliefs do you want to retire?

❖ What actions will you take to improve your own mental and emotional well-being?

❖ Who can you ask for help when you need it?

*Ask for help. Not because you are weak, but because you want to remain strong.*

~ Les Brown ~

# I Don't Deserve to Spend Money on Myself; I Need to Save It

# My Story

## Work and Money Date

"So tell me again," Greg began with his eyes closed as if that would help him process my decision-making methods better. "How did you decide to buy your condo?"

It was a beautiful Saturday afternoon. Greg and I were sitting on our plush, blue picnic blanket in Central Park with a spread of cheeses, crackers, and prosciutto in front of us. We were on the "Work & Money Date" from John and Julie Gottman's book *Eight Dates*. A few months prior we had attended their couples workshop in Seattle. Unsurprisingly, we discovered that our work and money mindsets were drastically different. In fact, it was a sticking point for our relationship. So we purchased the *Eight Dates* book to begin our open, curious conversations about this difficult topic.

I peered at Greg, his eyes still closed, waiting for my answer. "Well, I walked into the building and immediately knew it was the place. I saw some floor plans and picked one I liked on the third floor because three is my favorite number."

Greg's mouth opened as if he wanted to say something but wasn't sure what to say.

I shrugged, "I mean, I did look at a few other condo buildings. I didn't like them. Plus, this was 2005 when property prices were skyrocketing. Time was of the essence. And in my mind, it made sense to invest in property versus paying monthly rent."

Silence. I cut a large piece of triple-cream brie, put it on a Trader Joe's pita cracker, and took a bite.

"Is this the method you use to make all your big purchase decisions?" he implored.

"Method?" I swallowed my bite of brie. "If you mean intuition, yeah that's how I make a lot of decisions. I chose my car using my intuition."

Greg waited silently for me to continue.

"I was at a county fair, saw this beautiful car parked there, walked up to it, and really liked it. So, right then, I decided it was the car I'd buy."

"And then?" Greg nudged me to continue.

"Well, I walked to the back of the car and saw it was an Acura TL. Then I went home, researched local dealers, and emailed them for pricing. I negotiated through email and chose the dealer with the best price. Then I went, signed papers, and picked it up."

"Wait. So when did you test-drive the car?" Greg asked, shaking his head in bewilderment.

"I didn't."

Silence again.

"What?" I exclaimed. "When I know, I just know." I grinned and elbowed him. "Like how I knew when I first saw you!"

Greg shook his head, but a smile donned his face. "Well most people do a little research with large purchases."

I held both my hands up. "In my defense, I did *some* research and found that the TL had great resale value. I also figured a new car would break down less than my dad's hand-me-down car, which was in constant need of repair."

I bit my lip, wanting to further justify my purchase. "I took a second job on top of my full-time consulting job to pay for the car. I worked hard for it."

As Greg and I continued with our financial date, we uncovered more depth in both of our money mindsets: the stories we each held about how money works in the world, our individual beliefs about what we could or couldn't do with money, how much we're able to earn, how much we're entitled to spend, and, more broadly, how we judge and feel about money.

From an early age, I formed three primary beliefs about money.

## Money Belief #1: If You Can Save a Penny, Then Save a Penny.

While I was growing up, Sundays were my favorite days. Every Sunday morning, my mom and I would go to Safeway for groceries before stopping at McDonald's to get lunch.

"If you find a Safeway coupon for something you want, then you can buy it," my mom always promised me.

So every Sunday morning, I'd diligently sit at the kitchen table, scouring the Safeway coupon booklet that faithfully arrived in our mailbox every Thursday. This quickly expanded beyond the Safeway booklet to the Sunday *Washington Post* coupon books. My love for coupons and deals continued into adulthood.

"Guess what?" I asked Greg as I walked into our tiny New York City apartment.

"What?" Greg asked, looking up from his laptop to meet my gaze. He was sitting at our two-seater kitchen table.

"I got us Listerine. We've been out for a while. I was waiting for it to go on sale, and it finally did at CVS! Plus I had a dollar-fifty-off coupon!"

Greg laughed uncontrollably.

"What?" I exclaimed, puzzled by his laughter.

"I just can't get over the fact that you make good money at Google. You live in one of the most expensive cities. We eat at nice restaurants. You bought yourself a TL because you liked it. And yet, you get such joy over saving a few dollars on Listerine."

I furrowed my brow and pursed my lips, "Well I have to make sacrifices and save in order to justify buying things I want!"

Greg walked over to me and kissed my forehead tenderly. "You don't have to justify. Your happiness is reason enough."

I felt a warm rush of relief, but then my brain pulled me back to reality. *It doesn't matter what Greg says, you shouldn't spend on yourself*, it told me.

My mom's love for coupons and savings has, without a doubt, rubbed off on me. Perhaps it's the dopamine hit I received from all the years of cutting coupons and being rewarded with my favorite treats. Or maybe it's the association of saving money with mommy-and-me time.

The truth is, it's probably how I've come to justify that I deserve to spend money on myself and on purchases that feel "too luxurious." If I can save a penny, then I'll save a penny. Then it's okay to buy something nice for myself.

## Money Belief #2: If I Want Something, I Better Work Hard to Deserve It.

"If you save up enough money for an airplane ticket, you can go to Hong Kong," my dad finally relented after a long debate.

It was the fall of 1991. I was ten. My dad was paying bills while sitting at the desk in his bedroom. I sat cross-legged on the floor by his feet, looking up at him with my eyes wide and a big smile crossing my face from cheek to cheek. I couldn't believe it. I had finally persuaded him to let me go to Hong Kong!

I had heard all these stories from my parents and my sisters, who were born there, about what Hong Kong was like. "Food stalls everywhere," they would tell me. "Bakeries filled with egg tarts, pineapple buns, and red-bean-paste-filled goodies. Streets alive and bustling with people. And from atop Victoria Peak you can see the beautiful lights of Hong Kong." Their stories of Hong Kong made me feel left out. So I longed to visit and see what it was like with my own eyes; to experience what my parents and sisters had experienced during their time there.

No matter how many noes I received, I wouldn't give up. I'd offer proposal after proposal. My dad used to say that his stubbornness plus my mom's stubbornness equals a child with double stubbornness. I guess we know where I inherited mine!

Sitting by my dad's feet, I had just pitched the idea that if I could save enough for my own plane ticket, they should let me go. My dad finally relented.

"Great! How much is a plane ticket?" I asked him.

"About a thousand dollars."

*I'm gonna need more than coupons*, I thought to myself. *Time to work hard and save.*

And I did.

"I recommend this style with your name on it," I told a classmate as she browsed my look book of friendship bracelet samples.

"Oh I like it! How much?"

"Three dollars," I told her. "It takes more time to make it and more string."

At this young age, I was a crafter. And I was good at it. I made friendship bracelets, beaded earrings, hemp keychains, and more. When classmates started asking me to make them things, I realized there was a business opportunity. I had a skill. And there was a demand for it.

Thus, "Amy Yip Friendship Bracelets and Things" was born. Business was thriving! So much so that I had to hire a friend to help me.

I skipped lunch every week and would immediately place my lunch allowance, along with the money from my bracelet sales, into a shoebox. Alongside that, I kept a pink slip of paper where I tracked my progress towards the thousand dollars.

Just before my eleventh birthday, I took my shoebox to my dad.

"I've got it," I said.

"You've got what?" he asked, eyeing my shoebox.

"The money. For my plane ticket to Hong Kong," I said as I opened the box to show my dad the cash I'd saved.

My dad's jaw dropped. "Oh, Amy. You're not going to Hong Kong alone."

"Why not?" I shrieked. "You said if I saved a thousand dollars I could go. I even saved a little more just in case there's tax."

"You just can't. You can't fly alone."

"But you promised!" My heart sank. Tears streamed down my face as I felt the stabs of my dad's broken promise. I had gone hungry and relentlessly made bracelets every day for nothing.

"Amy, I didn't think you would actually be able to save a thousand dollars."

My dad ended up depositing the money into my college fund. Apparently $1,000 was too much cash for a kid to have in a shoebox for some reason.

Despite the disappointment, this experience instilled in me a belief that if I made proper sacrifices and worked hard, I could have permission to spend on myself. Within reason, of course.

During our Work & Money Date, Greg helped me uncover that this is the same belief that made me feel like I needed to work an extra job on top of my full-time consulting one when I bought my TL: I'm only allowed to enjoy things if I've worked hard enough for them.

## Money Belief #3: Money Is the Root of Evil.

"If he's such a great guy, why would he be charging people thousands of dollars to attend his events?" I argued as I stabbed at my pancakes. "Someone who wants to help people would just do so out of their good heart and not bankrupt people in the process. He just wants to make easy money off these people so he can pay for his own lifestyle."

Greg and I were at brunch debating Tony Robbins, an elite professional coach and speaker, and his multi-day, live events, which ran hundreds if not thousands of dollars.

"People have to invest in it to value it," Greg responded. "The more time or money you put into something, the more you value it. If his events were free, people wouldn't value them as much."

"Who told you that, your buddy Tony?" I retorted sarcastically. My eyes narrowed and I felt frustration bubbling in me as though I were a hot kettle of water.

"Well yes," Greg started, "but it's also in a lot of studies. People value what they pay for. It's why people value expensive, brand-name things. And if Tony didn't charge for events, he'd be a fraud because he's teaching people how to make money and live their best lives."

"Why would that make him a fraud?" I argued. "He'd be helping people. It would just show he has a big heart. A lot of people in the world do good for others without expecting payment."

"So you're saying that people can't charge money for their services *and* want to help people at the same time?"

"He's already rich enough," I bellowed. "He doesn't need more."

"Money is a tool, Amy. He uses his money to help people."

"Money is evil. And he's just greedy," I growled.

Greg had hoped to persuade me to attend an event with him, but instead I resisted. I refused to pay to attend and have my money go towards supporting someone who, I believed, was taking advantage of people who were desperate.

"Why do you think people who want money are greedy?" Greg asked gently. "Why do you think money is evil?"

My mind flew to all the arguments my parents had over money. They would yell angrily at each other, and I would run and hide so I didn't have to hear it. I remembered the worry lines that would crease their faces anytime the car broke down or another expense was added. One particular memory that had become imprinted in my memory bank was the time my dad had been laid off for over a month. He had no luck finding a job, and the stress of monthly bills without an income was weighing heavily on him. His mood was evidence of it.

"God dammit," my dad cursed angrily as he smacked his own head.

My heart stopped. My eyes widened. I couldn't breathe. We were sitting in the car outside of a Marriott hotel. I had gone with my dad to help him fill out a job application there and had just asked him the employment dates of one of his most recent restaurant jobs. He couldn't remember them.

"Dammit!" he spat. His eyes bulged with frustration.

I wanted to run, but there was nowhere to go. I cautiously moved my hand over his and whispered, "Please Daddy. Please stop. Don't be angry."

As if I had pulled him out of a trance, my dad gazed at me and softened. "I'm not angry with you, Amy," he said. "I'm just angry with myself for being so stupid. I need this job. We need the money for our family. And I'm so stupid. I can't even remember my employment dates. I don't know what's wrong with me." He sighed.

We eventually finished the application and turned it into the human resources office of the hotel. They interviewed and hired him on the spot. I felt a sigh of relief wash over me when I heard the good news. Employed dad meant no more moody dad.

I peered at Greg, the memories still lingering. "I just do," I said to him. "End of conversation."

I stubbornly clung to my mindset that money was the source of evil. It shouldn't be easy. It's supposed to be hard. And people who wanted easy money were just plain greedy. I didn't want to be one of those greedy people chasing money for money's sake. And I judged others for wanting more money, including Greg. I just couldn't see money as a tool. My personal experiences had blinded me into believing that I was right, and money was wrong.

## It's Time for My Relationship with Money to Change

My beliefs about money served me well in many regards. Throughout my life, I never carried debt and always paid off my credit cards. My credit score was always high, and I never felt like I deprived myself of too much.

At least not in my mind.

"Just buy it Amy," my mom yelped. "What's there to think about?"

I gawked at her.

We were standing in the Coach outlet store. I lovingly held a wine-red leather tote bag over my shoulder and glanced at the body-length mirror. The high-shine finish of the purse reflected the ceiling light. It was beautiful. And it was $185—*after* the outlet discounts. Just moments ago, I had been pondering all the things I could do with $185: pay my monthly gas bill, buy a week's worth of groceries, or even pay for two roundtrip bus tickets from New York to Maryland. This was merely a purse. I didn't *need* a nice purse. A

Target one would do just fine, though I didn't need one of those either; I had perfectly usable purses at home. But I really liked this tote. Really, really liked it. Did I mention that I also love red purses?

My mom shook her head. "I'll buy it for you."

"No! You can't. You worked hard for your money."

"And you didn't?" she questioned.

"Well not as hard as you and Daddy."

"Well your daddy and I worked hard so you could enjoy things like this. Stop thinking about it. If you like it that much, buy it. You can afford it. And you deserve nice things once in a while."

I chewed on my bottom lip. "I guess I did save nearly fifty dollars last weekend."

"Oh?" my mom asked.

"I went out for a friend's birthday Saturday night. I took the bus instead of paying for a taxi," I stated proudly. "It's slower, but I can read on the bus, and it saves me nearly twenty-five dollars each way."

"Saturday night?" my mom inquired while eyeing me. "What time on Saturday night?"

"Not late," I gulped, realizing my mistake.

"What time?"

"Umm. Around nine when I went to meet them," I muttered.

"And what time was it when you went home?"

"Umm. Oh around one in the morning." I stuttered.

"Was Greg with you?"

"No."

"Amy!" she nearly shouted. Wincing at the intensity of her voice, I glanced around the Coach store. Whew. Nobody was watching us. "Do you know how dangerous that is?" she continued. "You're a woman. Going home on a bus in New York City at one in the morning? That's dangerous. It's only twenty-five dollars for a taxi! Your safety is worth more than twenty-five dollars, Amy." She sighed. "You're buying the purse. And from now on, you're taking the taxi at night."

"But you used to always take the bus," I argued. "You always said to save money when you could."

"My situation was different," she breathed. "I didn't have money. I made eight dollars an hour. I had a family to raise. It would've taken me three hours to make twenty-five dollars. How long does it take you to make twenty-five dollars? Ten minutes? Fifteen minutes? Our circumstances are different, Amy. You need to learn to enjoy your hard work."

"I do enjoy my hard work," I muttered. "I bought a nice car. I travel the world. I eat things I enjoy."

My mom gave me a once-over. "So why are you so indecisive with this purse? Do you realize how much time and energy you've spent agonizing over this decision? You could spend that time working and you'd make up for buying the purse!"

Her words sucker punched me in my belly. Sure, I occasionally gave myself permission to spend on things that brought me joy, but only under the condition that I made sacrifices in other areas of my life. Only if it felt hard enough.

In truth, anytime I spent money on things I enjoyed, my stomach would knot, and guilt would envelope me like a bubble. A voice would whisper in my ear that I was wasting money on unnecessary guilty pleasures. It warned me, *If you keep on doing this, you'll become one of "those" people—the ones who are addicted to the nicer things in life. You'll become greedy and money hungry.* Most of all, I was afraid that if I spent on the finer things in life, I would disappoint my mom, the woman who had nurtured my coupon-cutting habits and proudly told people how great I was at saving.

But here she was telling me to spend money, to enjoy nicer things, and to not overthink it.

I took the purse off my shoulders and said, "You're right. I'll buy it."

My mom was right. Decisions like whether to buy a Coach purse shouldn't have been so difficult or taken such an emotional toll on me given how much I was making working at Google. The back-and-forth battles were an unnecessary waste of energy. Despite all the years of believing that my money mindset was the right one, the only one, and the one that my parents would approve of, it hit me that maybe I was wrong. Maybe there was another way of relating to money.

## Changing My Script

Despite knowing that there was a different, healthier way I could relate to money, I continued struggling to release myself from the deeply embedded beliefs I had. Years later, when I was exploring a possible shift in my career from corporate America into coaching, it became apparent that I had work to do on my relationship with money.

"I've always felt like money leads to greed," I explained to my coach Laura during our session.

I breathed. Then the words began to gush out like a river flowing at rapid speed. "I had an initial consultation with a potential coaching client. She asked, 'How much?' and I wanted to barf in my mouth when I told her twenty-five dollars. I'm still new at this. I'm not certified yet. Plus, if I can help people at a more affordable price or even for free, why wouldn't I do that? So many people can't afford food and I'm here charging people to help them. It just feels wrong. I know I can't run a business on free sessions or twenty-five-dollar sessions, but it feels so hard to ask for even that. There's no way I could ask for more. Nor do I feel right doing so."

Laura observed me without a word. I felt seen, and that felt uncomfortable.

"What would happen if you asked for more?" Laura inquired.

"Like how much more?"

"How much is an hour of your time worth?"

"I don't know. I've never thought about that." I tapped the table in front of me with my finger. "How do I figure that out?"

"Well, let's take a baseline. What do you make right now in your job at Google?"

As we calculated my hourly rate based on my salary, bonuses, and stock options, my jaw dropped at the number that appeared.

"One hundred ninety dollars an hour. That's a lot more than twenty-five dollars an hour," I muttered.

"Yes it is. And we haven't even counted all the benefits you receive."

"But I'm not experienced yet. And I'm still working on my certification," I justified. "I don't feel comfortable charging such a high rate."

"What's uncomfortable about it?" Laura asked.

"It just feels greedy still. I mean, what would people think? I say I want to help people, but I'm charging this outrageous fee that most people can't afford."

"It seems like you're saying it's an either or. *Either* you charge a lot and some people can't afford you, *or* you charge less and everyone can afford you. How might there be an *and* in there?"

"An *and*?" I tapped my chin thinking. Then suddenly the lightbulb came on. I had an aha moment. "I could charge more to those who can afford it, then donate my time to help people who can't?"

"What else?"

"I could offer a sliding scale."

"What else?"

"I could charge a higher fee, then donate money to a good cause!"

As we continued on with our coaching session, we came up with a variety of *and* options that I felt good about.

My mom's comments to me at the Coach outlet were the catalyst for me opening up to other money mindset possibilities. Laura's coaching guided me to transform my beliefs and relationship with money. They both helped me recognize that money isn't a positive or negative thing. Money is a tool, like a hammer or a screwdriver. And as a tool it can be used to do good for the world, if you so choose.

Over time, I shifted my beliefs.

> **Old belief:** I must save all my money.
>
> **New belief:** I can spend money on things I enjoy and still be smart about my money habits.

> **Old belief:** it's greedy and not fair for me to want more money when there are so many people in the world who are suffering and less fortunate than I am.
>
> **New belief:** money is a tool; having more money enables me to do more and contribute to making the world a better place for everyone.

> **Old belief:** money will make me evil.
>
> **New belief:** money doesn't change people but brings out more of who someone is; I'm kind, caring, and generous, and money will bring out more of that in me.

My relationship with money has evolved. I no longer get heavy chest pains from spending full price on things. Despite still loving coupons and a good bargain, I recognize that the time spent on bargain hunting and coupon-using isn't always worth it compared to the value of my hour.

I've come to accept that money isn't the source of evil and greed. People are the way they are, and money just brings that out.

Investing in myself and the things I love no longer carries guilt. The writing of this book is a testament to that. I had to decrease my number of paid clients in order to make time to write this book. All the hundreds of hours of writing weren't paid. It was hard to do, but it felt right.

Greg eventually got me to attend a Tony Robbins event. He's not such a bad guy. Robbins is actually inspiring, and I learned a lot from him. I even paid thousands of dollars to attend other events and read several of his books, including *Unshakeable: Your Financial Freedom Playbook*.

Change your beliefs, change your outcome.

# Mama & Papa Yip's Story

**金錢不是 萬能, 沒錢 萬萬不能.**

*jīn qián bù shì wàn néng, méi qián wàn wàn bù néng.*

Money is not everything, without money absolutely nothing.

## Setting the Scene

It's 7:30 p.m. on a Thursday. I just put my kiddo to bed for the night. I'm sitting in my home office. WhatsApp is ringing as I wait for my parents to pick up my call. They had originally planned to visit. Unfortunately, Greg and I caught a stomach bug at a friend's birthday earlier in the week. Logan ended up getting it too. I can't imagine my mom, a tiny, 95-pound woman, handling the stomach flu very well. She already struggles to keep weight on. So I told them not to visit. Of course my parents insisted on stopping by to drop off food that my mom had already made. So we did a contactless exchange earlier in the day and agreed to catch up on WhatsApp this evening.

My dad finally picks up, and I see his finger in the camera as he sets up the phone. He finally has it propped up against something, probably the box of tissues that has sat in the same spot on the kitchen table since we moved into that house thirty-five years ago. He asks how the baby is doing and whether I'm resting enough. I see my mom by the sink washing dishes. She doesn't turn around but mentions that they ate dinner early to talk to me. I pucker my lips and give them a virtual smooch to show my love and appreciation before we begin our conversation about money and money mindsets.

# What We Learned from My Grandfather

民以食為天.

*mín yǐ shí wéi tiān.*
Subjects think food is heaven.

"We grew up in China during the late '50s," Papa Yip starts. "At that time, China was a poor country. Many countries in Asia were poor. No money meant no food." Papa Yip leans in. His face fills my entire screen. His eyebrow lifts as he checks that I'm following what he's saying. Satisfied with my nods, he leans back into his chair. "Can you guess what a good day looked like for people in those days?" Without waiting for an answer, he continues, "Ending the day with a full belly was a good day. We were content with that."

"I've read that if you're just content, you stop taking steps forward. You stop striving. You lose your motivation. You might even start taking steps backward," I share. "So if you're content with something so simple as a full belly, how does that impact your motivation for something better? A better life?"

Papa Yip looks at me quizzically. "Being content doesn't mean you don't desire more, Amy. You can be grateful for a full belly, the little that you have, *and* you can have dreams of better."

There goes the "and" again. It makes me think of my many conversations with Laura, who always asked me to think with *and* instead of *or*.

"Take my father," Papa Yip continues. "His mother passed away when he was very young. His father remarried. This new wife never liked your grandfather. When he was twelve, she claimed that he raped her and demanded that he be kicked out of the home."

"She claimed a twelve-year-old raped her?" I shout, cutting off Papa Yip. "That's ridiculous!"

"Yes it was," Papa Yip nods in agreement. "Especially because your grandfather has always had a skinny, small stature. But his father didn't have the courage to stand up to this new wife." Papa Yip's eyebrows furrow. His lips press together. "Maybe he was afraid she would leave with their two children. Who knows? He took your grandfather to the riverbank, handed him a bit of money, and sent him away on a boat."

I wrinkle my nose. My lips twist in disdain. How could any parents just leave their twelve-year-old child? I cannot fathom that. What in the world was my great-grandfather thinking to send his child off on a boat because his wife said to do so? No balls.

I lean towards the screen as if that would ease my curiosity. "Where did the boat take him? What did he do?" I ask.

"The boat took your grandfather to a town called Hangzhou," Papa Yip begins. "He was homeless there, begging in the streets. The owner of a tailor shop saw your grandfather and felt sorry for him. The owner asked him, 'Little boy, why are you in the streets?' After he heard your grandfather's story, the tailor offered him an apprenticeship. Of course your grandfather accepted. As an apprentice you get a place to stay. Meals are provided. That's how your grandfather started as a tailor. He began with no skills, no education, no experience. He was content for a full belly and a roof over his shoulders. *And* your grandfather had a desire for more. He worked hard and was determined to have a better life."

"What happened?" I ask.

"Well," he said, "by the time I was born, your grandfather had over a hundred employees working for him. He owned tailor shops all over Shanghai. Your grandfather would just sit at home, and every morning an employee would come to provide him with a report on the state of his stores. I remember when it was time to pay employees their salary, they'd fill these huge burlap rice bags up with cash, the rice bags that hold one hundred pounds of rice." Papa Yip holds out his arms to show how big these bags were. "They'd fill those up with cash, bring them to the stores, and distribute salaries that way. Can you imagine just carrying a big rice sack full of cash around?"

Mama Yip pauses her dishwashing and turns around. I see a smirk cross her face as she exclaims, "Your grandfather was so rich that your daddy's butt was wiped with gold coins." She nods her head towards Papa Yip. "Right, old man?"

I raise my eyebrow and glance at Papa Yip quizzically.

Papa Yip laughs before sharing, "Your grandfather was extravagant. For my one-month birthday, he booked a few restaurants and held a three-day celebration. During those three days, if you went to one of those restaurants and told them my father's name and that he was celebrating his son's one-month birthday, then you ate for free. Just sign a receipt after you eat, and the restaurants would bring those bills to your grandfather to pay. Can you imagine how much he spent on my one-month birthday?

"When I was just a toddler, your grandfather would give me gold pieces to play with. The floor of our home was made of wood boards. I'd find cracks in the floor and drop the pieces into the holes."

"You just dropped gold coins through holes in the floor?" I exclaim. Papa Yip nods with a grin. "What did grandpa do about it?"

"He would just laugh and give me more out of his pocket."

"So how do you get the gold coins out of the floor?" I ask.

"You don't. Unless you tear the floorboards out," Papa Yip professes. "But your grandfather didn't care. That's how rich he was. He went from a homeless twelve-year-old, content with a meal and a roof over his head, to being rich. That's why being content doesn't mean you lose motivation. It just means you're grateful for what you have. You can still have desires and dreams for more. Your grandfather worked hard. Anything is possible with persistence and determination."

Papa Yip shakes his head. "The problem is that your grandfather spent a lot. He didn't know how to be frugal, how to save money. He went from over a hundred employees to being in debt when he passed away."

"What happened?" I implore.

"Well, communism took over China in the late 1940s," Papa Yip explains. "When that happened, it became illegal to run your own business. You could only be employed by the government. Your grandfather's friends advised him to go to Hong Kong to start his businesses there. At that time, Hong Kong was owned by the British, so their laws were different. But your grandfather refused to believe it. He would often say, 'I'm a businessman! It doesn't matter what government is in place, they couldn't possibly forbid people from running their own business!' But that's what happened in China. Business owners lost their right to their businesses. Your grandfather was among them. So month by month, as he paid for his family's expenses, his wealth disappeared. He finally went to Hong Kong to try to establish himself there, but it was too late."

Papa Yip pauses and glances at the floor. Sadness crosses his face. I wait patiently before he finally returns his gaze to the phone. His eyes are heavy. "Your grandfather got sick while he was in Hong Kong. By the time he passed away in November 1961, we were broke. Your grandmother and I had to borrow three hundred Hong Kong dollars just for his funeral. That wasn't enough to pay for a lot of the Chinese funeral traditions. So it was a simple ceremony."

Papa Yip's eyes gloss over. He sighs heavily before continuing, "Your grandfather worked so hard for his wealth. He lost it all because he didn't think about the long-term consequences, how to save. But the gift is that I learned a lot about money from how your grandfather built his wealth and managed his money."

"And I learned a lot from you," I whisper.

# Money Is Not Good or Bad, but a Reflection of an Individual's Character

身正不怕影子斜.

*shēn zhèng bú pà yǐng zi xié.*

A straight foot is not afraid of a crooked shoe.

Mama Yip comes to the table with a bowl of red-bean soup for Papa Yip, then settles into her chair.

After taking a sip of his soup, Papa Yip shares, "One of the greatest things your grandfather taught me was that money is a powerful tool. He always told me that if you can help others, you should help them."

Mama Yip chimes in, "Your grandfather was always doing good deeds. Always helping people."

Papa Yip nods. "When I was born, people sent gifts. Your grandfather refused to keep them. Instead, he donated the gifts to this shop that made coffins for the poor. Chinese believe that you can't pass to the next world without a coffin. So this shop made them coffins. After your grandfather made donations, all the people in our community said to him, 'You will have good karma for your deeds.' He responded, 'The good karma is for my son. These are his gifts.'"

Papa Yip throws up his hands and professes, "But I was just born. It's not like I had a say in donating the gifts. Your grandfather made that decision. The good karma should go to him. But that's the type of man your grandfather was. He cared more about other people. And he always said that money can help you to help people."

"You don't think money makes people evil?" I blurt out.

"Who said money makes people evil?" Papa Yip bellows. "That's silly. Money isn't evil. Money doesn't cause people to be evil. It merely brings their character out. Take Bill Gates. Look at how he spends his wealth. He's always donating to good causes. During the COVID pandemic he committed over two billion dollars to the global response. Some people use their wealth for good, some use it for evil. But that has nothing to do with money itself. It's merely a reflection of the person's character."

"I agree," Mama Yip replies. "If you want to help others, you need money. Even if you help with your time, your time is money. Like when you went to Ghana to volunteer at the breast cancer nonprofit. You were volunteering, but you still needed to pay for your own lodging, food, and transportation there. It cost you money to volunteer. If you didn't save up, how could you leave your job and go volunteer?"

"Even with the earthquakes in Turkey right now," Papa Yip adds, "people are donating to help the country. How are they able to donate? Because of money."

I'm surprised by their answers. All I can think about is how, growing up, they were constantly arguing and worrying about money. "Well I feel like money puts people in a bad mood. When they don't have it, they worry and get upset and argue," I say.

Papa Yip observes me. "Amy, money is just money. Money doesn't tell you to steal or murder or act unkindly to others. People do that. For example, Person A uses money to hire Person B to commit a crime. Did the money tell Person A to hire Person B to commit the crime? No. Person A is the one that made that decision. Money is not wrong. People are wrong."

"Anybody who tells you that money is the root of all evil doesn't have any money!" Mama Yip asserts. "Who's so stupid to think that?"

I wince, thinking, *Your daughter used to think that!* But I don't mention it. No need to go down that rabbit hole.

Papa Yip wags his forefinger and leans into the screen again. He likes to do this when he really wants my attention. "You, Greg, and Logan were all sick recently. How did money help you?" He answers his own question with "Money helped you by making you feel better and recover faster. You used money to buy medicine, to see the doctor, to buy Pedialyte. Even though health is the most important thing, having money can help you live a healthier life." Papa Yip leans back into his seat. His point is complete.

True. I was able to go to Walgreens and pick up what I needed without a thought of how much things cost. Nor did I have to worry about loss of income. I had the flexibility to reschedule meetings and clients to focus on taking care of my family. But my parents didn't have the same privilege. Doctors' visits and medicine meant taking money out of the family budget. Taking care of their family meant taking time off from their hourly jobs. The lack of money is what caused their arguments. The worry about money is what caused Papa Yip to get so angry at himself.

My eyes snap shut. My mind is whirling like a tornado. I purse my lips. Then the words come bursting out of me as I recount the story of Papa Yip filling out a job application outside of the Marriott.

"I didn't like seeing you upset over money," I sigh. "So I always hated money because it made you worry and get angry."

Papa Yip doesn't respond. Mama Yip slaps him on his shoulder, "Aiya. Your anger, old man."

After what feels like an eternity of silence, Papa Yip sighs. "I know I didn't respond well, Amy. I didn't know how to handle the situation and was frustrated at myself for forgetting something so stupid as my employment dates. It was important for me to get this application filled so I could start bringing income for our family."

"I understand that," I reply.

"Money didn't make me act that way. *I* acted that way. It wasn't money's fault."

Looking into Papa Yip's eyes, I can feel his love even through the screen. I can see that he's taking full ownership of his actions that day sitting outside of the Marriott; the actions that had scared the living shit out of little thirteen-year-old Amy. Hearing his words, I feel as if a hole within me is healing. This is what I've needed all these years.

# Frugality Does Not Equal Scarcity

常将有日思無日, 莫将無時想有时時.

*cháng jiāng yǒu rì sī wú rì, mò jiāng wú shí xiǎng yǒu shí.*

Be frugal in prosperity, fear not in adversity.

Mama Yip picks up Papa Yip's empty bowl and takes it to the sink. My attention turns to the entire scene around them: the thirty-five-year-old kitchen cabinets that are chipping away at the corners, the saucepan with a missing handle on the stovetop, my twenty-year-old sweatshirt on Mama Yip, and Papa Yip in his old Marriott work vest.

"You've worked so hard and saved money your whole life," I comment. "Why not use money as a tool to enjoy life? It's not like you have a lot of expenses. Why still be so cheap?"

"We're not cheap, we're frugal," Mama Yip states.

"I'm not cheap, but your mommy might be," Papa Yip proclaims with a cheeky grin. "Just the other day she refused to spend forty dollars on vitamins she needs because the price went up."

"A month ago they were only twenty-five dollars," Mama Yip exclaims. "How do you increase to forty dollars in a month? That's absurd. It's the principle!"

Papa Yip surveys Mama Yip. "Yeah, but like Amy said, we don't have many expenses. We don't need much. What's an extra fifteen dollars for vitamins?" He turns to meet my gaze and shakes his head. "In Chinese we say that this person can't think clearly."

Papa Yip inches his face so close to the phone that all I see are his nose and mouth. He whispers, "Can you order for your mommy later?" I nod.

"I heard that, old man!" Mama Yip shouts from the sink. "Don't buy it for forty dollars! It's not worth it."

"Okay, I won't," I agree. She said not to pay $40, but she didn't say I couldn't spend $41. . . I smile.

287

"Good," she bellows, walking back towards us. "See Amy, there's a difference between being frugal and being cheap. Being frugal is about seeing the big picture, knowing what you value and where you're willing to spend. It's about prioritizing things you find worthy. These vitamins aren't a priority to me. I'd rather spend my money elsewhere."

"So what's cheap?" I ask.

"Being cheap is wanting to save money no matter at what cost," she explains, taking her seat. "It's when you don't pay your fair share. Like your aunt who always comes out to eat with the family, orders everything, but never offers to pay. Being cheap is greediness; it's stealing other's fortunes. Like those people you hear about that'll do anything for an inheritance. People are cheap when they're afraid there isn't enough for everyone."

Mama Yip leans back in her chair before continuing, "We're frugal, not cheap. I've always been that way since I started working at age twelve. I was a garment beader making twenty Hong Kong dollars a month. Most of that went to my parents. They gave me just enough money for my bus rides to and from work."

"You didn't get any spending money?" I blurt out.

"No," Mama Yip shrugs. "But that's how I learned the importance of being frugal and saving for what you want. I wanted the freedom of having spending money. So I would take the bus halfway to work and walk the remaining thirty minutes. I saved ten cents on each trip. I never told your grandmother, though. If she knew, she'd take the money I'd saved away."

I grimace, thinking of how Papa Yip took away my hard-earned $1,000. I'm glad Mama Yip was able to squirrel away money without getting caught.

Not noticing my reaction, she continues, "I got better at my craft and started taking on private clients. I'd work on their garments in the evenings after work. That's when I started to really save a lot!" Mama Yip beams proudly. "I no longer had to reserve eating apples for special occasions. If I wanted an apple, I could buy an apple. With my savings, I bought fruit for all my siblings. That's what being frugal is about, Amy. Saving for things that you value. And I valued being able to treat my siblings."

Glancing at Papa Yip with a huge grin, Mama Yip professes, "Then your daddy tricked me to marry him when I was just twenty years old."

"Luckiest day of your life!" Papa Yip cuts in.

Mama Yip rolls her eyes in response. I laugh. I love seeing their silliness, especially after all the years they've focused on just working and saving.

As she returns her gaze towards me, Mama Yip adds, "Now I have my own family, and I value being able to treat my kids."

Papa Yip observes me and says, "You take after us, Amy. You save for what you want. Like the plane ticket to Hong Kong. Remember that?"

"Yeah," I nod my head. How could I forget that?

"Just the other day, your mommy found your arts and crafts box and your friendship bracelet book in the basement," Papa Yip continues. "She said, 'That stupid girl spent so much time in elementary school with this thin string making bracelets to sell for a dollar or two. It probably made her eyesight go bad!' You worked hard to save money little by little."

"And in high school you worked multiple jobs to save for a good college education because you knew we couldn't afford college tuition," Mama Yip adds. "That's being frugal, not being cheap. You prioritized and saved for what you valued. We just all value different things."

"Remember, Amy," Papa Yip notes as he wags his finger, "people in our day were content with just a full belly. That's why your mommy and I value being able to take care of our loved ones through their bellies. We spend minimally on ourselves so that we can make sure our loved ones end their day with a full belly." He points down to his round belly and grins. "And your mommy makes sure I have a very full belly."

Memories dance through my mind of all the years we were eligible for food stamps, yet my parents still found a way to send money to their family in China and Hong Kong. They've always prioritized taking care of others ahead of themselves. Just yesterday during our contactless food drop-off, my parents included groceries so I wouldn't have to go to the store while taking care of my sick family. When I opened up the grocery bags, I discovered, among other things, a few avocados and a dozen organic, free-range eggs—the expensive stuff that they don't ever buy for themselves.

Papa Yip starts coughing and gets up for a mug of warm water. I watch as he slowly hobbles over to the decades-old thermos they're still using. He has a knee brace on each knee. He never complains about the pain, but I know walking too much causes flare-ups. He recently asked me to help him buy new knee braces "on-the-line. Anything cheap is fine," he said. I bought him the best I could find.

It pains me to witness their "frugality" (at least that's what they call it) with themselves, even when it comes to crucial items such as knee braces or vitamins. Then they turn around and spend money on luxuries such as avocados and organic, free-range eggs for me. I sigh as Papa Yip shuffles back to his chair with his mug of hot water in hand. I notice the chip on the mouth of the mug and make a mental note to get him a new one.

"I appreciate the avocados and eggs you bought for me," I say, smiling softly.

Mama and Papa Yip nod to acknowledge they've received my appreciation.

# My Reflections Post-Conversation

How much is enough money? My dad told me a Chinese saying that has always stuck with me: "Want a thousand, have a thousand, want ten thousand, have ten thousand, want to be an emperor." The notion is that humans are never satisfied. And oftentimes, when we say things like, "I don't have enough" or "I'm afraid I won't make enough," we don't actually know how much "enough" is.

This reminds me of a client I worked with who was afraid to pursue a dream because there was a risk of "not making enough." When I asked her what would be enough, she didn't know the answer. When we dug in further, we discovered that beneath that "enoughness" was a fear of losing it all because as a child, her parents had lost it all. Overnight, she went from having everything to nothing. She's been caught in the grips of the fear of loss ever since, and this fear has prevented her from being able to enjoy money.

That's what I'm starting to realize. For many of us, not just me, our money mindsets were formed in early childhood as we observed and absorbed what we saw and heard from parents, friends, and others who influenced our upbringing: how they talked (or argued) about money and how money was spent (or not), as well as our own lived experiences of money (divorce, unemployment, illness) and of working (age of first job, types of jobs). All these experiences taught us how to think about money.

My parents were no different. My grandpa's hard work, wealth, then loss of wealth and eventual illness and passing impacted my dad's money mindset tremendously. My mom's upbringing, having to share an apple among six siblings and walking thirty minutes to work to save ten cents, impacted hers.

The beauty is that a money mindset is learned, which means it can be unlearned. My client was able to slowly unlearn beliefs and let go of her fears to form a new relationship with and start enjoying money. I was able to do the same. I unlearned my belief that money was evil and now recognize it and use it as a powerful tool for good.

Money cannot buy me happiness, but it can pay for things that bring me joy, such as travel and delicious food. Money cannot buy me love, but it sure does reduce the frequency of stressful financial conversations with my husband. Money cannot buy me more time, but it sure can afford me help— help that gives me back time so that I can focus on what matters most to me. Housekeeper? Check. Virtual assistant? Check. Nanny? Check. And with the extra time, I sleep, I work out, and I spend quality time being fully present with my kiddo, my husband, and my parents. My ability to ask my clients for what I'm worth allows me to donate and invest in causes that I believe in.

A few weeks after our initial conversation about money, my dad mentioned that he and my mom watched this Chinese show. He told me, "The TV show host said, 'If you're sick, then go see a doctor. If you wait, you may not recover. If you can eat, then eat. If you wait, you might not be able to eat it anymore.' And he's right! At our age, nothing is guaranteed. We've all worked so hard for so long; we need to stop being so frugal and learn to spend money on ourselves. We should learn to enjoy the last few years of our lives. Your mommy and I are trying to learn to do that, but old habits die hard."

I'm glad they're trying to change. And I do believe my parents *can* change their money mindset, at least a little. It's never too late, even for people in their seventies. And I'm determined to be by their side on this journey, encouraging them to enjoy their hard-earned wealth in these last years of their lives.

# A Date with Your Parents

## PRE-CONVERSATION PERSONAL REFLECTION

### Overview

The money messages you received from your parents are likely still having an impact on you today. They may influence whether you pick up the bill, whether you hold tightly to your paycheck or spend it immediately, and even how you feel when negotiating your salary or telling a new client your pricing. By understanding your money mindset, you will have greater agency in how you feel about money and the power it has in your life.

### Instructions

1. Spend some time journaling on these prompts:

   ❖ What did you see and hear about money growing up? Consider the following:

   ✦ What were your family's and/or parents' values and attitudes about money? Saving, spending, budgeting, donating?

   ✦ How was money talked about? Calmly? Or was there tension and fighting? What emotions did it bring up?

   ✦ How did you view these ideas as a child? What did you agree with? What did you disagree with?

   ✦ How do you feel about those teachings now?

◈ As a child, did you have an allowance? How did you view this as a child? Today?

◈ Did you work as a young adult? Why or why not?

◈ What does money mean to you personally? Why? Here are some starting ideas:

  ✦ Freedom
  ✦ Strength
  ✦ Power
  ✦ Self-reliance
  ✦ Luxury
  ✦ Safety and security
  ✦ Success
  ✦ Respect
  ✦ Control
  ✦ Confidence
  ✦ Less stress
  ✦ Comfort
  ✦ Happiness

◈ How do you think about the intersection of time and money? How do you feel when someone forgets a scheduled meeting with you or when they show up late?

◈ Tell your money stories.

  ✦ What is your most painful money memory?
  ✦ What is your happiest or best money memory?

2. Take a look at what you've written. As you gain awareness and understanding of your money mindset, you also gain greater agency to transform your money story.

   ❖ What's one thing from my family's money history that I want to replicate?

   ❖ What's one thing from my family's money history that I want to do differently?

## THE CONVERSATION

### Conversation Topic

Where your parents learned their money beliefs, how your parents' experiences influenced their money mindset, and what their relationship with money is today.

### Tips

These conversations can be hard, and potentially triggering. Priority number one is to take care of yourself. Remember to review the Conversation Tip Sheet on page 23 before your conversation.

### Conversation-Specific Suggestions

Conversations about money can be challenging, particularly if we have drastically conflicting beliefs. If you find that your money beliefs and values clash with those of your parents, remember that differences around money aren't about the actual dollars and cents but rather the meaning we place on money. There's no right or wrong way of thinking about or handling money. So be open to listening to your parents' experiences, beliefs, and values.

Make this date as low cost as possible while feeling comfortable and abundant, however you define comfortable and abundant. Dress up and sit in the lobby of a luxurious hotel. Or perhaps your parents, like mine, are content with just a full belly. In that case, order their favorite takeout food and pull out the finest tableware. If you're having the conversation virtually, have their favorite food delivered to their home.

## Questions For Your Parents

### *Lighter Questions*

- ◈ What is your first memory with money?

- ◈ Growing up, what did your family or parents believe about money and how it worked?

- ◈ What did your family or parents teach you about saving, budgeting, spending, and donating? What did you agree with? What did you not agree with?

- ◈ As a child, did you have an allowance? How did you view this as a child? Today?

- ◈ How do you spend money? What is worth it? What is not?

- ◈ What do you believe about people who have a lot of money?

- ◈ If you received a million dollars, what would you do with the money?

- ◈ What good deeds have you done with your wealth?

- ◈ What are the most important money lessons you want to pass on to your children and future generations?

## *Deeper Questions*

◆ When you were young, what were your hopes and dreams about money? How have they changed?

◆ When you were young, what were your biggest fears around money? How have they changed?

◆ What is the greatest money hardship you've been through? What did you learn from the experience?

◆ What is your happiest or best money memory?

◆ What does money mean to you personally? Why?

◆ Have you ever been fired from or quit a job? What happened?

◆ What would other people think of you if you had a lot of money?

◆ What would you believe about yourself if you had all the money you ever dreamed of?

◆ What are your current beliefs about money? *If your parents don't understand this question, you can use some of these examples and ask them if they agree with these statements. Feel free to add other statements to this list as well:*

  ✦ There's not enough money to go around.
  ✦ There's plenty of money to go around for everyone.
  ✦ Time is money.
  ✦ I'm bad with money.
  ✦ I can overcome any money obstacle.
  ✦ Money is always tight.
  ✦ I can always figure out my money problems.
  ✦ I can't afford to . . .

+ Saving money is easy.
+ I have to evaluate every purchase I make.

◈ Are there things you want that you don't allow yourself to have because of the cost? What are they?

◈ What do you wish you could do or want to do but haven't yet because it's too expensive?

## POST-CONVERSATION CONTEMPLATION

After the conversation with your parents, contemplate and journal on the following:

◈ What new insights have you gained about

+ who your parents are,
+ what their money mindset is, and
+ how they developed their money mindset?

◈ How might you help your parents live an "abundant" life, however you define abundant? Consider their answers to the last two Deeper Questions.

Using your new awareness and insights, how do you want to view financial success? What is "enough"? At the end of the day, financial success is a decision. When you make this decision with full faith, your behaviors will follow. Consider your answers to these questions:

◈ What do I want my life to look like?

◈ How would it feel once I've achieved this?

◈ What would change in my life?

The most important thing to understand is why all of this matters. A majority of people never sit down to consider why they have certain financial goals. But when you have a strong why, your behaviors will follow because your why gives you more than the reason; it serves as your purpose and provides you with continued motivation. Consider your answers to these questions:

❖ Why do you want your financial situation to change?

❖ Why would you like to earn more money?

❖ Why do your ultimate financial goals and dreams matter to you?

*Money doesn't change men, it merely unmasks them.*
~ Henry Ford ~

# MYTH 8

# It's Better to Be
# a Boy than a Girl

# My Story

## Mixed Messages

I was an accident. Unplanned. My parents came to the US in 1978 hoping for a better life and had left my two older sisters in Hong Kong with my grandparents while they established themselves in the US. Just two years after arriving in the US, my mom became pregnant with me.

"What do we do?" she had asked my dad.

After some contemplation, he responded, "We already have two daughters. This one has to be a boy. Let's keep it."

I was my dad's last hope for a son.

Boys are more desired in Chinese families. For one, they carry on the family name. And in rural areas of China, boys continue to be desired to help in the fields, as they're seen as stronger and more capable of such work. It's why in China, when there was a one-child policy, parents often abandoned their baby girls and left them to die so they could continue to try for a son.

Fortunately, my parents left China at a young age and didn't have to abide by the one-child policy. During the '60s and '70s, living in Hong Kong, a British territory at the time, then later in the US, they were free to have as many children as they desired. So after each daughter, my dad continued to hope for a son.

Apparently he fainted when I was born. He often jokes it was because "Three daughters and a wife! Too many women in the house!" Personally, I think it was because I came into the world as a baby girl full of passion, curiosity, and a lust for life. I also had a tremendously loud voice.

303

Unfortunately, much of my voice was muted as my sense of identity and worldviews formed. Growing up in a household of mostly women and a traditional father while trying to straddle the Western and Asian cultures, I received mixed messages about what a girl should be like. Specifically, what a

girl like me, the accident and last hope for a son, should be like.

My dad would cut my hair like a boy and explain, "Because you were supposed to be a boy." And so I believed that I needed to be more "boyish" to gain my dad's love and approval. So what did I do? I played soccer with the boys during recess and looked down on things like hopscotch and four square with the girls.

"Amy, why don't you play with the girls more?" my sister Jenny questioned. Ever since she could walk, Jenny loved to dress up and look pretty. At the mere age of twelve, she was already wearing makeup and following the latest fashions.

"I just like playing soccer with the boys more," I responded.

"That's so tomboyish."

"Well then, I guess I'm a tomboy," I asserted proudly. I took a liking to the word "tomboy." Perhaps it was because it contains the word "boy."

"Well if you keep acting too much like a boy, then boys won't like you," she taunted. With a flutter of her eyebrows, she walked away, leaving me to wonder whether her words were true. As much as I wanted to be boyish, I didn't want to be a boy because, well, I liked boys. In fact, I had a crush on a boy named Erick. So my sister's comment made me pause. I was confused.

The confusion deepened a few weeks later when my sister got angry with me and took it out on my coloring book. She tore it apart. Tears streamed down my face as I sniffed and wailed. It was my favorite coloring book.

"Stop being such a crybaby!" Jenny taunted me. "You're such a girly girl. Too emotional."

*Wait. Wasn't she the one who had told me not to be a tomboy? And now I'm not supposed to show emotion because it's too "girly girl"?* It was like trying to put two puzzle pieces together that just didn't fit.

My parents were no better at easing my confusion. In fourth grade, I told my parents I wanted to learn karate.

"Karate is for boys, Amy," my mom explained.

"Why?" I exclaimed.

"It just is. Not appropriate for a good Chinese girl. How about Chinese dance instead?"

"Uhhh . . . okay. Sure."

So my parents enrolled me in Chinese dance. During the first class, we were handed five foot-long, colorful, satin ribbons.

"Twirl and toss. Twirl and toss," the Chinese dance instructor shouted. "Large and flowing movements, girls. Let your ribbon float above you! Now flutter and flap! Flutter and flap. Let the music bring beauty to your dance!"

I lasted one lesson. Dancing around fluttering and flapping didn't feel like it would help me gain approval as "the son my dad always wanted." And yet, both of my parents had suggested Chinese dance in lieu of the "more masculine" karate.

*What in the world do my parents expect of me? Do they want a son or not?*

As I hit sixth grade and started leaning towards being more girly, dressing up pretty and actually spending time on my hair, my mom threw another curveball at me.

"My daughters must be strong and independent," she told me. "I know many women who financially rely on their husbands. Then, when their husbands mistreat them, they're left with no options. Stay in the relationship and they continue to endure mistreatment. Divorce and they're left in financial struggles. My daughters will be strong, powerful women who don't need men for financial security."

Months later, when my parents returned home from a parent–teacher conference, my dad admonished, "Amy, your teacher says you talk too much in class."

"What do you mean?" I questioned.

"She says you're always talking, you're loud, and always questioning her."

"Yeah. She says dumb things," I explained.

"Well you need to be obedient and listen to your teacher. She's the authority. Keep your head down, follow the rules, and don't rock the boat."

I bit my tongue as I filled with anger, frustration, and confusion.

So let me get this straight. When I was born, I was supposed to be a boy to carry on the family name, and my hair was cut like a boy for most of my childhood, yet I shouldn't play sports or learn karate because those are boy activities? But I also shouldn't get too emotional and cry because that's just being a weak "girly girl"? Somehow I need to be sure to do well and have a successful career so that I can be financially independent and not rely on men, but I need to stay quiet and keep my voice small? How does any of that even make sense?

## Girls Can Do Anything They Put Their Minds To

It was a Sunday afternoon. I sat cross-legged in front of the TV, but I wasn't paying any attention to what was on the screen. My attention was on my dad, who was behind me getting frustrated by the minute. From the corner of my eye, I had been watching him trying to fix our front door lock for the last hour. I could hear him muttering "dammit" beneath his breath.

Mustering up all the twelve-year-old courage I had, I finally turned to ask him, "Daddy, want me to try to help you?"

He peered at me, amused. "You're a girl, Amy. You don't know how to do these things."

I turned back to the TV, but I saw nothing. My eyes blanked as anger heated my blood. I felt a hard, black rock in my throat choking back the scream that wanted so desperately to escape me. But I knew better than to scream at my dad. Good Chinese girls don't do that.

I knew I was an accident. I knew I was supposed to be a boy, but I wasn't. And there was nothing I could do about it. But I could fix a damn lock even if I was a girl!

My dad's footsteps as he headed upstairs shook me out of my bubble of fury. I glanced at his back and saw him shaking his head. When he disappeared from my sight, I gazed back at the front door. The lock was still in disarray. The bathroom door upstairs clicked. I turned my gaze back to the TV screen, then back to the door, back to the screen, back to the door, then up the stairs.

Carefully, as if I were a ninja, I got up and walked quietly to the door and fiddled with the lock. I poked at the holes, the screws, and the knob, then picked up the screwdriver and started putting the lock together. Ten minutes later, voila! It was fixed. I patted myself on the back with a feeling of triumph as I returned to the floor in front of the TV, a big grin of satisfaction on my face. The joy of proving my dad wrong flooded over me like a beautiful sunset fills the sky.

Another ten minutes passed before my dad returned. As he got closer to the door, my heart pounded harder and harder. He studied the lock for what felt like an eternity before peering over at me.

"Amy, did you do this?"

"Yup. Girls can fix locks," I replied without turning away from the TV. I wanted to add "See? I told you I could help!" but I kept my mouth shut, knowing better than to rub it in.

At that moment, my mom walked out of the kitchen, a waft of freshly steamed fish and hot and sour soup following after her. "Are you done with the door yet?" she asked my dad.

"Uh," he hesitated, "yes. It's done."

"I did it, Mommy. Daddy was trying to fix it for over an hour. I asked Daddy if I could help him. He said girls can't fix locks. But when he went upstairs, I tried and I figured it out and I fixed it." The words erupted out of me like champagne bubbling out of an uncorked bottle.

The corners of my mom's eyes crinkled. Her mouth curved into a smile. "My daughters can do anything they put their minds to." Then she turned to my dad and wagged her finger at him. "You shouldn't be telling your daughters what they can and can't do just because they're girls. That's what you get."

I smiled and whispered to myself, "I *can* do anything I put my mind to." What my mom said sat with me for years to come.

## I'm Not Girly

I can do anything; I'm strong; I'm not a girly girl. That's what I believed throughout middle school and into my young adulthood.

Okay fine. You got me. It went beyond young adulthood into my late thirties.

My favorite color changed from pink, my favorite in elementary school, to blue. I chose to play sports instead of becoming a cheerleader. I even refused to have too many girlfriends.

*Most girls are too catty*, I thought. *They're drama queens and hate on each other, just like the girls in the book* Cat's Eye *or the movie* Mean Girls. *All they do is talk about each other behind their backs. Talk doesn't help you achieve anything meaningful. I'd rather hang out with chill guys.*

I began to associate masculine energy as powerful, strong, and capable. I abhorred the notion of being "girly," which I associated as weak, frail, and incapable; always needing help from others.

"You're a machine!" a guy who had been working out next to me at the CrossFit box said to me after we finished our Workout of the Day.

"Thanks!" I beamed. I embraced being called tough.

I was rewarded and recognized when I displayed my masculine energy characteristics. I thrived in academics and in my career when I focused on using logic, structure, and getting shit done. I received accolades and was quickly promoted in the corporate jobs that I held. And my dad became a walking ad of my successes, wearing merchandise donning "UCLA Anderson Dad" and "Google."

These rewards reinforced my behavior. I learned to push down emotions, compassion, and friendliness. I'd only cry in private, and even that would annoy me because I believed tears were weak. Oftentimes, to stop my own tears, I'd just bite my tongue until it hurt. I moved fast, I was independent, and I showed up with great passion and assertiveness. I hid behind my independent, Superwoman mask. "I don't need anybody's help" was my motto. I leaned on my masculine energy to succeed in this "man's world," and I blocked my feminine energy. In fact, I shunned the very notion of having any feminine energy at all. And I firmly believed that I was "just one of the guys."

"That's just who I am," I'd say.

"I wish you would just need me once in a while," Greg once professed to me.

"What do you mean?" I demanded, annoyed that he'd want me to be a damsel in distress.

"Well, you're just so independent. You don't ever ask me for help. It's like you really don't even need me. I want to feel needed."

"Isn't it better that I *want* you instead of *need* you?" I exclaimed. "I'm choosing to be with you. I'm not with you just because I need you to take care of me. If you want someone who's needy, well that's not me, and it never will be."

It logically made sense to me. I couldn't understand why he didn't get it.

Greg gave me a once-over, then said, "Well I think you might discover value from embracing your feminine energy." He left it at that.

I shrugged off Greg's suggestion. *I don't need to be more feminine*, I thought. *Other women just need to stop being such pussies.* A few weeks later, during a one-on-one with my manager, she shared feedback that contradicted my beliefs.

"You've been doing pretty stellar work, Amy," she shared. "You're leading the team in a profound way, you're driving impact, and you're innovating on so many dimensions."

"Thanks!" I beamed.

"I also have some feedback," she started.

My heart stopped. My mind started racing. What could her feedback be about?

"I've had a few of your colleagues tell me that it's difficult working with you," she explained.

*What? How am I difficult to work with?*

"In what way?" I asked cautiously.

"Well, you have a tendency to move fast. Not everyone moves at that pace. For example, in meetings where you're sharing your strategy, you've already moved on before everyone has had a chance to absorb it. Also, some people enjoy small talk, getting to know each other in meetings. You're not one of those. You go straight to business. So your coworkers feel like you're all business and they don't really know the human side of you."

"Okay," was all I could muster.

Through the grapevine, I found out these same colleagues said I was a bitch.

*Me? A bitch? How's that even possible? I bake goodies for everyone all the time! I'm like Betty Crocker. How could Betty Crocker be a bitch?* I vented to myself. *And it's not my fault they're slow and can't keep up. I don't have time to be chitchatting; I'm actually getting shit done!*

I blamed Greg for being too needy, for needing me to need him. I blamed these colleagues for being too catty, like the type of women I'd grown up learning to avoid. I can't help who I am. I'm not needy. I'm more of a dude than a girl. I get shit done. I'm independent. Why can't people just understand that's just how I am?

## Acknowledging the Truth: I Am More Than a Tough Cookie

The truth is, that's *not* "just how I am." My feminine energy was conditioned out of me. I was so conditioned into thinking, believing, and doing things a certain way that I truly thought that always being the logical, rigid, doer was my natural state of being.

In reality, it wasn't. I had just lost a sense of who I really was, and I didn't even realize it.

My first awakening to this possibility was at Burning Man, an annual week-long event that celebrates self-expression and community. Greg had insisted for some time that I explore more of my feminine energy. After receiving my manager's feedback, I was more open to exploring what this feminine energy was all about, though not without reservation. I was sure that being more "girly" wasn't for me. After all, the Chinese ribbon dance class was proof of it.

Dressed in tight silver shorts and a white crop top, I rode behind Greg on my retro blue bike. The lights I had decorated my bike with were flashing pink and blue as we biked across the playa after a dust storm cleared. The sun was setting on the horizon, the sky a clear, cloudless blue. Greg pulled over and pointed to a sign in front of a big, white, dome tent. I pulled over and leaned on my bike as I turned to see what he was pointing at.

"Tantra workshop for couples," he said. "We should try it."

"Tantra? Like sex?" I asked hesitantly. "I don't know."

"Tantra is a practice that allows life to live in you so you can fully connect with yourself," Greg said, gazing at me with a grin. "How about we check it out, and if you don't like it we can leave?"

I nodded, despite feeling resistant. *I can leave if it doesn't feel right*, I reminded myself.

We parked our bikes and locked them up, then walked towards the entrance of the tent.

The workshop leader welcomed us with a bow at the entrance as we walked in. She wore a long, shimmering-white satin dress with a hood and held a large white candle between her two hands. Her dark brown curls flowed down her back.

Greg and I grabbed seat cushions and sat as other couples streamed in.

"Welcome beautiful souls," the workshop leader sang warmly. "My name is Sonia. Tom here will be cofacilitating with me today. For the first part of our workshop, we'll be splitting the men and women. Women will stay here with me. Men will follow Tom to the tent next door. We'll come back together after."

My forehead creased as I raised an eyebrow towards Greg. He shrugged, then got up and followed the other men out.

After the last of the men disappeared and the tent flaps closed behind them, Sonia turned towards the women and said, "Tantra is often associated with sex, but that's an oversimplification and misconception. Tantra is the science and study of energy. It's about the liberation of energy and liberation of dormant potential energy. Today we're going to study and explore the feminine energy while the men will explore the masculine energy with Tom."

Sonia demonstrated feminine energy as she walked the room slowly. "Imagine your partner as a warrior. He's gone out to fight for his home, those he loves. What does he need when he returns home? To be nurtured and loved and held." She invited all in the room to follow her demonstration. "Walk around slowly, feel and embrace your feminine energy," she said. "Slow and smooth like the river waters. Welcome your warrior home with love and care."

I surveyed the other women as they flowed like the river, arms out, walking slowly and embracing their feminine energy. I felt like an oaf, awkward and out of place. *I don't belong here. I'm not even close to a flowing river; I'm more like a manic ocean.*

Sonia continued as she flowed among us. "It is common to judge the emotional experience as a weakness; to label certain emotions as good and others as bad. All emotions are merely expressions of energy. It is only when we give ourselves permission to explore an emotion, allow it to be expressed without identifying with it, that it is possible to release it."

"Feel emotion?" I muttered under my breath. I began eyeing the exit, contemplating how to make my escape, when Sonia flowed by me and whispered, "Just let yourself go. Find the courage to let go and feel yourself flow." And then she disappeared, flowing back into the river of other women.

"I don't need to find my courage. I *am* courageous," I growled, glaring after Sonia. "I'm not quitting."

I closed my eyes and took a deep breath, envisioning the flow of water in a slow-moving river. Sensing into the love my mother has always held for me, I reached into the depths of my soul for the nurturing love that has been and always will be a part of me. Images danced into my mind: my mom holding me when I was sick, my sister protecting me from bullies, me at two years old pulling a blanket off the bed to put over my dad who had been napping on the sofa. I let go. And I flowed.

The men returned. One by one they waited at the entrance as their partners guided them into the room. When I saw Greg, I took my place, candle in hand, and flowed to the entrance to lead him into the room with gentle, nurturing love. Each woman led her partner to his seat at the center of the tent. The men sat in a circle, facing out towards the tent walls. The women took their places, seated and facing towards their partners.

Over the next hour, the women rotated from man to man, practicing different modalities of nurturing, feminine energy. Without a word, we each gently held the hand of the man in front of us between our own hands and let our love hold him. Rotate. We gazed into the eyes of the man in front of us without losing eye contact. Rotate. We'd sit with the man, then whisper what arose in our hearts into his ear. Rotate.

We rotated and made our way around the circle. I vividly remember one complete stranger I sat across from. I gazed into his eyes and sensed strength and love within him, but fear was holding that strength and love back. I whispered to him, "You're stronger than you know, and you're full of love that the world needs from you."

Tears fell from his eyes. "Thank you. Thank you for seeing me," he breathed.

After we made our way around the circle once, I finally returned back to Greg. We sat in silence, staring into each other's eyes. He was fully present with me. My warrior. I was his nurturer, his tender partner, welcoming him home. Tears welled in my eyes. I didn't bite my tongue to stop them. I let them flow. Tears of joy. Tears of love.

Something magical happened at that moment: I learned that I *do* have feminine energy, and I discovered its strength. It was the beginning of my journey to continue exploring more about the balance of my feminine versus masculine energy.

## Out-of-Balance Energy

I've learned in my journey that, for most of us, our masculine and feminine energies are out of balance.

Let me clarify. This isn't about male versus female. It's not about sex or gender. It's about energies, like yin and yang or the two poles of a magnet. Whether you're a bodybuilder or a beauty queen, a lumberjack or a caregiver, we all have both types of energy regardless of sex or gender.

Unfortunately, we live in a world where masculine energy is over-valued and where progress, structure, and logic are more respected and admired than empathy, patience, and intuition. So we're constantly keeping our masculine energy on, but on the flip side, we're pushing away our feminine energy, even denying its existence. As a society, we've completely blocked and lost touch with our feminine energy. We are out of balance.

I certainly was. I was constantly draining my energy trying to keep up this facade of independence and strength for the sake of gaining acceptance. I was burned out and exhausted from being off-balance, and I was unhappy because I wasn't in a harmonious, natural state. I believed power to be a masculine energy. Words like "protecting," "controlling," "dominating," and "asserting" often came to mind. This is one form of power.

But then I learned that feminine energy possesses power too.

(Mic drop.)

Over the last few years, through coaching, therapy, ayahuasca, and becoming a mother, I've come to accept that true success and power comes from learning to use your feminine and masculine energies in harmony to balance the yin and the yang.

There's power in asserting and speaking, like voicing my request for my husband to watch our kiddo so I have time to write this book. There's also power in listening and connecting, like staying open to hearing my parents' stories and experiences.

Power comes with doing and taking action. But there's also power in just being and pausing. There are times for logical thinking and times for intuitive feeling and creativity. Being able to balance the dance, I've been able to reawaken my full potential.

Today, I am me. I can be *and* I can do. I can nurture *and* I can protect. I am intuitive *and* I am logical. I no longer carry the facade of a strong independent Asian woman who doesn't need others. I've learned to support others and lean on them. And it feels so much lighter and true to who I am.

Oh, and I've also returned home to my favorite color: pink.

# Mama & Papa Yip's Story

國無二君, 家無二主.

*guó wú' èr jūn, jiā wú èr zhǔ.*

A state cannot have two monarchs, or a family two heads.

## Setting The Scene

It's a Wednesday afternoon. My kiddo is napping. Ever since I let my parents know that Logan would be starting daycare soon, they've been stopping by with increased frequency "to drop off food." Though they don't outright say they're coming over to see their grandson, they've coincidentally timed their visits during his wake windows. Yesterday, my mom called to ask if I needed sweet and sour chicken or radishes, which happened to be on sale. I didn't need any of it, but I told her, "Sure, that sounds nice. Come by before Logan wakes up so we have time to chat."

So here they are in my apartment. My mom is pulling out the various plastic produce baggies and Chinese takeout containers, explaining to me what's in each and when they'll go bad as she places them onto the counter. My dad has gone out to the car to get more bags and boxes of things they've brought over. Greg eyes me quizzically. He loves my mom, but he's told me quite a few times that he's been eating too much of her food. I smile at him with a toothy grin and mouth "I love you." He shakes his head and leaves the scene. My dad returns with the last of the food and sets it down for my mom to unpack. After he hangs up his coat and washes his hands, he joins me at the kitchen table with a bottle of Deer Park water in hand.

# Traditional Beliefs about a Woman's Role

男主外, 女主内.

*nán zhǔ wài, nǚ zhǔ nèi.*

Men are responsible for external affairs, women are responsible
for internal affairs.

Holding up his forefinger as if about to lecture a university class, Papa Yip begins, "For thousands of years, dating back to Confucian times, Chinese have believed that a man's role is to focus on the outside and a woman's role is to focus on the inside. Men are the providers, the protectors. Women are focused on home life. Their primary purpose is to bear children, preferably boys to maintain the descent line."

I cringe and resist the urge to roll my eyes at this outdated philosophy. I want to stay open-minded to what Papa Yip has to say.

"It's like that Korean guy you dated," Papa Yip explains. "The one who wanted you to be a stay-at-home wife. He has the same traditional philosophy."

I shudder at the memory. Oh I remember him. We dated in business school. He was hoping to get into investment banking. I was studying brand management. We were both recruiting for internships when he said to me, "You don't have to work so hard. You're going to be staying at home anyway after we have kids."

"I'm going to be what?" I choked.

"Well, I want my kids to be cared for by one of their parents. I don't want them with a stranger. I'll clearly be making more money than you since I'm going into banking. So you'll have to be the one who stays at home."

"Why would I be getting my MBA if my long-term plan was to be a stay-at-home mom?" I demanded. Clearly, the relationship didn't last much longer after that conversation.

I study Papa Yip before asking him, "What did you think about him wanting me to quit my career? To stay at home?"

318

"Well," Papa Yip begins, "on the positive side, he seemed to have a sense of responsibility for his family's finances, taking care of his family as the head of the household. On the negative side, he didn't seem to respect women. If you married him, he probably wouldn't listen to you or your opinions. There would be no discussion, no negotiation. His way would be the only way."

I smirk. "So what you're saying is that he's old-fashioned."

"Well in today's world, things are different," Papa Yip explains. "A man should still be the primary breadwinner, be the protector of the house. But a woman can be the support. If the man doesn't make enough money, she can work to supplement his income. But her primary focus should be on teaching and disciplining the children, all things within the house."

My mind travels to the fall of 2021 when I was five months pregnant. Greg and I had just returned to the US after living abroad for over a year and a half. On top of preparing for our baby's arrival amidst the COVID-19 pandemic, we had to figure out where we were going to settle. Greg was still job hunting, while I was an entrepreneur without the benefits of paid maternity leave. I was stressed by our financial instability and even considered returning to a corporate job.

Papa Yip vocally shared his opinions at the time: "Greg needs to know his role as the man of the household and do whatever is necessary to financially support his family. Get a job at Starbucks. Go work for FedEx. All he's doing is job hunting. He should use some of that time to bring money into the family while he looks for a corporate position. What does he do with all his time anyway?"

A stressed, emotional ball of energy, I didn't respond very well to his criticisms. "Well what if he wants to be a stay-at-home dad?" I retorted.

"No," Papa Yip shook his head adamantly.

"Why not? I used to make more money at Google than most two-income households. I could easily find a job and support our family, and Greg could focus on taking care of the kids and the house."

"That's not a man's role," Papa Yip declared. "A man should be the head of the household. The provider."

I was so frustrated by Papa Yip's closed mindset that I refused to listen anymore. I clenched my jaw and stalked off without another word. Since that conversation, Papa Yip and I never delved deeper into his perspective on why he was against Greg being a stay-at-home dad. Until now.

Shaking myself from my memories, I study Papa Yip's timeworn face in front of me. Despite his old-fashioned beliefs that women should focus on the home and the children, I fondly remember him giving us baths every night and helping us with our homework. He later even started washing the dishes and doing laundry.

"Why were you opposed to Greg being a stay-at-home dad?" I ask pointedly.

Papa Yip sighs. "Amy, one day your kids will be at school. Other kids will ask 'What does your daddy do?' How embarrassing would it be for your child to say, 'Oh my daddy stays at home. He cooks and cleans.' What would other kids think?"

"They would probably be jealous and wish their dads were at home spending time with them," I retort. Growing up, I certainly would've enjoyed more time with Papa Yip.

"A man can have a respectable job *and* spend time with their children," Papa Yip states.

"So why did you push your daughters to get educated and work so hard?" I ask. "Why does it matter if, as a woman, my primary focus should be the household?"

"Education and work experience gives you knowledge and skills," Papa Yip explains, "something that nobody can ever take away from you. But just because you have knowledge and skills doesn't mean you have to work a job. If your husband is successful enough and you can financially afford to stay at home, then why not?"

"Because maybe I have dreams and goals that I don't want to give up!" I exclaim, thinking of all the women clients I've worked with who at one point in their lives had given up their dreams to let their husbands pursue theirs. They had put aside their goals to focus on the family because "it made sense to do so."

"Maybe there are things I want to do with my life," I add. "Your daughters are all brilliant and successful. Wouldn't it be a shame for them to give all that up?"

Papa Yip surveys me before sharing, "My father always said, 'Even if a woman can fly like a bird, she's still a woman.' In a lot of old Chinese movies, flying was the top skill anybody could have. But in your grandfather's mind, even if a woman had the top skill, she is still only a woman, not a man."

"And what do *you* believe?" I ask flatly.

"I am your grandfather's son. I'm influenced by his beliefs."

"Your daddy is basically saying he thinks the same way," Mama Yip snaps as she shuffles over to the kitchen table. Her nose crinkles and she shoots Papa Yip a dirty look.

"So that's why you thought I couldn't fix the door lock," I mutter.

"Lock?" he asks curiously. I remind Papa Yip of the lock I had fixed when I was twelve despite him saying that girls couldn't do such a thing.

"Even the doorknob we have right now, your daddy didn't change that," Mama Yip provokes. "Your sister changed it."

"Well look at the home-building industry," Papa Yip argues. "How many women do you see in home-building and construction?"

"You don't see women in that field because they're smarter, more educated than all the men who go into that field," Mama Yip retorts as she hovers over Papa Yip in his chair. "Women don't have to do that kind of hard labor work." Her forehead creases and her eyes fill with annoyance as she continues, "Your daddy always talks about all the things your grandfather would say. Well what about women who have ruled? Empress Wu who ruled during the Tang dynasty for forty years and turned China into one of the greatest powers in the world! Or all the other things women have done better than men? He has nothing to say about that!"

Papa Yip winks at me and says, "I think your mommy has some opinions she wants to share. I'm going to go take my vitamins." He gets up to let Mama Yip take a seat next to me, then walks over to the counter as Mama Yip settles into the chair.

# A Strong Chinese Woman's Perspective

婦女能頂半邊天.

*fù nǚ néng dǐng bàn biān tiān.*

Women hold half the sky.

"Your daddy is old-fashioned," Mama Yip thunders. "In today's world, how many households can thrive under a man's single income? Even if his income covers all the expenses, don't you have to save money for your future? If you earn then spend it all, earn then spend it all and you save nothing, then how will you ever retire? That's why most families are multi-income households now. You need that in order to retire."

Mama Yip sighs and gazes at me before continuing. "I've always wanted my daughters to be self-reliant. I know too many women who have cheating or abusive husbands. The women are scared to leave because they don't have an education or work experience. They don't know how they'll survive without their husbands. It's a horrible place to be in, to feel stuck like that!"

"I remember you always telling us how important it was to be independent and not financially rely on a man," I note. "What's your opinion about your daughters becoming stay-at-home moms?"

"It would be a shame!" Mama Yip exclaims. "Each of you worked so hard to be where you are today. I'd rather you hire help than leave your career. Get a nanny. Get a housecleaner. I think you lose your freedom relying on a husband financially. And being stuck at home all day long is too restrictive in my opinion. But at the end of the day, it's your choice. If you want to leave the workforce, that's fine. If your husband forces you to do so, then I don't approve." Mama Yip wags her finger to emphasize her disapproval.

I smile. Well I sure know where I got my "girl power" attitude from.

Mama Yip waves her hand around as she continues, "And women need to speak up more. This isn't the ancient Chinese dynasty period from thousands of years ago where women had to stay quiet. You have to speak up and stand up for yourself. Even if it's your boss. So what if they fire you? You can always get another job. Don't ever let people treat you wrong because you're a woman."

"Wait a second," I begin. "What about in sixth grade when you and Daddy told me not to talk back to my teacher? You told me I had to listen to her."

Mama Yip looks confused. I jog her memory.

"Oh! That time," she laughs. "Well you can't really quit school. You know we intentionally chose to live in a district with a top-ranked public school system. Our top priority was that you girls receive a good education. We wanted you to do well in school. That's why we said to listen to your teacher. Jobs are different. You can quit a job. You can find a new boss."

Mama Yip studies me fondly, then adds, "That was pretty audacious of you to talk back to your teacher. You're kind of like me."

"How so?"

"I talk back all the time," Mama Yip beams. "I was working in the deli of a supermarket chain. My boss kept trying to assign me more work, things that weren't part of my job. One time I said to him, 'I'm not making that food.' He asked why not, and I said, 'It's not my job, and I don't have time.' My colleagues were all shocked that I would talk to the general manager like that. I just said to them, 'Why can't I? It isn't my job to make that dish.' I stood up for myself. In the end, the general manager still liked me because I did my job well and fast."

I know how hard Mama Yip worked. She was always a fast learner and efficient. She had to be. She worked two jobs while managing our entire household, including doing the laundry, chauffeuring, cooking, buying the groceries, and more. We also depended on her for our family insurance. At times she even brought in more income than Papa Yip. He wasn't always pleased that his role of primary breadwinner shifted to a "supporting role" as he calls it.

"So what do you think about a woman who brings in more financially than her husband?" I wonder curiously.

"If the woman is earning more, the husband needs to use it as motivation to do better himself," Papa Yip chimes in as he totters back to the kitchen table. I can tell his knee is bothering him again. He takes a seat next to Mama Yip. "He needs to work harder and chase up to her salary."

I roll my eyes. Oh, the male ego.

Mama Yip frowns at Papa Yip. "I think it's bad to compare and compete with your spouse. You shouldn't get upset and jealous of each other's successes. You should be happy for each other," she states.

I nod in agreement. In my late twenties I dated a guy who was always comparing and competing with me. When we first started dating, he told me how much he abhorred running. He had participated in a 10K race and never wanted to run another one ever again. That is, until I ran my marathon, after which he immediately signed up for a marathon himself and started training. In his words, "I can't let you outdo me."

On top of that, I later discovered that he had signed up for a cybersecurity professional learning program, despite his earlier comments on hating school. At the time, I was a cybersecurity professional and had just received my Certified Information Systems Security Professional certification. It was one of the hardest and longest certification exams in the cybersecurity field. I had also just been admitted to UCLA Anderson for business school. "I feel like I need to do something or I'll fall behind you," he had commented. I didn't want to be in a relationship that involved just competing with each other.

"That's why I love Greg," I proclaim. "He's always supportive and proud of my achievements. I just got notified that I'm one of three finalists to keynote at this large conference. He's excited for me and celebrated with me even though I haven't even been selected yet."

"That's what a marriage should be like!" Mama Yip exclaims. "Men who compete with their spouse just lack confidence. When will you find out if you got selected?"

"Early next week."

"They'll pick my daughter," Mama Yip reassures. "No doubt about it."

"I appreciate that, Mommy," I gush. "Even with me writing this book, Greg is supportive. He watches Logan so that I can have time to write." I wink at Papa Yip and add, "But don't worry. He's not becoming a stay-at-home dad. Just on weekends."

Mama Yip leans towards me and says, "A lot of men stay at home to watch kids now. If a man doesn't have a job, or even if he just enjoys the stay-at-home role and it makes financial sense, then who cares? It's better to have a parent watch the child than a stranger. I had a friend whose son-in-law did that. He watched the kids, grocery shopped, cooked, and cleaned the house. This was thirty years ago too! Who cares what people say? If you think it's good and you're happy with the choice, that's all that matters."

Boom. Mic drop. I love my mama. Clearly, my parents have very different perspectives.

Mama Yip peers at Papa Yip and softens. "Your daddy loves you girls, Amy," she says. "He might not tell you how he really feels, but he's proud of your successes. I know he'd be upset to see you give it all up too. He says stupid things because he's a man. My father was the same way. He kept things inside and never showed his true emotions."

I raise my eyebrow at Papa Yip. He raises his eyebrow back and grins.

## Expectations of What It Means to Be a Man

男人漏血, 不漏眼淚.

*nán rén lòu xuè, bù lòu yǎn lèi.*

A man sheds blood, not tears.

Papa Yip takes a sip of his water. "There's always a public version and a private version of people," he starts. "When I was a child, a lot of men were very different outside the home versus inside the home. Take your grandfather. He was a businessman. That meant a lot of negotiations. If the negotiations went sour, there was a lot of fighting and killing. But at home, he was different."

Papa Yip pauses as he gazes out the window. "One time we were walking and I got tired. I shouted to your grandfather, 'DiDi! I'm tired. I don't want to walk anymore.' Without a word, he picked me up and carried me on his back, despite his own failing health. He would do anything for me."

Papa Yip's eyes glisten, but he doesn't cry.

Growing up, Papa Yip always taught us that crying was bad luck. I never saw him shed a tear nor express sadness or grief. The only emotion he ever showed was anger.

"Did you ever see Grandfather shed a tear?" I ask curiously.

"Of course," Papa Yip replies.

I lean in to indicate that I want to hear more.

"It was late 1950s," Papa Yip starts. "I was about eleven. Your grandfather was living in Hong Kong, trying to establish his business. Your grandmother was working odd jobs in Shanghai. So they had me stay with my maternal grandmother. This particular day, my father had just returned to Shanghai to visit us. On the rickshaw ride home from the train station, my father asked me, 'Do you like staying with your grandmother?' I indignantly said, 'No! She doesn't treat me well!' He wanted to know why, so I told him.

"You see, every week my mother paid my grandmother for me to live with them. The payment covered my lunches and dinners, but not breakfast."

I grimace. *Additional fee for breakfast? What is this, boarding school? Aren't Chinese all about family first? Community support? How could you charge your grandchild for breakfast?*

Before I can ask, Papa Yip goes on. "Every weekend, my mother visited me and gave me a weekly breakfast allowance. One weekend, she couldn't make it. So I had no money left for breakfast. On Monday morning, I scooped myself a bowl of the pao fan, this porridge of leftover rice that my grandmother had made. Before I even finished it, my grandmother started scolding me. She accused me of eating their food and called me selfish and disrespectful. It was difficult to swallow those nasty words."

Papa Yip's eyes narrow and his nose crinkles. "After what she said to me, I refused to ever eat her breakfast again. The problem is, I had no money for food that week."

I peer at Mama Yip. She's leaning in, just as interested in this story as I am.

"The next morning, I arrived at school and my belly was rumbling," Papa Yip continues. "I thought, 'What should I do?' Then I had an idea! I ran over to the waterspout and drank water until I no longer felt hungry." Papa Yip pauses for dramatic effect. "But as soon as I peed, I was hungry again! So back to the spout I went for more water!" Papa Yip roars with laughter. "After a few days, I got accustomed to no breakfast and didn't feel hunger anymore." He pats his belly.

"You were a stubborn one!" I laugh.

"He hasn't changed one bit," Mama Yip teases.

Papa Yip smiles in acknowledgment. "So when my father and I were sitting in the rickshaw together, I explained what happened. I told him my grandmother was unkind and yelled at me." Papa Yip's voice quavers as he finishes. "That's when I saw my father pull out his handkerchief. He turned his head to look away, but I saw him wipe a tear from his eye."

Papa Yip turns his own head to look away. As he does, I see a glimmer in his eye. I can sense both his fondness and sorrow.

"Are you tearing up, old man?" Mama Yip rubs his head playfully.

"No!" he exclaims.

I instinctively get up and give Papa Yip a hug and kiss his cheek. "I love you, Daddy."

Tears start streaming down his face. Mama Yip hands him a tissue and touches his shoulder. It's the first time I've ever witnessed Papa Yip crying. And one of few times I've seen Mama Yip outwardly show Papa Yip affection.

My heart softens.

At some point Papa Yip learned that, as a man, he had to hide his internal state from the outer world; that he couldn't express his emotions, a feminine energy quality. Perhaps, he's finally unlearning his old beliefs and discovering that it's okay to feel emotions, to cry, just like I did.

# Decent Lines

有其父, 必有其子.

*yǒu qí fù, bì yǒu qí zǐ.*

Where there is a father, there is a son.

Papa Yip wipes his eyes and glances at Mama Yip's hand on his shoulder. "You know your mommy always acts hard, but she's a softy," he says. "When people aren't looking, she's very affectionate."

"Yeah, yeah," Mama Yip snorts, removing her hand and smacking his arm.

"She is!" Papa Yip exclaims. "Why do you think I married her? All men want their wives to be warm and loving."

I think of all the years I wore my tough armor, refusing to soften because I thought being a boy was better, that masculine energy was better.

"If men want women to be affectionate, if men want warmth and love from women, then why are Chinese so obsessed with having a son?" I ask. "A son wouldn't be loving and affectionate like your daughters, you know."

"It's a traditional belief from thousands of years ago," Papa Yip explains. "Chinese have always considered not bearing a son, a male heir, to be one of the worst things imaginable. Family descent lines get passed from father to son. Without a son, the line ends. My elder brother has three daughters. I have three daughters. My younger brother has no children. No sons to carry the Yip family name. So this is where our Yip family line ends."

I nod and say, "That's why you wanted me to be a son."

"I took a gamble!" Papa Yip laughs. "I thought surely after two daughters, number three would be a son. Our doctor told us there was a 70 percent chance you were a girl. But in the early '80s, technology wasn't accurate at predicting a baby's sex. A doctor told my friend and his pregnant wife that they were having a girl. Ended up being a boy. So I was hoping our doctor was wrong too."

Mama Yip smirks, "But the doctor was right. So your daddy has three daughters."

"Is that why you always gave me a boy haircut?" I inquire. "Because you wished I was a boy?"

"It wasn't a boy haircut!" Papa Yip defends. "It was a mushroom cut. A lot of little girls had a mushroom cut."

"I always got made fun of."

Papa Yip smiles and says, "I thought you looked cute."

Mama Yip cuts in, "Your daddy might always talk about wanting a son, but he always brags about his daughters."

I raise an eyebrow. "Oh?"

"I don't ever brag about my daughters!" Papa Yip tries to keep a serious face but ends up breaking into laughter. He studies me before saying, "Your mommy is right. All of my daughters are extremely successful. You all have your own children. You're healthy, financially stable, and happy. That makes me content and happy."

I grin and walk over to Mama and Papa Yip. "And if you had a son, he wouldn't be doing this," I say, kissing their cheeks and giving them big fat hugs. They both laugh and openly receive my affection, a big shift compared to where we started before all these conversations.

"True," Papa Yip beams. "That's why you need to give me a granddaughter. All I have are grandsons."

I roll my eyes at the irony; he wanted a son and had three daughters, now he has five grandsons and wants a granddaughter.

# My Reflections Post-Conversation

Old beliefs and habits die hard. Generation after generation, gender expectations have been passed down, including the notions that a son is better than a daughter and that women should not be educated nor work.

But just because old beliefs and habits die hard doesn't mean they can't and won't ever change. It's like trying to redirect a large ship. It'll happen in due time with persistence and patience. And we can all play a role in helping redirect the ship.

What comes to mind for me after this conversation with my parents?

1. **Everyone has different belief systems and worldviews.**
   This is true even of our parents. But that's not necessarily a bad thing. Diversity of thought can be a strength. Take my parents, for example. My mom is much more open-minded when it comes to gender equity, which makes sense being that she's a woman, and a very strong-minded woman at that. My dad, on the other hand, still holds many of the beliefs that were passed down from Confucian days. They challenge each other, and their different perspectives are what came together to influence how my sisters and I were brought up. Each of us was exposed to our parents' differing opinions, and each of us was able to decide which of those perspectives we wanted to take into our own lives and which we wanted to leave behind. And though I don't agree with my dad's beliefs, I do respect and appreciate his desire to take care of his family.

2. **Show. Don't tell.**
   As a new mom, I've been reading a lot about how to teach children. A common theme is to have parents model the behavior they want to see

330

in their children. I believe this also works for children who want to influence their parents. Pushing our beliefs onto our parents won't change the way they think. I've had many arguments with my dad in the past about gender roles and even called him sexist during those exchanges. Clearly, it didn't work to change his way of thinking.

What we *can* do is model openness and understanding by showing curiosity as to why they think the way they do. Modeling openness over time, perhaps a long time, will lead to their becoming more open-minded. In truth, it's only with understanding that we can influence others.

My dad has actually come a long way since I was child, when he was much more headstrong in his beliefs about gender roles. Today, he's open to my mom's opinions. He respects his daughter's achievements. And on occasion, he even mentions how impressive his wife and daughters are. Perhaps it's the fact that his wife and daughters have shown him what women are capable of through their own successes and feats. From raising a family while working full time to playing sports and trekking mountains, and from building their own thriving businesses to becoming sought-after speakers, he sees, with his own eyes, the strength of women. We've shown instead of told. And as I smother him with hugs and kisses, I always point out that with a son he likely wouldn't have all the love and affection he gets from us. He agrees with that.

Show. Don't tell. Open their eyes by letting them experience it.

3. **I can do my part in helping redirect the ship.**
   While I can't control the whole gender equity ship, there are things that are within my control. I can continue to have these conversations with my parents with an open heart and open ear. I can share things I learn about gender equity to give them a different perspective. And most importantly, I have an opportunity to raise my son differently. I will teach Logan that he can play with whatever toys he wants (and so can girls); dolls are not just for girls, and cars are not just for boys. I will teach Logan to process and express his emotions. I will teach Logan to respect

women. I will expose him to women's sports. And most importantly, I will model what it means to be kind, respectful, and accepting of others. Perhaps by the time Logan is a father, things will be completely different in how the world views gender roles.

# A Date with Your Parents

## PRE-CONVERSATION PERSONAL REFLECTION

### Overview

We all have both feminine and masculine energy. It isn't based on sex or gender identity. Feminine and masculine energy can be thought of as a yin and yang or the two poles of a magnet. Together they create balance and wholeness, and they complete each other. Both qualities are necessary. Neither is better than the other. To be whole, balanced, and truly powerful, we need to be able to tap into both of these energies. But for most of us, our energies are out of balance. From a young age, we absorbed information about gender roles from our environment. We learn from our parents, our teachers, our institutions, our communities, and society at large what it means to be a girl and what it means to be a boy. In turn, many of us developed our ways of being in the world to conform to these expectations. Whether you're cisgender, gender non-conforming, or something else, understanding how your beliefs have been shaped, how your energies are being expressed, and whether you're staying true to yourself or masking certain energies to conform will help you decide what you want to carry forward and what you want to retire.

### Instructions

1. Read the following statements. Take notice of the automatic thoughts and beliefs that surface. Reflect and journal on what you make of this.

◈ Women should do the cooking in the house.

◈ Men should do the fixing in the house.

◈ Men are better at math and science.

◈ Women are better at communication.

◈ Men should hold the door open for women.

◈ Women are more emotional than men.

◈ It's okay for men to cry.

◈ Women face more barriers to succeeding in business than men.

◈ Women should be able to serve in combat roles in the military.

◈ Children should be able to turn to their fathers for emotional support.

◈ Raising a child should be primarily a woman's job.

◈ Feminine energy is powerful.

◈ Masculinity means you cannot show any emotions.

**BONUS**: Watch Justin Baldoni's 2017 TEDWomen talk called "Why I'm Done Trying to Be 'Man Enough'."

2. Oftentimes, scripts are passed down from generation to generation about masculinity versus femininity; men versus women. Based on what showed up for you with the prompts from Step 1, reflect and journal on the following:

◈ Where do your gender scripts come from?

◈ What do your gender scripts say about masculinity versus femininity; men versus women?

3. Reflect and journal on the following:

   ❖ How does your script serve you?

   ❖ What does your script cost you?

   ❖ Which parts of your script do you want to keep?

   ❖ What parts of your script do you want to change?

   ❖ What's the first small step you can take towards making this change?

## THE CONVERSATION

### Conversation Topic

What your parents believe about a woman's role versus a man's role, where their beliefs come from, and how these beliefs have shifted (or not).

### Tips

These conversations can be hard, and potentially triggering. Priority number one is to take care of yourself. Remember to review the Conversation Tip Sheet on page 23 before your conversation.

### Conversation-Specific Suggestions

Bring photographs or articles that depict or challenge stereotypical gender roles, expectations and inequities. For example, photographs of famous women leaders, inventors, scientists, or athletes throughout history. Bonus if it's a woman from your parents' home country, someone they may recognize. Or bring images of men serving in caretaker roles or exhibiting strong emotions other than anger.

You can also bring articles about the atrocities in countries such as Iran and Syria where there is tremendous gender inequality. You may want to send these days or weeks before the conversation so that your parents have time to read and absorb before you chat. Kickstart the conversation by showing these artifacts and posing the question, "What do you think about that?"

You can also show your parents the "Why I'm Done Trying to Be 'Man Enough'" video. If they don't speak English, turn on subtitles in their native language.

Bring your feminine energy (we all have it) to move with the flow of the conversation, focusing on inclusion, connection, listening, and having an open mind as you listen to your parents' experiences and perspectives.

## Questions For Your Parents

### *Lighter Questions*

◆ What were your first memories of learning about gender and gender roles? Tell me more about that.

◆ What did you learn about gender roles in school? At home? From movies, books, and/or TV shows?

◆ Do you prefer working with men or women? Do you prefer to have a female or a male boss? Why?

◆ How do you feel about women going to college?

◆ How do you feel about women prioritizing career achievements over family?

◆ Has your country ever had a woman leader? Does the gender of a leader make a difference?

❖ What role should a mother play in parenting and raising children? What role should a father play? What role did you take? Are there ways in which you wish your role could have been different?

❖ Are men better at some things than women? Are women better at some things than men? Why do you believe this?

❖ What emotions are okay for women to express? For men to express? When is it okay for men to cry? Why?

## Deeper Questions

❖ How do you define gender? What does gender mean to you?

❖ What are the differences between men and women? What does it mean to be a man? To be a woman?

❖ Growing up, how were you expected to behave because of your gender? How did you feel about these expectations? Did you ever challenge them?

❖ Did you ever do anything that went against gender role expectations of people in authority (such as teachers or your parents)? Tell me about it.

❖ Have you ever questioned your beliefs about gender and gender roles? What would it look like if you did?

❖ Considering your beliefs about gender roles, what do you think about me as a [gender] and how I live my life?

❖ What things should I stand up for and when should I stay quiet?

❖ Which emotion(s) do you try to avoid? Why do you try to hide from this emotion?

❖ Have you ever cried? Tell me about it.

## POST-CONVERSATION CONTEMPLATION

After the conversation with your parents, contemplate and journal on the following:

- ◈ What new insights have you gained about
  - ✦ who your parents are,
  - ✦ what their scripts say about gender and gender roles, and
  - ✦ how their upbringing and environment shaped their scripts about women versus men, femininity versus masculinity, and gender roles in the world, at home, and in the workforce?
  - ✦ Based on what you've uncovered, do you believe your parents might lean more towards masculine energy or feminine energy? What makes you believe that? How might you help your parents live more in balance between their masculine and feminine energies?
  - ✦ How might you live in greater balance between your masculine and feminine energies?[17]

*Know the masculine, but keep to the feminine.*
~ Lao Tzu ~

---

[17]  Visit https://amyyipcoaching.com/UnfinishedBusiness-Resources for a feminine–masculine energy resource along with other book resources.

# DATES WITH MY PARENTS: HOW IT'S GOING

When I reflect on my days as a toddler and a preschooler, I fondly remember the warmth of my mom's snuggles and kisses when I awoke. Having her nearby made my day start out just right. I remember the joy when my dad came home after what felt like an eternity at work. When I heard his keys jingling in the lock, I'd run to the door, excited to jump into his arms of safety. I never wanted to leave my parents' side.

At some point, as if I had amnesia, I forgot their love for me. I forgot my love for them. I lost my way. I don't even remember how or when the ground beneath our relationship collapsed. But it did.

It happens to most of us.

Since we were in our mother's womb, we've had an unwavering bond with our parents. A connection that ran as deep as the ocean. When we entered the world, we felt safe snuggling in their arms. Their presence brought us giggles and squeals of joy. A kiss from them made a tingling warmth arise in us. We were attached and in love with our parents. We looked up to them, literally and figuratively.

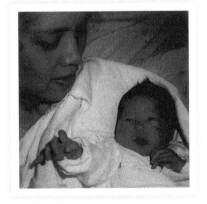

Then what happened?

We grew up. And through that growing up, it's as if we lost consciousness of the sacred love and bond between parent and child. But things don't have to be that way.

My conversations with my parents have taught me that I always have a choice.

I can choose to try, or I can choose to give up.

I can choose to belong, or I can choose to leave.

I can choose to love myself, my parents, my children, my partner, and the lady that yelled at me to go back to my own country when I was just three, or I can choose to hold grudges and be angry.

I choose to try. I choose to love. I am not at the mercy of my circumstances. I am at choice.

As my dad said, we all need to come together. Humanity needs to come together. It's not just about being Asian or White or Black. If we really want to do something different, we have to see ourselves as a larger community and come together versus separating. We need to love more. We even need to love the people who hate us and treat us badly. That's how we're going to change the world.

I choose to love more. Especially my parents, the two people who gave me this life.

Just before I started writing this book and was living overseas, I came across an app called "See Your Folks."[18] The tool calculates how many times you'll see your parents before they're expected to die.

When I filled in the form and hit "Show My Results," this is what it calculated:

---

[18]    http://seeyourfolks.com/.

Fourteen. Based on my parents' ages and the number of times I saw them every year, fourteen is what this tool calculated.

Though the number felt scary low, I couldn't bring myself to want to see them more. I resisted seeing them. I resisted calling them. I felt like any interaction with them involved lectures, criticisms, and judgments. So I resisted our relationship.

Then, I mustered the courage to have my first deep conversation with my parents. We continued these conversations over the last few years, and that has triggered a tremendous shift in my perspective about what it means to spend time with them, to see them. No longer do I feel the familial pressure to see them. No longer do I sense the resistance to see them; the nagging feeling that I'll just come out the other side feeling worse off after lectures, criticisms, and judgments from them.

Now I see this fourteen and rejoice at the number of times I have left, the number of opportunities I'm blessed with to be with the two people who gave me life, the two people who brought me into the world, the two people who gave up their dreams and made sacrifices so that I could live the life I have now.

I am returning home to the sacred place I was in once before, the place where there's a deep bond between parent and child. I never fully understood this bond until I had my own little one. The irony of having him in the midst of these conversations is that it brought me greater awareness of what it's like to be the parent in this relationship versus the child. I can see what my dad meant now when he explained that a child will never understand what it's like to be a parent, nor the love a parent has for their child, until they become a parent themselves.

I look at Logan each and every day as he grows up. I know he'll likely meander off the road and forget our bond, forget this love we share right now while he's just a toddler. But I also look at him and know that I will do my best to protect this bond for as long as I can and hope that he returns home like I have.

I lost my way. I forgot the love that my parents and I shared. Now, after years of conversations, I've returned home. I feel as if I've awakened from a dream and I'm home again. I'm not that young girl running to the door as my dad's keys jingle in the lock, but I am that girl who runs to my dad to give him a hug and ask how I can help with his latest technology questions. I'm not that young girl wondering whether my mom loves me because she doesn't vocalize it, but I am that girl who *knows* my mom loves me because she's always making sure I have a full belly. And I am the daughter who showers them both with reminders that I love and appreciate them.

I know now what I didn't know before, or perhaps what I just never thought about: My parents are human beings too. They have dreams. They have fears. They love me unconditionally. I want to make the best of the few moments I have left with them.

It was never easy to have conversations with them. It still isn't. I still get triggered. But it is and will continue to get easier.

This is not the end. It's just the beginning. These conversations I've had with my parents over the years are just the beginning of a new way of being, a new way of relating to a deeper, more loving relationship with my parents, with your parents, with all of our parents.

If you remember Ida, my client who in her mid-50s began asking questions about her father's history and life experiences, she sent me this message today:

That first conversation with my dad was a turning point for me. I have been visiting my folks just about every week for the last couple of months. Sometimes I imagine a bunch of possible arguments or conflicts that might arise, but I tell myself that there's always some kind of gift, most notably my amazing relationship with my kids, and walk through the door with a smile. The last three visits have been stress-free and very pleasant! I wouldn't be here without you! Thank you!

This is not and was never going to be easy. But it can be better. Let's all finish our business.

# AFTERWORD
# BY GREG MUELLER

When my wife first asked me to write the afterword for her book, I was flattered but surprised. "I'm honored, and of course I'm happy to do it if that's what you want. But wouldn't you rather find someone whose parents were immigrants? Why would your readers want to hear from me? I'm the Whitest guy ever, remember?" I asked skeptically.

Amy explained that I had a more objective perspective on the changes that occurred as a result of her work, which made it potentially interesting and useful for others to hear. I realized that although at times I participated in the process, I also stood outside of it. I reflected on her decision to write this book and how it impacted her, her relationship with her parents, and ultimately, our marriage.

I admire many things about my beautiful wife, and not the least of which is her courage to embark on this journey. Writing any book must be a harrowing, vulnerable experience. Writing one in which you expose the intimate details of your relationship with your parents for all to see takes big (figurative) balls. And of course, there's the conversations themselves. Perhaps I'm projecting a little, but I know I'm not the only one for whom interactions with parents can be frustrating, even in the strongest relationships. We just know them too well . . . or at least we know a certain version of them that we've determined to be the "real" one. And we have a list of things about this person that we judge to be faults or character flaws, or things they do or say that we judge to be wrong, unjustified, or unfair. Amy decided to practice suspending these judgments and open to the possibility of greater understanding and compassion towards her parents. She decided to be curious again.

As Amy observed her parents' past and present behavior without seeking to judge, but rather to understand, she saw the ways that it was often rooted in love and that it was always the best they could do with the resources they had. Her curiosity allowed her to empathize with them, and this empathy led to healing and a stronger connection.

And as she stated in her story, it took time and effort. Curiosity and empathy aren't personality traits, nor are they innate talents. We all have the capacity for them, but they're like muscles in that they grow stronger when we use them and weaker when we don't. It was so important for Amy that people realize it's okay if this seems like an impossible task. Our curiosity and empathy muscles might be a bit weak, and our relationships with our parents might be a massive weight. But wherever our starting point, if we exercise them, they can and will get stronger. Amy's have become quite jacked in this process, and all of her relationships have reaped the benefits.

Her interactions with her parents have transformed. Before this project, she often called them out of guilt or a sense of obligation. Now she looks forward to calling them and does so almost daily, allowing them to check in on their grandson. Beyond quantity, the quality of the conversations has changed. I can hear more laughter, more playfulness, and more respect in her tone of voice when she talks with them on the phone and in person. Of course, arguments and frustrations still occur. But they're less intense, less frequent, and shorter-lived.

Our own relationship has benefited from this work in several ways as well. As she practiced showing love to her parents in the ways that they most readily received it, she also built habits around providing me with the verbal and physical touch that pushes my buttons the right way. I used to feel silly and desperate asking for her to be more affectionate with me, so I rarely did. Now I get random hugs and back scratches during the day, which is super awesome. I don't know whether she'll admit it, but it seems to be quite natural for her. She may not be as fluent as a native speaker in all five love languages, but she's at least conversant.

She also recognizes her own needs more clearly and is much, much more prone to ask for my help and straight-up tell me what she needs. This is good, because I am a dim-witted male and sometimes I need that. It's astounding how many conflicts have been avoided because of this. On top of it all, I get to serve my wife and feel needed. Win–win.

I've also sensed a shift in how Amy sees herself as a Chinese American woman and the role those descriptions play in her identity. Due to Amy's work in the DEI space and our common interest in societal issues, race-based topics came up often in our conversations. More often than not, they would lead to arguments and usually ended with both of us feeling invalidated, mis-understood, and upset. I can honestly say that the tone and result of these conversations has taken a complete 180-degree turn for us. It helps that I've done a lot of work on my own ability to listen and empathize in this area, but I have a much greater sense that Amy also wants to listen to what I have to say, even though I'm an attractive White man. She used to tell me she wished I could understand, and then tell me I never could. Now we have a true dialogue and end our conversations feeling heard and with new perspectives to consider. Amy loves all of who she is, but she's lost the need to constantly defend it or define herself in any particular way. In my opinion, this makes her more powerful and effective in the work she does.

In short, my wife is amazing. But she didn't have to be in order to grow in the ways that she did. She just needed to make a few decisions. First, she had to decide that her parents were worth it and that she was worth it. Then she had to decide that no matter what ignorant or hurtful things her parents had done in the past, they were always doing the best they could with what they had and that she'd also done ignorant and hurtful things in her life as well. Once she made these decisions, she was free to drop the burdens of keeping score, feeling defensive, and harboring resentment and replace them with curiosity, empathy, and compassion. It took time, and naturally she'd revert back to judgment from time to time, but she kept moving forward, step by step, and still does to this day.

Amy has picked up many tools and resources along her personal development work and coaching journey. She has just shared many of them with you. If you make the same decisions Amy made, you can make use of these tools and transform your relationship with your parents. It's not easy, but you don't need certain innate talents or special circumstances. And you can do this even if, for whatever reason, you can't have a relationship with them. Even if you're unable to get them to share, even if they're no longer here, you can still look at them through a new lens, forgive, and heal. Changing even one side of the relationship—your side—changes the relationship. You have that power.

So if after reading Amy's story you have new insights or a sense of excitement or hope, don't let days, weeks, and months go by and allow those feelings to fade and the insights to dim. Take the first step and give them a call, or schedule one. If you're an adult, the vast majority of the time you will ever spend with them is likely over. The remaining time will go by in the blink of an eye.

One last thing: My parents aren't immigrants and are different in many ways from Amy's, but they still did and do things that frustrate me. Amy has inspired me to stop trying to change them and start trying to really understand and accept them. If you have a partner, family member, or friend who struggles in any way in their relationship with their parents—immigrants or not—share this book with them.

# WORKS CITED

Brown, Brené. *Rising Strong*. London: Vermilion, 2015.

Ganguly, Kunal K. "Life of M.K. Gandhi: A Message to Youth of Modern India." *Indian Journal of Medical Research* 149, supplement (January 2019): 145–151. https://doi.org/10.4103/0971-5916.251672.

Gottman, John. "The Art and Science of Love." Presentation, the Gottman Institute, Seattle, WA, October 20–21, 2018. https://www.gottman.com/couples/workshops/art-science-of-love/.

Greicius, Julie. "The Benefits of Touch for Babies, Parents." Stanford Medicine News Center. September 23, 2013. https://med.stanford.edu/news/all-news/2013/09/the-benefits-of-touch-for-babies-parents.html.

Hamill, Jonathan, Jaime Hallak, Serdar M. Dursun, and Glen Bakera. "Ayahuasca: Psychological and Physiologic Effects, Pharmacology and Potential Uses in Addiction and Mental Illness." *Current Neuropharmacology* 17, no. 2 (February 2019): 108–128. https://www.ncbi.nlm.nih.gov/pmc/articles/PMC6343205/.

Jolij, Jacob, and Maaike Meurs. "Music Alters Visual Perception." PLoS ONE 6, no. 4 (April 2011): e18861. https://doi.org/10.1371/journal.pone.0018861.

Jung, Carl Gustav. *Modern Man in Search of a Soul*. Translated by William Stanley Dell and Cary F. Baynes. London: Psychology Press, 2001.

McNichols, Nicole K. "The Vital Importance of Human Touch." Psychology Today. August 3, 2021. https://www.psychologytoday.com/us/blog/everyone-top/202108/the-vital-importance-human-touch.

Newman, Benjamin, Jennifer L. Merolla, Sono Shah, Danielle Casarez Lemi, Loren Collingwood, and S. Karthick Ramakrishnan. "The Trump Effect: An Experimental Investigation of the Emboldening Effect of Racially Inflammatory Elite Communication." *British Journal of Political Science* 51, no. 3 (February 17, 2021): 1138–1159. https://doi.org/10.1017/S0007123419000590.

Pierce, Shanley. "Touch Starvation Is a Consequence of COVID-19's Physical Distancing." Texas Medical Center. May 15, 2020. https://www.tmc.edu/news/2020/05/touch-starvation/.

The Gottman Institute. "About John & Julie Gottman." Accessed April 13, 2023. https://www.gottman.com/about/john-julie-gottman/.

U. S. Census Bureau. "Arizona - Race and Hispanic Origin: 1860 to 1990." Internet release date September 13, 2002. Accessed March 1, 2023. https://www2.census.gov/library/working-papers/2002/demo/pop-twps0056/table17.pdf.

# ABOUT THE AUTHOR

Amy Yip is a Somatic Life Transformation and Mental Fitness coach, keynote speaker, author, and self-confidence trainer.

She works with women of color to strengthen their mental fitness, heal their intergenerational wounds, and have agency to let go of all the 'shoulds' so that they can be the authors of their own life stories. Her mission is to empower AAPI women to be seen, to be heard, and to f-ing rock the boat.

In January 2020, after 16+ years of building and leading global teams in organizations including Google, Clorox, and Booz Allen, Amy left the corporate world, sold everything, and took a one-way flight to Ghana with her husband to volunteer at a breast cancer nonprofit and travel the world. COVID-19 shifted their plans; they got stuck in Ghana for seven months.

One of Amy's greatest learnings is this:

**Your mindset, *not* your circumstances, makes all the difference in your happiness and success.**

Through this lens, she works with leaders, including corporate executives, nonprofits, and social entrepreneurs, to find their voice and the courage to speak up, build self-confidence, navigate change, and discover what they *really* want next in their lives and careers.

Amy is an International Coach Federation Professional Certified Coach, a Certified Hudson Institute Coach, a Certified Strozzi Institute Somatic Coach, and a pioneer Mental Fitness Coach certified through Positive Intelligence.

Amy received her MBA from the UCLA Anderson School of Management, and her BS in computer science and BA in communications from the University of Maryland.

Amy resides in Maryland (ten minutes from her parents!) with Greg, her best friend and husband, and her son Logan, the cutest kid ever.

To learn more visit: **amyyipcoaching.com**
Connect with Amy on LinkedIn: **@amycyip**

# B CORP CONTENT FOR BACK MATTER OF PUBLISHED BOOKS

Publish Your Purpose is a hybrid publisher of non-fiction books. Our mission is to elevate the voices often excluded from traditional publishing. We intentionally seek out authors and storytellers with diverse backgrounds, life experiences, and unique perspectives to publish books that will make an impact in the world.

## The B Corp Movement

Dear reader,

Thank you for reading this book and joining the Publish Your Purpose community! You are joining a special group of people who aim to make the world a better place.

### What's Publish Your Purpose About?

Our mission is to elevate the voices often excluded from traditional publishing. We intentionally seek out authors and storytellers with diverse backgrounds, life experiences, and unique perspectives to publish books that will make an impact in the world. Beyond our books, we are focused on tangible, action-based change. As a woman- and LGBTQ+-owned company, we are committed to reducing inequality, lowering levels of poverty, creating a healthier environment, building stronger communities, and creating high-quality jobs with dignity and purpose.

Certified

Corporation

As a Certified B Corporation, we use business as a force for good. We join a community of mission-driven companies building a more equitable, inclusive, and sustainable global economy. B Corporations must meet high standards of transparency, social and environmental performance, and accountability as determined by the nonprofit B Lab. The certification process is rigorous and ongoing (with a recertification requirement every three years).

### How Do We Do This?

We intentionally partner with socially and economically disadvantaged businesses that meet our sustainability goals. We embrace and encourage our authors and employee's differences in race, age, color, disability, ethnicity, family or marital status, gender identity or expression, language, national origin, physical and mental ability, political affiliation, religion, sexual orientation, socio-economic status, veteran status, and other characteristics that make them unique.

Community is at the heart of everything we do—from our writing and publishing programs to contributing to social enterprise nonprofits like reSET (https://www.resetco.org) and our work in founding B Local Connecticut.

We are endlessly grateful to our authors, readers, and local community for being the driving force behind the equitable and sustainable world we are building together.

To connect with us online, or publish with us, visit us at www.publishyourpurpose.com.

Elevating Your Voice,

*Jenn T Grace*

**Jenn T. Grace**
Founder, Publish Your Purpose

Printed in the USA
CPSIA information can be obtained
at www.ICGtesting.com
JSHW022112301023
51152JS00001B/2